TO RUN
AFTER
THEM

THE UNIVERSITY OF ARIZONA PRESS
Tucson, Arizona

TO RUN AFTER THEM

Cultural and Social Bases of Cooperation in a Navajo Community

LOUISE LAMPHERE

About the Author . . .

LOUISE LAMPHERE spent fifteen months in 1965–66 on the eastern Navajo Reservation studying kinship cooperation and norms. She developed *To Run After
Them* from her fieldwork on the economic and ritual activities that are concrete
manifestations of cooperation among kinsmen in the modern Navajo community she
calls Copper Canyon. Earlier research interests led her to the Rimrock Navajo to
study religious learning and residence patterns. Between 1968 and 1975 she was an
Assistant Professor of Anthropology at Brown University. In 1971–72 she was an
Academic Visitor at the London School of Economics. She has also been a Fellow
at the Radcliffe Institute and joined the faculty at the University of New Mexico in
January 1976 as an Associate Professor of Anthropology. She is the author of
numerous journal articles and chapters in books and is co-editor of the book,
Woman, Culture and Society.

THE UNIVERSITY OF ARIZONA PRESS

Copyright © 1977
The Arizona Board of Regents
All Rights Reserved
Manufactured in the U.S.A.

Library of Congress Cataloging in Publication Data

Lamphere, Louise.
    To run after them.

    Bibliography: p.
    Includes index.
    1. Navaho Indians—Social life and customs.
I. Title.
E99.N3L35   301.45′19′7079135   77-22352
ISBN 0-8165-0594-2
ISBN 0-8165-0369-9 pbk.

To the Navajo People (Diné)

With the hope that they may continue to preserve
the principles of sharing, generosity, and cooperation
that distinguish their way of life

Contents

CONTENTS

REFERENCE MATERIAL

CASE REPORTS

TABLES

ILLUSTRATIONS

Figures

Maps

Preface

~~~~~~

To Run After Them alludes to the Navajo concept of cooperation, which is expressed in phrases like "I'll help him" or "I'll run after him" (*bíká 'adeeshghoł*) and "After me they are running along" or "They are helping me" (*shíká 'anájah*). *To Run After Them* is a study of the economic and ritual activities that are concrete manifestations of cooperation among kinsmen in a modern Navajo community. Fieldwork for this study was conducted in a Navajo community located on the Navajo Reservation, north of Gallup, New Mexico, between June 1965 and September 1966. In order to protect the anonymity of my informants, pseudonyms are used throughout, and the community is called Copper Canyon. I have analyzed my data on day-to-day activities and ceremonials in terms of three aspects of Navajo life: (1) the cultural concepts relating to cooperation and authority; (2) the structure of domestic groups, kinship relationships, and matrilineal clanship; and (3) the organization of a wide variety of activities, using case material to reveal the principles that account for actual participation in specific tasks.

To understand patterns of aid and reciprocity, it has been necessary to examine aspects of Navajo life that are the opposite of cooperation: gossip and witchcraft. I even have included case material that mentions drinking, quarrels, sickness, and death. These are "dangerous" topics not publicly discussed, which might lead some to view my analysis as emphasizing the negative side of Navajo culture. But Navajo life is no more full of conflict and difficulty than life in other segments of contemporary American society. In fact, many signs of stress (for example, the increasing suicide, homicide, and alcoholism rates) clearly are related to the pressures of Anglo-American society. Anglo institutions—schools, hospitals, churches, government agencies, and certainly Anglo business interests—dominate the reservation and continue to shape the life of the Navajo.

In response, the Navajo, like other native Americans, have been struggling to free themselves from the control of outsiders—government agents, politicians, teachers, missionaries, and even social scientists. In the early 1970s Navajo Tribal Chairman Peter McDonald advocated Navajo control of their resources and of educational, health, and commercial institutions on the reservation. Navajos also have started community-controlled schools (such as the one at Rough Rock), criticized the role of the traders on the reservation, and proposed plans for Navajo control of Bureau of Indian Affairs facilities. The Navajo are beginning to find ways of realizing their desire for self-determination and are gaining a place as an ethnic minority in a plural society.

To Run After Them, in focusing on Navajo ideas of help, aid, and cooperation, stresses the features of Navajo culture that would be lost if the Navajo were totally assimilated into the competitive, individualistic, and hierarchical institutions of Anglo-American society. That the Navajo have been able to maintain a form of family life and kinship organization based on values of generosity and egalitarianism is indeed a credit to the strength and resilience of the Navajo themselves. The importance of strategies for recruiting aid and the utilization of a flexible network of kin for the exchange of goods and services—two other qualities of social life stressed in this study—may not be unique to the Navajo or to other native American groups. Similar patterns of social organization, though in different cultural contexts, are found among the urban poor and working classes of the United States and Europe in both black and white ethnic populations (Stack 1974, Bott 1957, Young and Willmott 1957). *To Run After Them*, then, is part of a growing body of information on the ways in which groups who lack access to economic resources and political power are able to provide for their own needs and maintain a sense of cultural integrity.

Acknowledgments

∽∽∽

Many persons and organizations have helped make this study possible, and to them I gratefully express appreciation. Financial support for three years of graduate study at Harvard and additional funds for fieldwork were provided by a National Institute of Mental Health Fellowship and Research Grant Attachment.

I owe thanks to Evan Lewis, the trader at Copper Canyon during the early 1960s, for introducing me to various aspects of the community and for helping me with all sorts of daily problems. He also was kind enough to provide data on income for Copper Canyon residents who trade at his store.

Through the years I have been extremely grateful to David F. Aberle for consultation on problems of Navajo kinship and for suggestions about conducting fieldwork among the Navajo. His knowledge of social organization on the reservation is much greater than mine, and I have profited from his wide experience and comments concerning data from other communities. I also would like to thank Robert Young of the University of New Mexico for his help with the meaning and spelling of Navajo vocabulary relating to social groups. Mary Shepardson, Blodwen Hammond, Jerrold Levy, and Gary Witherspoon all have generously provided drafts of their own work on Navajo social organization and have read and critically commented on papers that I have sent to them. Though specialists in Navajo kinship do not always agree, they are more than willing to listen, debate, and exchange data with those presenting another point of view.

I am indebted to George Collier of Stanford University for the use of his Kin Program and for the time and effort he spent processing my census data. Especially I wish to thank E. Z. Vogt and David Maybury-Lewis, my advisors at Harvard University, for their careful reading and commentary on initial drafts of my doctoral dissertation from which this book was developed. Cora Dubois and T. O. Beidelman also were extremely helpful at various stages in the planning and implementing of this study. Several of my fellow graduate students at Harvard—Joan Bamburger, Robin Ridington, Nancy Howell, and Gordon Finley—read various portions of the thesis and provided helpful comments. Cecil Cook, another Harvard graduate student, deserves credit for initially interesting me in the problem of Navajo social organization.

I am particularly grateful to Terry Reynolds, long-time colleague and friend, for her assistance during my fieldwork and her suggestions and comments concerning my data. Our conversations were especially important in helping me formulate many of the ideas contained in this study.

During the years in which I was rewriting many portions of this study, many of my colleagues substantially contributed to my thinking and read and criticized various drafts of chapters. At the University of Rochester, I was particularly indebted to Alfred and Grace Harris and to Robert Merrill, who introduced me to data and theory on social networks. At Brown University, colleagues George Hicks, Karl Heider, Philip Leis, and Nancy Leis provided valuable comments and suggestions. I owe thanks to Dean Yager for patiently reading this book in manuscript form, and to Peter B. Evans for help with copy editing and proofreading. I also am indebted to the staff of the University of Arizona Press for their efforts in bringing about the publication of this study.

Finally, I am grateful to the Navajos of Copper Canyon. Without their interest in someone who wanted to learn about their way of life, this study would not have been possible. They provided me not only with rich and fascinating data but also with many memorable experiences.

LOUISE LAMPHERE

Abbreviations

~~~~~~

Throughout this book the following abbreviations are used. Other abbreviations for kin relationships are derived from those below.

M	mother
F	father
Z	sister
B	brother
D	daughter
S	son
ZD	sister's daughter
ZS	sister's son
BS	brother's son
FF	father's father
MZS	mother's sister's son
FZDD	father's sister's daughter's daughter

Part I

INTRODUCTION

Chapter 1

Copper Canyon Community

~~~~~~

The present-day Navajo Nation is a society within a society, an ethnic minority of more than 130 thousand American Indians, most of whom live in and around the eighteen-million-acre Navajo Reservation in northern Arizona and New Mexico. Over the past five hundred years the cultural and social patterns of the Navajo have changed tremendously. The Navajo arrived in the Southwest as hunters and gatherers and acquired a mixed pastoral and agricultural economy as a result of contact with Pueblo and Spanish populations. After the Southwest became part of the United States, the Navajo way of life was seriously disrupted by the U.S. Cavalry campaign, which resulted in the capture and incarceration of more than eight thousand Navajo at Fort Sumner between 1864 and 1868. This attempt to pacify the Navajo and turn them into "civilized" sedentary agriculturalists was a failure. The Navajo were given a reservation incorporating much of their previous territory and were allowed to reestablish their fields and build up their flocks. During the last half of the nineteenth century, Anglo-American society began to make inroads into reservation life through the establishment of trading posts, missions, and government boarding schools.

During the 1920s oil was discovered on the reservation, and the creation of a Tribal Council to sign leases brought the beginning of tribal government modeled after Anglo-American institutions (Kelly 1968: 48–75). The BIA-sponsored stock reduction program of the 1930s forced an unwelcome transformation of the Navajo economy. With the imposition of grazing areas and the limitation placed on size of flocks, it was no longer possible to maintain a subsistence economy based on herds and fields. Since World War II, change has accelerated so that the economy has become a mixed one. The traditional pursuits of sheepherding, agriculture, and production of native crafts have declined, while income from welfare payments and from sporadic employment (for example, railroad maintenance and migrant farm labor) has increased. A substantial number of Navajo have moved to urban areas or have taken wage jobs in some of the small government and trading centers, which are expanding rapidly on the reservation. As a consequence of the Navajo-Hopi

Rehabilitation Act (passed by Congress in 1950), the Navajo have access to Public Health Service hospital care, their children are educated at county day schools or BIA boarding schools, and roads have been vastly improved. The reservation has become dominated by institutions from Anglo-American society: hospitals, schools, trading posts, and, more recently, factories and shopping centers, which the Navajo do not control.

In the midst of all this economic change, the Navajo population is becoming more and more heterogeneous. Not only is there an incipient "generation gap" between school children and their elders, but adult Navajos are developing varied orientations toward the dominant society, depending on whether they are peyotists, members of a Christian sect, tribal or government employees, teenagers, or urban migrants. The United States is, after all, a heterogeneous society, and the Navajo are being pulled into various sectors of it. Those who take wage jobs in such centers as Window Rock, Shiprock, Tuba City, and Fort Defiance are drifting toward the middle class, while those who move to Los Angeles, Denver, Chicago, or Albuquerque are thrust in amongst the urban poor. The bulk of the population, however, remains in the rural areas of the reservation and is, in many respects, taking on the characteristics of the rural poor in the United States, while at the same time retaining their identity as Navajo and maintaining many traditional patterns.

Thus, most Navajos continue to live on or near the reservation in extended family hoghan clusters which have been arranged in a dispersed settlement pattern. Within a local area, families tend to use the same school and trading facilities. Because of the growth of the modern local-government system of "chapters," these areas are becoming "communities," increasing the interaction and cooperation between unrelated families.

This book is a study of one modern Navajo community, Copper Canyon, as it was in the mid-1960s. On one hand, it is a contribution to the study of Navajo social organization, that is, the patterns of family and kinship that compose everyday Navajo life; on the other hand, it is a contribution to the study of small-scale rural ethnic communities that are in turn part of larger complex societies. Relationships at this local level are "face to face"; they are "multiplex" social relationships characteristic of most tribal and peasant communities studied by anthropologists (Gluckman 1955). Family, kinship, and neighborhood ties are important and can be partially analyzed with anthropological constructs specifically developed for such communities—for example, the notion of a developmental cycle of domestic groups. But constructs developed for the study of urban social relationships, notably those of "set" and "network," can be adapted to elucidate the principles behind social organization in a changing rural setting. In the following chapters, a variety of anthropological constructs will be used in order to discover principles of social interaction in one kind of face-to-face community, which in turn can suggest comparison with other commmunities. At a more specific level, my analysis should have implications for reinterpreting data from other Navajo settlements.

Anthropological Studies of Navajo Social Organization

Anthropologists have written a great deal about the Navajo, so much so that another community study might seem superfluous. However, although there are data from several areas of the reservation at several points in time, these studies have produced contradictory analyses, especially in relation to kinship and family

patterns. Are these contradictions due to qualitative differences in social organization among communities, or are they due to differences in the theoretical orientations of anthropologists? One problem, for instance, is that of defining the major
social groupings among the Navajo. On one hand, the view that Navajo society is
matrilineal and matrilocal and is structured in terms of the nuclear family, the
matrilocal extended family, the "outfit," and the matrilineal clan has become a
standard stereotype found in text books on American Indians (Josephy 1968,
Spencer and Jennings 1965). On the other hand, several anthropologists have emphasized the flexibility and variant patterns to be found in Navajo social life (Aberle
1963, Shepardson and Hammond 1970). This view emphasizes that the extended
family is not always matrilocal and that matrilineal clans are dispersed with no
social functions except the regulation of marriage. Furthermore, there has been
disagreement on the issue of defining the "outfit." Kluckhohn and Leighton (1946)
first proposed the term, and Ross (1955) and Levy (1962) subsequently used this
concept in interpreting their own community data. Collier (1966) and, following
her, Shepardson and Hammond (1970) argued that outfits are lacking at Navajo
Mountain. Collier has proposed the notion of a "cooperating group;" Shepardson
and Hammond use "matrilineage." Adams suggested the term "resident lineage"
in his study of Shonto (1963). Aberle, in a general analysis of Navajo kinship,
discussed the "Local Clan Element" as having some of the same functions that
others attribute to the outfit (1961). More recently Gary Witherspoon (1975) has
revived Kluckhohn's and Leighton's definition, but has set it within a genealogical
context, defining an "outfit" in the Rough Rock-Black Mountain area as those
camps (subsistence residential units) where personnel trace their relationship back to
a common female head.

In addition to studies that have focused on social organization, much also has
been written about the cultural aspects of Navajo life. Navajo myth, ritual, values,
and world view have been described in many publications, but these aspects of
culture have been studied in the abstract, apart from their relationship to social
interaction. As a consequence, the links between beliefs and ideas and the structure
of social relationships have not become apparent.

These difficulties suggest the need for another analysis, one that addresses itself
to the unsolved problems of Navajo social organization while, at the same time,
relating social organization to aspects of Navajo culture (the ideas, beliefs, and
concepts through which Navajo interpret their world). Such an analysis can best be
achieved, I would argue, through the use of detailed data on everday activities from
one community. It is just this sort of detailed case material that is lacking in many
studies and that is necessary to produce a coherent and complete "picture" or
"observer's model" of how the cultural and social system works.[1] It will become
apparent in the following chapters that the Navajo, like many other people, do not
have a highly schematic "actors' model" of their own kinship system and social
structure.[2] The anthropologist is thus left with the necessity of using an observer's
model to interpret the patterns in his or her data. This observer's model, however,
should not ignore the concepts of the people under study. Rather, it should be
constructed carefully using these concepts and remaining as faithful as possible to
them. This study, then, concerns the mundane daily events of Navajo life, or what I
have called "cooperative activities," that is, those tasks or aggregates of tasks that
require the joint effort of several adults, usually those related by kinship and marriage. Of a potentially wide range of activities, I will concentrate on tasks that,

during the course of my fieldwork, were often performed and that are an integral part of everyday Navajo life. They include: transportation-related activities, agricultural and livestock chores, and tasks necessary to carry out the nonritual aspects of ceremonies and funerals. The study has four purposes:

1. To suggest an observer's model of the Navajo cultural ideas that relate to cooperation and to giving and receiving aid from genealogical relatives, clan kin, and neighbors.
2. To propose an observer's model of domestic group structure and kin relations beyond the domestic group based on a careful consideration of the Navajo's own concepts about living arrangements, kinship, and clanship. The model will also account for variation and flexibility in the structure of kin groups and the use of kin ties.
3. To show how these two models (cultural and structural) can help analyze cooperative activities and the way in which individuals get help in concrete situations.
4. In conclusion, to assess the literature on other Navajo communities and to suggest alternative ways of interpreting Navajo culture and social structure.

Theoretical Framework

Any observer's model is based on certain distinctions about how to conceptualize what people do and say. Four important terms I will use are: cultural system, social system, social structure, and social organization. The distinction between a cultural system and a social system has been made by Parsons and Shils (1951), Geertz (1957, 1964), and Schneider (1968). Geertz defines a cultural system as a set of "shared conceptions" through which behavior is defined and interpreted. These concepts and ideas are "extrinsic sources of information in terms of which human life can be patterned—extrapersonal mechanisms for the perception, understanding, judgment, and manipulation of the world" (1964: 52). As cognitive and expressive symbols, they provide a "template" or "blueprint" for the definition and organization of social processes. The social system, on the other hand, is the "ongoing process of interactive behavior, whose persistent form we call social structure" (Geertz 1957: 33).

Two aspects of the social system can be emphasized. On one hand, social structure consists of the formal properties of interaction, the system of statuses and roles, and the organization of groups. Among the various definitions of social structure are those used by Levi-Strauss (1963), Leach (1954), Evans-Pritchard (1940), and Radcliffe-Brown (1952). Social structure, particularly as construed by Leach, has a highly "cultural" component since it is based on norms or "ideal rules" derived from native statements, that is, shared conceptions for interpreting behavior. In this book I will use the term social structure to describe persisting dyadic ties, roles, and groups which organize a population, though the categories by which these groups are defined are usually "cultural," or in the minds of the actors rather than the observer.

In contrast to structure, an emphasis on process and individual choice leads to the treatment of social organization. Firth, in distinguishing between social structure and social organization, stated: "One may describe social organization, then, as the working arrangements of society. It is the processes of ordering of action and of relations in reference to given social ends, in terms of adjustments resulting from the exercise of choices by members of the society'' (1964: 45).

The failure of past studies of Navajo kinship is that authors, in an attempt to give a generalized picture, have looked for structural features rather than organizational ones and have been frustrated by the endless variation and flexibility mentioned above. Generalizations must be derived from concrete situations or ''working arrangements,'' thus calling for abundant use of extended case material, or what Van Velsen has called ''situational analysis.''[3]

This approach assumes that the norms and concepts that guide behavior do not form a consistent system but are often vaguely formulated and discrepant. Furthermore, they are manipulated by members of a society to further their own aims, without necessarily impairing its enduring structure (Van Velsen 1967: 146). A close analysis of concrete cases is a useful method of revealing the process of optation. An individual in any one situation has a variety of relationships with other individuals, and the relationships themselves may be governed by different norms. From these possibilities, he chooses to activate those that will best serve his aims. As Van Velsen points out, ''The particular relationships and norms selected are likely to vary in regard to the same individuals from one situation to another and in regard to similar situations from one individual to another'' (1967: 143).

Cooperative activities, because they involve interaction between kinsmen and because they are highly recurrent, provide the abundant case material necessary to carry out ''situational analysis.'' The setting for my study of cooperative activities, the community of Copper Canyon, is a Navajo settlement on the eastern part of the reservation where I conducted field research from June 1965 to August 1966. Although I will utilize the extensive anthropological literature on the Navajo to support my analysis, concrete examples will be drawn from the daily lives of the Navajos with whom I lived and in whose activities I often participated.

The first section of this book concerns the cultural system that underlies cooperation. I first focus on the ''actors' view'' by describing Navajo concepts of authority and cooperation as they emerge from the literature and from conversations with Copper Canyon residents. Using case material I show how public occasions and face-to-face interaction (involving gossip and witchcraft accusations) are used by Navajos at Copper Canyon to continually define and communicate concepts of cooperative and uncooperative behavior. This interpretation, or ''observer's model,'' goes beyond Navajo views of cooperation, gossip, and witchcraft but allows us to discover important relationships between ideas and beliefs (the cultual system) and patterns of aid among kinsmen (the social system). Next I deal with the relationship of cooperation and authority concepts to situations where aid is requested. Here close attention is given to accounts from Navajo informants and to situations I observed in outlining the way Navajos make requests and accept or refuse them.

The social system as found at Cooper Canyon is viewed first in terms of its structural aspects, using two anthropological constructs to create a model of Navajo social relationships: (1) the developmental cycle of domestic groups as first proposed by Fortes (1949) and later used by Goody (1956), and (2) the concepts of ''set'' and ''network'' as used by Barnes (1954) and more recently by Bott (1957), Epstein (1961), Mayer (1966), and Mitchell (1966). Careful attention is here given to the ''actors' model,'' and I discuss concepts of kinship and living arrangements as elicited in interviews with Copper Canyon residents in order to define two

Navajo domestic groups: the household and the residence group. However, I go beyond Navajo views to use the notion of "developmental cycle" to account for variations in size and composition of households and residence groups. Navajo categories that might be used to analyze cooperation beyond the domestic sphere are lacking, so, in the absence of an "actors' model," I propose an "observer's model," which seems to impose the least amount of rigidity on the data and which accounts for the flexibility in patterns of aid among members of different domestic groups. Rejecting certain previously used terms such as "outfit," cooperating group, and matrilineage, I introduce the concepts of "set" and "network." It should be clear that the Navajo do not "have" sets or networks anymore than they "have" outfits or matrilineages, but these two concepts are more productive tools for analyzing the way kin ties are used than are other constructs based on the notion of bounded groups. Navajo categories of clanship are also discussed, and I show how the dispersal of clan members in various parts of the community inhibits the organization of cooperation solely along lines of matrilineal clan affiliation.

In three chapters on cooperative activities, the organizational aspects of Copper Canyon life become apparent, and I show how cultural and structural models can interpret a wide variety of situations. Actual methods of handling such problems as hauling wood and water, herding and shearing sheep, plowing fields, and arranging a ceremony or funeral are presented. Case material is used to show how the residents of Copper Canyon use authority and cooperation concepts (aspects of the cultural system) and kin ties within the residence group or a set of genealogical kin (aspects of the social system) to perform these tasks. Principles of recruitment are specified, which show under what conditions an individual will use ties within the residence group, ties to more distant primary and secondary kin, ties to neighboring clansmen, or ties to nonrelated neighbors.

The last chapter critically assesses the published literature on the Navajo in terms of the results of my observer's model derived from the study of cooperative activities. I suggest that past emphasis on religion, mythology, and values has ignored those aspects of the cultural system (e.g., concepts of authority and cooperation along with notions that define request-making situations) that most directly link ideology and behavior. In the study of social structure or organization, anthropologists have emphasized the matrilineal aspects of Navajo society and have concentrated on the definition of social groups, thereby failing to provide an adequate framework for analyzing variation. A more productive approach is one that emphasizes only domestic groups (carefully defined in terms of Navajo concepts) and utilizes the notion of a developmental cycle. The organization of activities beyond the domestic sphere is more accurately handled in terms of the "set" and "network," since an analysis based on these concepts, although not conceptualized by the Navajo themselves, does reflect the actual process of recruitment and better accounts for the type of kin and neighbors who participate.

Selection of a Community

Since World War II, the impact of Anglo-American institutions on the Navajo has accelerated changes already taking place during the earlier periods of contact. Some of the most important changes follow.

1. A decline in the traditional economy and an increase in income from welfare and wages has occurred.

2. With increased medical facilities, the death and infant mortality rates have declined, and these rates, though still higher than for most groups in the United States (Kluckholn and Leighton 1946; 1962 ed.: 51–52) are still low enough to allow for substantial population growth. The population has increased to over 130 thousand, while the land base of the reservation has remained the same.

3. As education has increased, many younger Navajos have been encouraged (through various government programs) to migrate to urban centers throughout the West and to border towns near the reservation or agency communities on the reservation. These young people often return to their home communities after several years, but increasing numbers are remaining away from their kin, except for sporadic visits.

4. American technology has brought the use of transistor radios, and, in homes which have access to electricity, there are television sets, refrigerators, and even electric frying pans. The biggest changes have come with the use of the pickup truck and car as the major means of transportation. Motor vehicles have increased the mobility of the Navajo, giving them more access to off-reservation shopping centers and hospitals and facilitating travel to distant residence groups for the exchange of goods and service or to attend ceremonies, peyote meetings, or funerals.

These changes are most readily apparent on the eastern portion of the reservation, where population density is greatest, off-reservation migration has been substantial, and greater contact with Anglo-American society exists. Since most community studies of Navajo social organization have been conducted in off-reservation communities or on western portions of the reservation, it seemed wise to choose an eastern reservation community, so that an "observer's model" of cooperative activities and social organization would fit this situation as well as other communities already studied.

Kluckhohn and Leighton (1946; rev. ed. 1962), Kluckhohn (1966), and others connected with the Harvard Values Project have provided data on the off-reservation community near Rimrock, New Mexico. Information on this community dates back to the post-Fort Sumner period and has been used, along with land-allotment records and Kluckhohn's genealogies, to reconstruct the formation and fission of domestic groups and the growth of the community (Reynolds, Lamphere, and Cook 1967).[4] However, Rimrock's isolation from the rest of the reservation and the land-allotment system makes this and other off-reservation communities unique and slightly peripheral to trends on the reservation at large.

Western portions of the reservation were added to the original treaty reservation between 1868 and 1900 (Kelly 1968: 16–36). Thus, some areas were settled as late as 1890, are less densely populated, and are more traditional. Studies of the western Navajo include those by Malcolm Carr Collier at Navajo Mountain and Klagetoh (1966), William Adams at Shonto (1963), James Downs on Black Mesa near Piñon (1964), and the Cornell Medical Project at Many Farms (Richards 1963). At the time of my fieldwork, several investigators were in the process of completing studies of social organization in various western Navajo groups: Jerrold Levy near Tuba City (1962), Mary Shepardson and Blodwen Hammond at Navajo Mountain (1970), David Aberle near Piñon (1967), and Gary Witherspoon (1966–68) in the Rough Rock-Black Mountain area. In contrast, there has been comparable extensive research in only one eastern reservation community, Fruitland (Sasaki 1960, and Ross 1955). This is a recently formed agricultural community located on a government irrigation project, which makes the data on social organization less relevant to other parts of the reservation. Shepardson has studied political organization in Shiprock (1966, 1971), and Aberle (1966) has done fieldwork on the peyote religion in the eastern reservation communities of Mexican Springs, Aneth, Red Rock. To my knowledge, neither researcher gathered extensive data on kinship.[5] An excellent summary of social organization data and anthropological "models" in these and other communities is contained in E. B. Henderson's and Jerrold Levy's survey of community studies (1975). Not only does this monograph contain data from unpublished studies but compares social organization features and economic data from a wide range of communities.

The choice of an eastern reservation community, then, was calculated to provide data that would complement information already collected on Navajo kinship and social organization. In the final chapter, where the literature on Navajo kinship is reviewed in detail, I argue that contradictions among various interpretations of Navajo social organization are a result of the theoretical predilections of anthropological observers rather than the result of fundamental differences in local patterns of social organization. Differences in residence patterns, domestic group composition, and patterns of aid can be accounted for under one general model. Changes in the past few decades are due not to a "breakdown" of a predominately matrilineal system but to shifts in patterns already part of a flexible social structure in response to changes in population density, microecology, and Anglo-American technology.

Research Procedures

Two summers of field investigation carried out in the Navajo community of Rimrock gave me experience in living with Navajo families, some knowledge of the language, and a sense of the unsolved problems of Navajo social organization. Data on Rimrock residence patterns and land use (Reynolds, Lamphere, and Cook 1967), for example, showed a great deal of variation and led to my choice of the eastern reservation community of Copper Canyon as an area for more extensive fieldwork.

I had briefly visited Copper Canyon during the summers of 1963 and 1964 and had two contacts there: the Mormon trader, whose family resided in Rimrock, and the family of a Navajo woman temporarily living in the Rimrock area in 1963. On coming to the community in June 1965, the trader helped locate Sarah, a female interpreter with a good command of English, the divorced daughter of the chapter president. I had learned in Rimrock that it is best to work with an interpreter of the same sex, since being seen with a male of the same age always provoked rumors of being "married to him," or "living with him." The parents of the Navajo woman I had known in Rimrock (John Begay and his wife) provided temporary housing in their winter cabin.

During the summers of 1965 and 1966 I was accompanied by Terry Reynolds, a Ph.D. candidate in Anthropology at the University of British Columbia. In 1965 she and I concentrated, with Sarah our interpreter, on learning some of the Navajo language and on becoming acquainted with the area. I also obtained census and genealogical information and mapped hoghan sites. These data were later processed by computer, using the Kin Program (Collier and Vogt 1965), which produced a listing of the population by matrilineage with maps showing the residence location of lineage members.

In the fall of 1965 I began living with my interpreter in the extended family camp of her parents. It soon became evident that the Copper Canyon area was divided into many clusters of kin, and an entree into one extended family did not necessarily bring opportunities to get to know others. This is, in part, related to the dispersed settlement pattern that separates residence groups in the area, but of more importance is the fact that interaction is mainly with close relatives, while other relatives are rarely visited or are seen only at public gatherings.

At the request of another woman, Edna, I began living with her during her husband's absence from Copper Canyon to engage in railroad maintenance work. It was only then that my role as an outsider in a community with internal subdivisions became apparent. For instance, the chapter president's family (which I had considered an upstanding traditional family, since he was a singer in addition to holding a political position, and his wife was a good weaver) had a reputation for bootlegging and drunkenness.[6] My interpreter's two sisters were rumored to be "prostitutes."[7] The family had confined much of their drinking to the days when I was away from the community, so their reputation seemed exaggerated to me. I discovered later that these attitudes toward Sarah's family were part of the general view Edna and other peyotists held of traditional families, and that I, in turn, was being associated with their alleged activities simply by living with them. The importance of these attitudes and their communication through gossip will be discussed in my analysis of the cultural system of cooperation.

For many months Copper Canyon Navajos had a difficult time understanding the purpose of my stay in the community. I usually explained my presence in terms of my desire to learn the Navajo language and the necessity of living with the Navajos as part of my education. Most Navajos, on the other hand, tried to place me in one of the Anglo female roles with which they were already familiar. However, my living arrangements and day-to-day activities indicated that I was not a nurse, teacher, or trader's wife, the three most obvious roles I might have occupied. Some thought that since I was often with another woman (Terry Reynolds) I was a Mormon missionary, as these missionaries often travel in same-sex pairs, visit families, and learn the Navajo language. Others thought that I was a Communist spy, a fact that I gradually became aware of as Navajo acquaintances took the trouble to tell me stories about female Anglo spies living in the vicinity during and since World War II. The local Navajo policeman, Sam, had often told the story that I was sent up from Cuba to gain training as a spy, a fact he told me laughingly when I first met him in person. I gave a speech at a local chapter meeting in December which undoubtedly helped clarify my purposes for staying at Copper Canyon. In general, the longer I remained in the community and the more Navajos I lived with, the less suspicion there was. Those who knew I accepted Navajo customs and was willing to contribute food and labor to daily household chores began to defend me and explain my presence when others asked. I also provided transportation to hospitals, trading posts, and stores in Gallup which often made my friendship valuable. I found that the most congenial way to relate to Navajos was to attempt to fit in with their own system of "generalized reciprocity" (see Chapter 2). Rather than paying informants by the hour, I contributed groceries, household help, and transportation in return for staying with families and participating in Navajo life. Thus I became drawn into the system of requests for aid, either by being asked for favors or by transporting those with whom I lived to make requests of others.

The experience of living first with Sarah and then with Edna convinced me that it is essential to live in a variety of residence groups in order to study social organization in a society with a dispersed settlement pattern. Edna, her close relatives, and neighbors provided me with a whole new set of social relationships from those I had been exposed to at Sarah's camp, and I discovered that members of one residence group rarely know much about residence groups where they have no relatives. I found that by establishing close relationships with members of a number of residence groups whose members were not related, I could tap several different sources of information at the same time. During the second summer of my stay I was able to live with one family and make visits to several others during the same day to discuss community events, happenings within the residence group, and other gossip.

The residence groups in which I lived represent variations in size and composition, ranging from a nuclear family camp to an extended family camp of five households. They were selected from all religious orientations so that I had an opportunity to attend traditional ceremonies, peyote meetings, and Latter-day Saints and Pentecostal church services. The genealogical and clan relatives of members of these residence groups extended over most of the community so that I was able to gain some knowledge of cooperation in most residence groups. Since I did not live with a family in Black Mesa or Crumbled House Mesa, my knowledge of residence groups in these two neighborhoods comes only from their relatives who lived in other neighborhoods and from visits to "sings" in these camps.

Table 1.1 gives a summary of the families with whom I lived.

TABLE 1.1
Data Pertaining to Families With Whom Author Lived

Type of Camp	Religious Orientation	Principal Informants	Camp Number
Extended family (two households)	Traditional	John Begay and wife	28 (winter)
Extended family (four households)	Traditional	Sarah, her parents (the chapter president and his wife), her married sisters	35 (winter & summer)
Extended family (two households)	Peyote	Edna and Mike, and Edna's mother	46 (winter & summer)
Nuclear family	Peyote and Mormon	Lucy and Kevin	14 (winter & summer)
Nuclear family	Pentecostal	Stella and Thomas	49 (winter & summer)
Extended family (four households)	Peyote	Iris, Jake, and Sam Grant's mother	57 (summer)
Extended family (five households)	Peyote	Nellie and Lester, Nellie's married daughter and three married sons	13 (summer)

My close association with members of these residence groups constituted my own "network" of social relations, which in turn tapped the ego-centered networks of my informants and provided me with an opportunity to observe activities with their close kin, neighbors, and clan relatives. This research strategy of living with several families is not only adaptive to the dispersed settlement pattern of the Navajo but clearly advantageous for collecting the kind of data on Navajo culture and social organization that I came to regard as important during the course of my study.

As a way of studying the Navajo social system, I had originally planned to investigate the determinants of residence group composition by gathering data on the norms governing residence choice, the resources each residence group controlled, the residence histories of a sample of community members, and cooperative patterns found in various residence groups. I soon found that eliciting norms and obtaining detailed residence histories was a difficult and unfruitful task. Navajos were much more interested in day-to-day events than in explaining factors surrounding past residential movements. I began to realize that the most vital aspects of social life were those concerned with cooperation, that is, getting and receiving help in accomplishing particular tasks. Cooperative activities thus became the focus of my study.

My efforts to learn the Navajo language, begun during the summer of 1965 and continuing throughout my stay, were particularly helpful in gathering data on the cultural aspects of cooperation. Although I never became a fluent speaker, I could understand preliminary conversations and the general topic of most discussions. I was able to ask appropriate questions[8] and record words and phrases crucial to understanding ways of asking for aid (presented in Chapter 3) and Navajo categories for social groups (presented in Chapter 4). I feel that many investigators of Navajo social organization have neglected this sort of linguistic data and, as a consequence, have presented analyses that are not congruent with the Navajo's own conceptions of kinship and domestic life.

As my knowledge of conversational Navajo grew, I was able to record actual requests for aid, to observe disputes, and to hear gossip. Being on hand when conflict arises or is discussed is crucial, I feel, for studying Navajo society. Navajos are reticent to give complete details of events that have happened several days or weeks before, since the reporting of disputes contradicts the view that cooperative life should be harmonious. Accounts, thus, tend to be extremely vague and imprecise, only alluding to the fact that norms may have been broken, rather than giving explicit details that might be interpreted as accusations. However, informants were quite willing to explain what was occurring immediately after an event that I had witnessed, since they felt I was already familiar with the situation and could easily understand their interpretation and possibly take their side in a dispute. (The relation between disputes and gossip will be further amplified in Chapter 2.)

In addition to acquiring data on cultural categories, disputes, and gossip, I was able to obtain complete and detailed information on a variety of activities. Data for almost all residence groups on transportation resources and means of hauling wood and water were obtained from a survey made by the Community Development Aide in connection with his work for the Office of Navajo Economic Opportunity. I participated in sheepshearing and sheepdipping so that I could observe the composition of cooperative groups organized for these purposes. I attended as many ceremonies as possible to observe what tasks had to be accomplished and which relatives were helping. I was often available to provide free transportation, which gave me more opportunities to attend sings and peyote meetings than might have otherwise been the case. Like the Navajo women I accompanied to ceremonies, I often contributed groceries (for example, flour, potatoes, or coffee) and "pitched in" to help with cooking or cleaning-up chores.

Toward the end of my stay I was able to help with two Squaw Dances and could observe how requests were made and carried out in larger ceremonies. Gathering data on twenty different ceremonies was particularly valuable for comparing several instances of cooperation for the same type of sing. During my stay, eight Navajos at Copper Canyon died, and I was able to attend or find out about their funerals and the cooperative activities surrounding them. These data are interesting in light of the recent changes in funeral arrangements and in demonstrating the importance of relatives outside the residence group.

The anthropologist is always confined to activities appropriate to a society's definition of sex roles, and the sex of the investigator has a direct impact on the kind of data that can be collected. Being a woman was an advantage among the Navajo for this type of study. On one hand, the Navajo division of labor is extremely flexible so that Navajo women (and by analogy the female anthropologist) can participate in a wide variety of productive tasks including sheepherding, shearing, and dipping and almost all agricultural activities. On the other hand, much of the cooperation at ceremonies focuses on food preparation, which is done in women's work groups. Thus I was barred from relatively few activities (notably housebuilding, log cutting, shallow-well digging, and other "heavy" tasks), and I had easy access to activities that would have been more difficult for a male to observe.

In sum, during the first six months of fieldwork, I developed for myself the role of part-time "daughter" within the families where I lived and for whom I provided specific goods and services.[9] This allowed me to pursue the research strategy of participant-observation, supplemented by intensive interviews with selected informants on cultural categories and by the collection of aggregate social and economic data on the whole area. In turn, the role of participant-observer proved advantageous for collecting the detailed case material that serves as a basis for this analysis of cooperative activities.

The Copper Canyon Area

One of the major methodological problems that I encountered during my early months at Copper Canyon was that of defining a population for study. As noted earlier, the Navajo live in a dispersed settlement pattern consisting of clusters of dwellings—eight-sided hoghans or cabins—that are scattered over an area. How the population in any particular section of the reservation is to be subdivided and whether these subdivisions might fit some sort of "community" organization is thus problematic. The indigenous bandlike political structure that existed prior to 1868 was extremely fluid (Hill 1940) and provides no principles with which to classify hoghan clusters into larger aggregates. Only a few Navajo populations (such as those near Rimrock and Cañoncito, New Mexico) are surrounded by alien cultures that cut them off from other Navajos and create a bounded population. Some Navajo groups (such as the one at Navajo Mountain, Arizona) are isolated because geographic features provide natural boundaries from neighboring Navajos. However, in the Copper Canyon area, as is generally the case throughout the reservation, a map of hoghan sites reveals no regular patterns of nucleation. Where one subpopulation begins and another ends is extremely unclear.

Aberle has attempted to solve these ambiguities by designating a community as a set of facilities used by a Navajo population. Implicitly, this amounts to defining a community in terms of frequency of interaction, or as those who "come together and separate again" (Arensberg 1961: 258). On the Navajo Reservation, facilities that the Navajo frequently use and that provide centers of interaction include schools, trading posts, and government offices (Aberle 1961: 106). Through the Bureau of Indian Affairs (BIA) and the Navajo Tribe, a system of local "chapters" was instituted in the 1930s and reinstated in the early 1950s after a period of inactivity. There are ninety-seven chapters on the reservation, each with an elected president, vice-president, and secretary. During the past few years the Navajo Tribe has built modern chapter houses in many areas, complete with butane heat, electricity, and kitchen equipment. The chapter house, then, can provide another important facility or center for interaction.

Following Aberle's lead, it is important to discover what facilities are used near Copper Canyon and by which Navajos. A complex is located at the crossroads of a paved highway to Gallup and a gravel road (paved in the 1970s) that traverses the nearby mountains; this small set of buildings consists of a trading post and cafe, a chapter meetinghouse, and a Pentecostal mission. In the mountains are a summer chapter house and dipping vats, which are used during the months when the Navajo move to higher elevations to plant fields and provide better pasture for flocks. These two sets of facilities, one used year-around, and one during the summer, are centers of interaction for many of the Navajos who live in hoghans and cabins scattered throughout a ten-mile square area. The problem, then, becomes one of defining the boundaries of a population rather than its central focus.

Despite Aberle's suggestion, populations that use the same school and trading facilities are not isomorphic. Grade school children attend a variety of schools. Those who live north of the grazing district fence attend a public school ten miles north of the Copper Canyon trading post, if they are near the highway[10]; others attend a BIA boarding school fifteen miles away. Those south of the fence go to a boarding school twenty-five miles to the south. High school students are sent to off-reservation boarding schools where they are classmates of students from other parts of the reservation or from other Indian tribes. Thus the school system cross-cuts the population and divides it into several segments rather than uniting it.

There are three trading posts in the area, other than the one at Copper Canyon. Navajos tend to trade at the nearest store, although there are exceptions; a trader may discontinue an account at any time, and because of unpaid bills or a disagreement with the trader a Navajo may seek credit at another store. Any Navajo with a potential source of income may establish credit at a trading post, with the result that husbands and wives with independent incomes or members of the same residence group have separate accounts, not necessarily with the same trader. Although the boundaries of the Copper Canyon trading area extend to a large number of families, within these boundaries are those who trade elsewhere, making the use of trading facilities a poor criteria for defining a community.

Since about 1965, chapter organizations on the reservation have become consolidated, becoming centers of decision making and program implementation. Observations made during the first several months of my stay at Copper Canyon confirmed this pattern, so that I found chapter membership provided the best starting point for defining a "community." The Copper Canyon chapter meets regularly to discuss and organize various Navajo Tribe and government-sponsored projects (including Tribal Works Projects,[11] Head Start and Vista Programs, and sheepdipping and vaccination programs). Families on the border between two chapters are discouraged from attending meetings in both places, so adults are registered and allowed to receive benefits in one chapter area only. I have used the 1963 chapter census, taken under the auspices of the Navajo Tribe as the basic Copper Canyon population, revising it in terms of later births and deaths and adding a few hoghan clusters because of their spatial and kinship ties with other families in the census. Here I have followed Jerrold Levy's analysis (1962) of western Navajo communities and looked for boundaries defined by kinship and natural features rather than arbitrarily limiting the population to the chapter census.

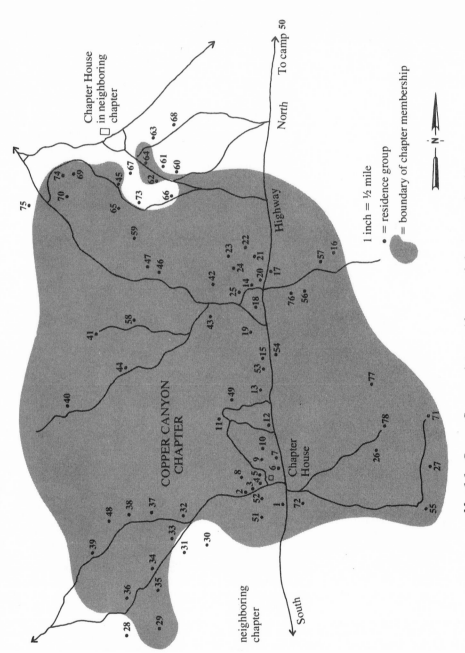

Map 1.1   Copper Canyon winter residences and chapter membership

Chapter House in neighboring chapter

Chapter House

COPPER CANYON CHAPTER

neighboring chapter

To camp 50

North

Highway

South

1 inch = ½ mile

• = residence group

= boundary of chapter membership

-·N·-

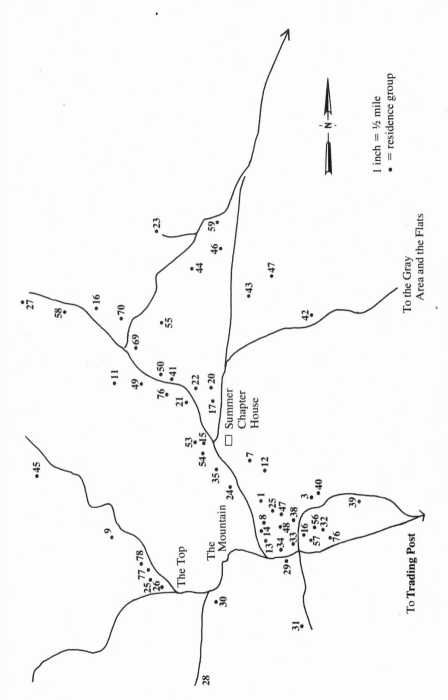

Map 1.2 Copper Canyon summer residences

Map 1.1 shows the membership of the Copper Canyon chapter in terms of winter residences. Map 1.2 shows summer residences. I have focused on the winter area in initially defining the community, since the winter dwellings are used seven to nine months of the year, and recent improvements, including cemented exterior walls, tar-paper roofing, and, in some cases, the installation of electricity, indicate that these cabins are considered more permanent.

In addition to the residence groups of Chapter members indicated on Map 1.1, I have added the residence groups of their siblings who live in two dry-farm areas: Black House Mesa and Crumbled House Mesa (Camps 60, 63, 66, 67, 68, and 73). This places the northern edge of the Copper Canyon community at a ridge of hills, a natural boundary which divides kin groups.

On the south, where there is no natural boundary, the district fence has become one. I have added five residence groups which are located on the south side of the fence. Members of two groups (Camps 28 and 35) move near the Copper Canyon chapter house during the summer, making their connection with the rest of the community clear. Members of the other three residence groups (Camps 29, 30, and 31) belong to the adjacent chapter and live nearer members of this chapter during the summer. However, I have included them in my study since they trade at Copper Canyon and have important relatives in the community.

Boundaries on the east and west raise no problems, since a large wash (ten miles east of the trading post) effectively cuts off Copper Canyon families from other Navajos, and the mountains form a barrier on the west.

Defining a Copper Canyon community is relatively simple compared to defining communities in other parts of the reservation where trading posts, schools, and government facilities cross-cut both kinship networks and chapter membership, creating an incoherent picture. At Copper Canyon there are problems in defining the edges of the community, while in other areas the center or focus may be difficult to delineate (Levy 1962: 792).

It is important to emphasize that the boundaries I have proposed are not fixed in any permanent form. Residence groups located at the edges of the community, as I have defined it, have many contacts with those living in adjacent areas. Rather than a nucleated village or hamlet pattern, Navajo settlement is regulated by the growth and expansion of domestic groups which tend to fill an ecological area (Levy 1962). As I will show, using the concepts of set and network, it is accurate to characterize Copper Canyon and the surrounding region as an unbounded series of domestic groups linked by ties of kinship and marriage. The idea of a Copper Canyon community is thus based partly on anthropological necessity and partly on recent acculturative influences. On one hand, the anthropologist must limit the population to be studied if uniform data are to be collected; on the other hand, the growth of the chapter system has increased interaction between distant groups, providing a basis for a community that is recognized by the Navajo themselves.

Ecology

The Copper Canyon Navajos see their environment as divided into four ecological zones. The geologic and climatic characteristics of the area determine the differences in land features and vegetation that form the basis of the Navajo distinctions. Map 1.3 shows the ecological zones, Navajo place names, and settlement patterns.

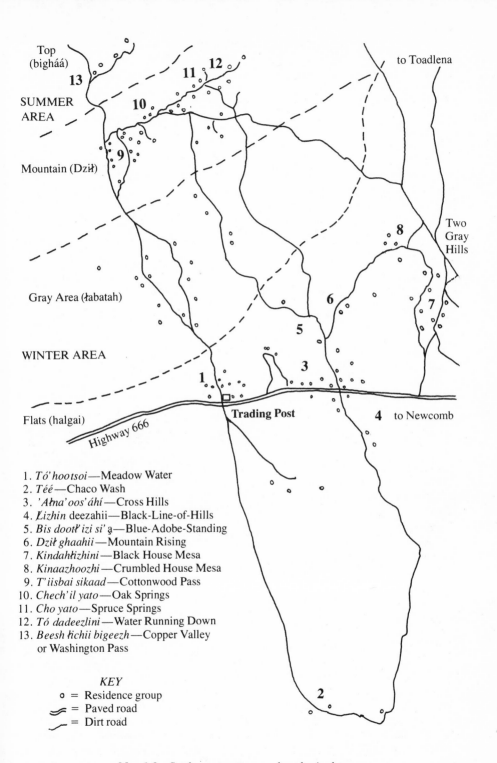

Top
(bighá́á)
13

SUMMER
AREA

Mountain (Dził)

Gray Area (łabatah)

WINTER AREA

Flats (halgai)

Highway 666

11 12

10

9

to Toadlena

Two
Gray
Hills

8

6   7

5

3

1

Trading Post   4 to Newcomb

1. *Tó' hootsoi*—Meadow Water
2. *Téé*—Chaco Wash
3. *'Ałna' oos' áhí*—Cross Hills
4. *Łizhin* deezahii—Black-Line-of-Hills
5. *Bis dootł'izi si'ạ*—Blue-Adobe-Standing
6. *Dził ghaahii*—Mountain Rising
7. *Kindahłizhini*—Black House Mesa
8. *Kinaazhoozhi*—Crumbled House Mesa
9. *T'iisbai sikaad*—Cottonwood Pass
10. *Chech'il yato*—Oak Springs
11. *Cho yato*—Spruce Springs
12. *Tó dadeezlini*—Water Running Down
13. *Beesh łichii bigeezh*—Copper Valley
    or Washington Pass

KEY

o = Residence group
⌇ = Paved road
⌒ = Dirt road

Map 1.3 *Settlement pattern and ecological zones*

THE FLATS

The flat, plainlike area (5,500 to 6,000 feet) is called the Flats (*halgai*). *Halgai* is a general term for any flat region or valley, but near Copper Canyon it signifies the region from the trading post eastward to a large wash and northward along the front line of hills. Navajo names for subareas, or neighborhoods, in this zone include:

1. Meadow Water (*tó hootsoi*)—a spring near the trading post and its surrounding area.
2. Chaco Wash (*tééh*).
3. Cross Hills (*'ałna'oos'áhí*)—a series of mesas which cross each other, three miles north of the trading post.
4. Black-Line-of-Hills (*łizhindeez'áhii*)—a ridge of hills parallel to and east of the highway, six miles north of the trading post.
5. Blue-Adobe-Standing or Blue Mesa (*bis dootł'izhi si'á*)—refers specifically to a small peak, but more generally to the surrounding area, including fields on the Blue Mesa Irrigation Project.
6. Mountain Rising (*dził ghaahi*)—a hill which rises from the plains adjacent to Blue Adobe Standing.
7. Black Houses or Black House Mesa (*kindałizhini*)—refers to the dry farm area eight miles north of the trading post and one mile west of the highway.
8. Fallen-in-House of Crumbled House Mesa (*kináázhoozhi*)—a dry farm area one mile west of Black House Mesa.

This zone is flat with some broken land, cut by washes; there are a few cotton-wood trees (*t'iis*), but the main ground cover consists of sagebrush, rabbit brush, Russian thistle, greasewood, chamiso, and grama grass. Water is not plentiful, and most Navajos must haul it from the windmill near the trading post, though there are at least six improved permanent springs or wells in the zone. Shallow man-made depressions, natural lakes, and troughs attached to wells provide water for live-stock. In the early 1970s new water resources, in the form of deep wells and large storage tanks, were being developed through a Navajo Tribal Program. This has opened the possibility of water being transported by pipeline to individual residence groups.

Fields are found in three neighborhoods: Blue Mesa, Black House Mesa, and Crumbled House Mesa, where water is diverted from the spring run-off to irrigate fields before planting, using ditches built around 1950 as part of a government-sponsored irrigation program. Wood must be hauled from the mountains; each household uses one or two pickup-truckloads of wood during the winter months.

THE GRAY AREA

The landslide area (6,000 to 7,000 feet) is called the Gray Area (*łabatah*), or as one informant translated the term, "rocky, hilly places." This foothill-like area extends along the mountains for some twenty-five to thirty miles. In the lower elevations are few trees, but at higher elevations the pinon (*chá'oł*) and juniper (*gad*) distinguish the Gray Area from the Flats, where cottonwoods are present. Other plants such as sage, cactus, rabbit brush, and Russian thistle grow in both zones. Most of the area is rough broken land caused by geological erosion, although some flat areas provide fair range and, on the upper edge of the zone, a wooded region provides poor range.

Water resources in the Gray Area are poor, and the fifteen winter residence groups haul water from the spring near the trading post (a distance of several miles). A few depressions (natural and man-made) and two temporary well sites provide adequate water for livestock. The wooded areas at higher elevations provide a good source of firewood, especially during winter months when snow makes the mountaintop inaccessible. Only one open flat area is used for dry farming, and the fields are not always planted. Two residence groups with winter homes on the Flats have another set of hoghans in the Gray Area which they use during spring months so that their flocks can graze on early grass.

THE MOUNTAIN

The Mountain (*dził*) is the term for the bench area (7,200 to 8,000 feet) between the Gray Area and the meadowland at the summit.[12] As one approaches the Mountain from the Gray Area, the pinon trees become taller and there are stands of ponderosa pine (*ńdischíí*), oak trees (*chéch'il*), and aspen (*t'iisbáí*, literally "grey cottonwood"). This bench consists of open pasturelike areas interspersed between woodland, with a steep wooded area rising directly in back of the bench, separating it from the summit of the pass. Navajo terms designate the following subareas, or neighborhoods:

1. Clump of Aspens (*t'iisbáí sikaad* or Cottonwood Pass)—originally meant a small grove of trees, but is now applied to a wide meadow area at the foot of the pass.
2. Oak Springs (*chéch'il yató*)—a spring about one mile from Cottonwood Pass near summer chapter house.
3. Spruce Springs (*ch'ó yató*)—a spring one mile northwest of Oak Springs; the term designates the spring and surrounding area.
4. Water Running Down (*tó dadeezlíní*)—a small creek running into a steep wash about one-half mile from Spruce Springs; it also designates the surrounding homesite area.

Water is plentiful; at least ten springs, improved through the Shallow Wells Program, provide water for home use and for livestock; numerous unimproved springs and small streams can be used to water livestock. Most families plant fields in the open pasturelike areas near their summer residence sites. These fields are not irrigated, since melting spring snows and summer rainfall afford adequate moisture.

THE TOP

The summit of the mountain range is referred to as the Top (*bigháá*). The area (elevation 9,000 to 9,365 feet) consists of flat meadows, filled with shallow lakes in the summer, and surrounded by wooded areas. A large meadow at the pass summit and the area two miles north are inhabited in summer by Copper Canyon Navajos, with other sections being controlled by members of adjacent communities. Compared to the Mountain (that is, the bench area), on the Top there are more aspen (*t'iisbáí*), spruce (*ch'ó*) and douglas fir (also *ch'ó*) but fewer ponderosa pine (*ńdíshchíí'*). Several springs provide water, meadows provide excellent grazing land, and a few scattered fields are planted. Timber resources on top and in the bench area are used for houses and fence repair. Firewood from fallen or dead trees is collected near home sites for summer consumption and hauled to lower elevations for use during the winter.

IMPLICATIONS FOR SOCIAL STRUCTURE

The Copper Canyon area ecology has important implications for social structure, since the four zones provide Navajo residents with a map for interpreting their seasonal movements and for locating various clusters of kinsmen with respect to each other. Navajos see the zones as divided into two pairs: the Flats and the Gray Area, which are used for winter residences, and the Mountain and the Top, in which summer residences have been built. Place names within these areas—especially those on the Mountain and the Flats, the most populated summer and winter zones—designate either a neighborhood where several clusters of hoghans are found or the specific location of one extended-family camp. An individual uses the names of the zones and various place names in everyday conversation to communicate where he or she is going or lives, or where another Navajo's house or fields are located. The place name attached to a residence site is often used to refer to the head of the extended family that lives there, so labels like "Cross Hills Lady" (*'Asdzáán 'ałna'oos'ahí*) or "Yellow Hills Lady" (*'Asdzáán łitso dahask'idi*) designate not only a particular person but also where she lives. Some neighborhoods are composed mainly of genealogical kin (for example, a set of grown siblings, their spouses and married children) while others contain several extended families, who are either unrelated or connected by marriage and distant clan ties.[13] The complex relationship between neighborhood, kinship, and cooperation is an important aspect of this study.

Population and Population Movements

Seasonal movement follows the patterning of the washes and arroyos, so that the community is aligned on a northeast-southwest bias, rather than in the east-west direction of the main road that crosses the mountains. In general, those persons living near the trading post move to Cottonwood Pass, or on Top, at the southernmost limits of the Copper Canyon population. Those who live several miles north of the trading post move to the middle of the bench area near Oak Springs and the chapter house, while those near Mountain Rising and Crumbled House Mesa move to the north end of the Copper Canyon settlement near Spruce Springs and Water Running Down. Most Black House Mesa families remain on the Flats to take care of their fields and fruit trees. There are exceptions to these trends; for example, if a couple living near one set of relatives in winter gains access to a residence site near other relatives, the result is that their summer position in the community does not correlate with their winter one.

The major changes in settlement pattern since 1938 are due to an increase in population from four hundred or five hundred to the 1966 population of one thousand (750 resident and 250 nonresident individuals).[14] A decrease in the death rate, including infant mortality, and the increasing migration of young couples to wage jobs on other parts of the reservation and in western cities, means that the Copper Canyon population consists of a large number of school-age children (many of whom are in boarding schools during nine months of the year), some middle-aged couples, and a few old people. The old women (ages sixty to seventy-five years) outnumber the old men, as is true for other parts of the reservation (Hillery 1965).

As a consequence of population expansion, dwellings of adult offspring have been built in the same area as their parents, increasing the hoghan density near the trading post and in other areas. There has been a movement away from the area between the highway and the wash, with some families moving along the edge of the highway. More hoghans seem to have been built in the Gray Area, but habitation areas in the mountains have remained the same except for an increase in the number of dwellings. Some movement within small areas is to be expected, since Navajo destroy a house if someone has died inside, and either build a new hoghan at least fifty yards away or move near another set of relatives, abandoning the old site.

An increase in population density, movement toward highways, and increasing out-migration to reservation towns and off-reservation urban areas are trends pertaining to the Navajo Reservation as a whole. Shepardson and Hammond give information on population growth in Navajo Mountain (1964: 1039–40; 1970: 13) that fits with Levy's observation that land on the western part of the reservation has been filling up over the past two generations (1962: 790). This is also the case in Rimrock (Reynolds, Lamphere, and Cook 1967: 189). Increased density and fewer sheep may mean that seasonal movement is also on the decline (Levy 1962: 791), as it is in Copper Canyon. At the same time there has been a growth of population (in residence group settlement pattern) around Agency towns, as documented for Tuba City by Levy (1962: 796–98). On the whole, I would guess that these trends are less advanced for western sectors. For instance, population density in the west is still lower than for the reservation in general. Navajo Mountain has a density of 0.84 per square mile, as compared with 1.6 for the western reservation, and 3.2 for the entire reservation. Although I do not have comparative statistics, I suspect there is more out-migration in the eastern portion and possibly more rapid growth of central and eastern towns like Window Rock, Ft. Defiance, Shiprock, and Crownpoint. Movement toward highways may be more advanced in the east also. I have observed this tendency in both Rimrock and Copper Canyon but would suspect that communities like the Kaibito Plateau, Navajo Mountain, Shonto, and Pinon are less affected.

Economy

Like the economy of other Navajo communities, the Copper Canyon economy since the 1930s has changed from a pastoral-agricultural base to one primarily derived from wage work and welfare. Ties to the traditional economy remain, however, since most residence groups own sheep, cultivate fields, and take part in the transhumant pattern. The major events of the yearly cycle include sheepshearing, sheepdipping, plowing, and harvest. Railroad work and other wage jobs are a much less conspicuous part of the seasonal routine, even though they, along with welfare, are the greatest source of income.

Early trading post records from 1929 show a community income of $20,238 from sale of lambs, wool, woven rugs, and cattle (which for a population of four hundred would amount to $50 per capita). This does not include the value of agricultural and pastoral products consumed at home. By 1940, income was probably close to that estimated by Young (1961: 213) for the Navajo population as a whole: $81.89, per capita, per year.

From 1938 to 1966, the number of sheep owned by Copper Canyon families had declined from 3,972 to 2,228 head and the number of cattle from 246 to 184 head. There were only thirty-six herds in 1938, while in 1966 there were forty-three herds, and average size had declined from one hundred sheep to fifty. The overall decrease in livestock, in combination with increasing population, means that more families in the 1970s own no livestock at all. Fewer fields are planted, and though income from weaving has increased, fewer rugs are produced than in the past. Table 1.2 shows the 1966 community income for Copper Canyon, based on data from the Copper Canyon trader for sixty-five of the seventy-eight residence groups, or approximately six hundred individuals. The per capita income from all sources is $357.75.[15]

TABLE 1.2
Copper Canyon Community Income, 1966
(65 Residence Groups: 600 people)

Source	Number of Camps*	Income	
Livestock—2,228 sheep and goats	43	$ 10,930	
—185 cows		5,010	
Weaving	41	14,460	
Welfare	42	51,976	
Railroad work	23	40,738	
Other wage	27	68,039	
Tribal Works Project and Shallow Wells	—	23,500	
		$214,653.00	total income
		$ 357.75	per capita income

Note: The above estimate does not include various social welfare benefits from the Navajo Tribe and United States Government amounting to $124 per person per year (Young 1961: 228).

*Number of residence groups where members derive some income from this source.

The major characteristic of the economy is its mixed nature. Nuclear families may have one source of income, but the general tendency is for an extended family residence group to depend on a traditional source of income (livestock and/or weaving) in addition to one or more nontraditional sources (railroad work, other wage labor, or welfare). Members of almost every family participate in the Tribal Works Program and earn one hundred dollars for ten days of work, although families of chapter officers work more often than others.

Diversity in economic pursuits is made easier because of the seasonal variation in activities, as shown in Table 1.3. Aside from herding, which is a daily task, the major work of the traditional pastoral-agricultural economy (including the shearing of flocks and the clearing and plowing of fields) falls in the spring, during the months of March, April, and May, culminating in the move to the mountains in May or early June. Other important events in the yearly cycle are: the birth of lambs from January to April; sheepdipping and vaccinating in June and July; and harvest, which begins in August, when green corn and melons are eaten, and culminates in September or October, when the remaining corn and squash is removed.

Most men who work on the railroad are away during the spring season and also in the fall and early winter. This diminishes the number of males in the community, but extended family residence groups are large enough and herds and fields are small enough so that spring shearing, plowing, and planting can still be handled. Both ceremonial activities and Tribal Works Projects occur during slack periods in the pastoral-agricultural cycle. Increased ceremonial activity takes place during the summer season of Squaw Dances (the Enemyway Ceremony) and during the fall months when the Night Chant (*yeibichai*) and Mountain Chant (Fire Dance) are held. Both times are ritually dictated, which does not account for the flurry of five-day sings held in January, February, and March. Their clustering may be atypical and due both to the greater amount of sickness during winter months and to the lack of pressing economic pursuits. In sum, agricultural, pastoral, and ceremonial activities are spaced so as not to conflict with each other; some recently introduced wage activities (e.g., the Tribal Works Program and some railroad work) are fitted into the slack periods of the yearly economic cycle. Since traditional economic tasks afford some of the most readily available data on work which requires the joint effort of kinsmen—tasks such as sheepherding, shearing, and dipping, and the cultivation of fields—these will form an important part of my analysis of cooperation within and between residence groups.

The Copper Canyon economy is similar to that in other communities and reflects changes that are taking place on the whole reservation. The decline of the agricultural and pastoral economy was already advanced for the entire reservation in 1958, according to figures presented in the revised edition of *The Navaho* (Kluckhohn and Leighton 1962: 60). The transition to a wage and welfare-dominated economy is mentioned even for western Navajo communities such as Shonto in the 1950s (Adams 1971), due to the work available on railroads. This source of wage income has declined, and Aberle suggests that figures on the economy for the present period, if available,

> ... would show a rise in terms of on-reservation wagework, because of ONEO funds (about $11,500,000 in 1968), Tribal public works programs, Federal building programs, and increase in the number of school employees. Welfare would also rise. The percentage derived from farming and herding would fall. Yet under present circumstances, ... many Navajos will not give up and dare not give up their farming and herding, although on a dollar accounting basis it is relatively trivial. Instead, the characteristic pattern for Navajo families is the necessity to depend on a multiplicity of income sources, no one of which yields a stable and predictable income. (1969: 236)

More than their elders, the younger generation, after leaving school, want permanent wage jobs and are willing to migrate from their local communities and take jobs such as those at the Fairchild plant in Shiprock or the General Dynamics plant in Ft. Defiance, those aforementioned by Aberle, or those available off-reservation. Outmigration in Rimrock and Copper Canyon are compared in Chapter 4, suggesting that there may be more in eastern reservation communities than in off-reservation communities. Shepardson and Hammond's data on Navajo Mountain

TABLE 1.3
Copper Canyon Annual Cycle, 1965–66

Month	Climate	Moving	Livestock	Agriculture	Wage Work	Ceremonial Activities	Chapter Activities	School
Jan.	Snow		Lambs born			Increase in 5-day sings & peyote meetings (from Jan. 20)	Tribal Works Projects (Jan. 2–15; 17–30)	Christmas vacation (through Jan. 4)
Feb.	Snow		Lambs born			Increase in 5-day sings & peyote meetings	Tribal Works Projects (Feb. 2–18)	
March	Winds		Lambs born	Burn weeds, clear ditches on the Flats	Railroad (beginning March 15)	Increase in 5-day sings & peyote meetings (to March 20)	Tribal Works Projects (March 21–31)	
April	Last snow: April 20		Lambs born; shearing begins April 20	Irrigate fields on the Flats (April 1–20); plow 2 weeks later (beginning April 10)	Railroad			Easter vacation (April 2–9)
May	Dry	Move to the Mountain (from May 20)	Shearing through May 10; castrate lambs May 1–15 (after shearing)	Plow (through May 20; plow fields on the Mountain (May 1–31)	Railroad			

Month								
June	Dry	Move to the Mountain (to June 6)	Dipping (June 7, 8, & 9)	Weed the fields	Railroad	Squaw Dances (begin June 15)		School out (June 3)
July	Rain		Vaccinating		Railroad (to July 15)	Squaw Dances	Shallow Wells (July 3–11)	
Aug.	Rain			Begin corn eating (Aug. 15)		Squaw Dances	Shallow Wells (Aug. 16–30)	School starts (Aug. 28)
Sept.	Dry; first frost, Sept. 15	Move to the Flats		Corn eating (through Sept. 1); begin harvest (Sept. 15); piñons begin (Sept. 28)		Squaw Dances through Sept. 30; yeibichai & Fire Dances (begin Sept. 20)	Shallow Wells (begin Sept. 29)	
Oct.	Dry; first snow, Oct. 18	Move to the Flats		Harvest (through Oct. 12); piñons	Railroad	Yeibichai & Fire Dances	Shallow Wells (through Oct. 8)	
Nov.	Snow			Piñons (through Nov. 10)	Railroad	Yeibichai & Fire Dances (through Nov. 27)	Shallow Wells (Nov. 3–18)	
Dec.	Snow				Railroad			Christmas vacation (begins Dec. 17)

NOTE: Rug weaving is done continuously throughout the twelve months.
The first day of the month, welfare checks are distributed; the first week of the month, commodities are distributed.

'(1964; 1970) suggest that western communities might be more conservative in this matter also.

Religious Activities

In 1966, there were three religious orientations among Copper Canyon residents.

TRADITIONAL CEREMONIES

Members of forty-one of seventy-eight residence groups adhered to traditional religious beliefs and attend Navajo curing ceremonies. An illness is first diagnosed by a diviner (usually a hand trembler) who discovers what is making the patient sick and prescribes the correct ceremony as a cure (Kluckhohn and Wyman 1940). Ceremonies include Blessing Way and thirty-eight different chants (hatáál or "sings"), many of which have two-night, five-night, and nine-night forms. A chant is performed by a "singer" (hataałii) who has learned the requisite songs, ritual, and medicines. The choice of a particular practitioner depends on such factors as the diagnosis of the diviner, the singer's knowledge of the requisite "sing," his proximity to the requesting residence group, and his reputation as a successful curer. Three practicing singers and one Blessing Way curer live in Copper Canyon; several men and women practice "hand-trembling" (ńdilnííh) as a form of divination. Many families go outside Copper Canyon to get an appropriate singer, although often this only means traveling to one of the adjacent areas. Most "traditional" men and women drink, and drunkenness has increasingly become associated with native ceremonies, leading to inaccuracies in the 'ritual and quarrels among participants. As previously mentioned, members of the other two religious factions (many of whom are converted drunks) condemn the "traditionals" for this behavior.

THE PEYOTE CULT

The second orientation is the peyote cult or the Native American Church, which drew adherents from twenty-three of the seventy-eight residence groups. Peyotists do not see any conflict between their beliefs and either the Christian or the Navajo religion. They often participate in sings or hold them for family members, and some attend the Latter-day Saints services conducted by two young resident LDS elders. (Other LDS participants are drawn from the traditional population.)

Nonmembers say that taking peyote is just like being drunk. Peyotists are aware of such gossip and are sensitive to criticism. Between 1940 and 1967, the use of peyote on the reservation was illegal. In the mid-1960s, the Navajo police no longer disrupted meetings, but members of the Native American Church were still somewhat secretive about their activities (Aberle 1966). There are important similarities between peyotism and traditional Navajo religion. The primary aim of both is curing, or the restoration of a balanced state of affairs, and the role of the peyote road man is parallel to that of the singer. Particular to peyotism is a transcendent view of the supernatural (God) and the notion of membership in an organization (the Native American Church) (Aberle 1966: 195–98).

THE PENTECOSTAL CHURCH

Members of the local Pentecostal church make up the third religious faction in the community. The church (located about one-half mile from the trading post) was established in the early 1960s and is under the leadership of a young Navajo man who married a woman from Copper Canyon. Membership has increased to include individuals from thirteen residence groups. The Wednesday and Saturday night meetings consist of praying, hymn singing, testimonials, and preaching. Music is provided by an electric guitar, drums, piano, and tambourine. Several female members dance during hymn singing and speak in tongues while praying. The Pentecostal movement presents an interesting contrast with the traditional and peyote orientations. Pentecostals stress a rejection of the traditional Navajo religion and emphasize the process of conversion. Although there is an order of worship, there is no ritual; the minister, rather than performing a set of prescribed actions, preaches and leads the group in singing and prayer. There are some elements of curing and restoring "pleasant conditions" (*hózhóníí*), but the emphasis of meetings is on communication with the supernatural and salvation. Pentecostals are condemned by traditionals and peyotists for their refusal to participate in Navajo ceremonies, to help in preparatory activities, and to contribute food.

Membership in religious factions tends to follow kinship lines. Residents of the same camp usually have the same religious orientation, although there are a few cases of traditional/Peyotist or traditional/Pentecostal residence groups. There are no cases of Peyotist/Pentecostal households in the same residence group. It is difficult to determine whether antagonism and gossip between factions is due to previous distance between families, or whether antagonism concerning religious beliefs and practices has created distance. I suspect both factors are at work and are mutually reinforcing. Religion, in the form of frequent Pentecostal meetings, peyote meetings, and traditional ceremonies, provides the basis for much of the social interaction at Copper Canyon involving a large number of Navajos. Peyote meetings and traditional sings, unlike Pentecostal meetings, require a considerable amount of nonritual activities, such as the preparation of food, all of which are organized on the basis of kin ties. Thus patterns of aid that surround the ceremonies of these two religious orientations will provide crucial data for the analysis of cooperation in later chapters.

Political Organization

In the traditional Navajo political system, which functioned before the period of Navajo captivity at Fort Sumner (1864–68), there was no centralized authority. The tribe never convened as a group but was bound together by common language, customs, and territory (Shepardson 1963: 47).

Two local leadership roles were that of the *naat'áani* ("one who talks well," or peace leader) and the *naatíni* (war or raid leader). The *naat'áani* often addressed his relatives and neighbors at ceremonies, offering solutions to specific problems or admonishing the people to live peacefully and work hard. He sometimes acted as a mediator in disputes and may have organized farming activities (Hill 1940: 26). Despite ethnographic references to the elective nature of the role, the *naat'áani's* leadership was undoubtedly based on group consensus rather than an actual democratic election. His authority was situational and noncoercive, extending informally to several residence groups united by ties of kinship and marriage, and operating according to the principles outlined in the following chapter.

The war leader (*naatíni*) organized raids against non-Navajo groups in order to acquire plunder or retaliate for previous raids. He knew the appropriate sings which could protect the warriors from harm (Hill 1936). His leadership was also situational but more prescribed by ritual than that of the *naat'áani* whose role stressed cooperative and dispute-settling functions.

Traditional authority roles have been replaced by the organization of the Navajo Tribe into a corporate body, the formation of the Navajo Tribal Council to administer tribal affairs, and the chapter system to deal with local problems. Tribal police and courts provide a method of enforcing decisions and sanctioning behavior. Elections are held every four years for tribal chairman, vice-chairman, and delegates to the council from each of the eighteen districts of the reservation. (The history of modern tribal government has been described by both Shepardson 1963, and Aberle 1966.)

Close parallels exist between present-day Navajo leaders (both the tribal chairman and councilmen and local chapter officers) and the role of *naat'áani*. These include emphasis on such qualities as an exemplary character, oratorical ability, personal magnetism, and proven ability in practical matters, all attributes of the *naat'áani* role (Hill 1940: 25). On the local chapter level close contact is maintained between officers (the president, vice-president, and secretary), their relatives, and fellow community members; chapter officers often make speeches at weddings and other ceremonies and act as mediators in disputes, both functions of the *naat'áani*. Although officers are elected, their authority is situational, consensus-based, and nondirective. Outwardly, these roles are defined in terms of the town-meeting official; however, in practice they incorporate important aspects of the traditional kin-based authority system of which the *naat'áani* role was a part.

Some local chapters have been centers of factional disputes similar to those that paralyzed the Tribal Council (Shepardson 1971). Factions have tended to polarize around religious orientations such as peyotists, Christians, and traditionals. Factionalism has been avoided at Copper Canyon, where members of the three religious groups are brought together in the chapter organization; chapter politics has not been monopolized by any one group but has represented a balance of all three. Disputes occasionally have occurred in meetings, and sides have been taken, sometimes along religious lines. However, polarization has not been great enough to block action permanently on an issue. The balance of the three groups can be seen in the list of chapter officers and committee members in Table 1.4. It may appear that the chapter organization was in the hands of the traditionals, since the three most

TABLE 1.4
Chapter Officers and Committee Members at Copper Canyon

Officer	Religious Affiliation
Chapter President	Traditional
Vice-president	Traditional
Secretary	Traditional (held by peyotist until December 1965)
Treasurers	Two Pentecostals
Community Development Aide	Peyotist (previous chapter Secretary)
Recreation Committee	Three peyotists, in addition to the two Pentecostal treasurers (three additional members elected later, including the chapter president's son and daughter and one other traditional)

important officers came from this group. This would underestimate, however, the importance of the treasurers, the ex-chapter secretary, and committee members, who represented the other two groups. In addition, the number of traditionals is not out of proportion to their number in the community as a whole.

The most active members of the chapter came from five clusters of kin (the relatives of the chapter president, vice-president, Community Development Aide, and two treasurers). New positions were often filled with members of these kin groups. For instance, the bus driver and two female aids elected to assist with the new preschool were relatives of chapter officers, as were two of the new members of the recreation committee.

It is important to stress the limited nature of the political organization, both traditionally and at present. With the dispersed settlement pattern, most activities and decision making take place in domestic groups (i.e., the household and residence group). Before 1868, larger gatherings consisted of ceremonials and raiding parties, both of which were situational and provided limited areas of action for the *naat'áani* and *naatini*. The contemporary chapter organization is also limited; even if its effectiveness were impaired by disputes between individuals of different kin groups or religious orientations, daily life would go on as usual. In fact, most disputes are between members of residence groups and are not characterized by alignments within the whole community. Although the chapter organization has helped create the notion of "community" and increased interaction among members of an area, it has not centralized Navajo life or superseded the importance of domestic and genealogical relatives or clan affiliations. Rather the kin ideology of cooperation and authority, and kinship behavior, have affected the chapter organization and the definition of chapter officer roles.

This general introduction to the Copper Canyon community indicates the impact of Anglo-American institutions on the economic, religious, and political life of these Navajos. The changes that have come to Copper Canyon since 1940 can be briefly summarized. The population has doubled, but twenty-five percent of that population was, in 1966, living outside Copper Canyon. The net increase in population density within the same land base has meant that hoghan clusters in the summer areas are more closely crowded together, although fewer families are moving up to the Mountain during the summer. The winter residence areas are also more crowded, and more hoghans and cabins have been built closer to the roads. Since the stock reduction program, there has been a decline in the importance of sheepherding. Flocks are small and provide only a fragment of community income. Agriculture has declined, and the community has become increasingly dependent on income from sporadic wage work and various forms of welfare. Education in Anglo-controlled schools has been accepted, and almost all children under sixteen years of age attend a local county day school or a BIA boarding school.

Christianity has influenced the community both through Pentecostal and Latter-day Saints' missionary activities and through peyotism, which combines elements of native North American Indian religions with those of the Christian faith. Democratic elections and a town-meeting form of government have been adopted in local politics, even though traditional conceptions of authority have been retained. The chapter organization has become a center of many government and tribal programs and has increased the integration of the Copper Canyon area as a community.

Similar changes are apparent throughout the reservation as a whole. Even communities in the western region have shown an increase in population (Shepardson and Hammond 1970: 13) and a transformation to a wage economy, though perhaps with less out-migration (Adams 1971: 78). Schooling, missionary activity, and chapter-centered programs have increased. Access to cars and pickup trucks has meant that even the more traditional areas of the reservation are becoming less and less isolated. Thus the differences between western and eastern reservation communities are of degree, yet important to consider in the comparing data from different communities studied at different points in time.

Despite the changes that have taken place in the last three decades in Copper Canyon, residents are still traditional in many ways. Navajo is the main language of every household; pastoral and agricultural activities are still important; and Navajo religion, along with belief in ghosts and witches, flourishes. Kinship continues to play a crucial role in the organization of daily tasks even in the midst of material modernity, making a study of kinship and cooperation relevant to an understanding of present-day Navajo society.

Part II

CULTURAL
SYSTEM

Chapter 2

Cooperation and
Autonomy Concepts

~~~~~~

The title of this book, "To Run After Them," is a paraphrase of Navajo terms for helping or giving aid, as in the sentence, "I'll help him," or literally translated, "I'll run after him." The terminology of cooperation is an important aspect of the Navajo cultural system that, along with Navajo concepts of autonomy, has crucial significance for an analysis of economic and ritual activities. This chapter draws on other anthropological studies and on conversations with Copper Canyon residents to offer an interpretation of Navajo ideas about cooperative and uncooperative behavior,[1] autonomy, and authority relations. My observer's model of the cultural system of cooperation is partly based on the notion of "generalized reciprocity" used by Sahlins in the analysis of exchange systems (1965). This anthropological construct allows me to elucidate the general properties of the Navajo cultural system as it relates to cooperation and to suggest comparisons with other tribal and hunter-gatherer societies, particularly in native North America.

The general discussion of Navajo concepts of cooperation and autonomy will be followed by a section stating the ways in which these concepts are communicated during public occasions and in face-to-face interaction situations. Finally, I will illustrate, using case material from Copper Canyon, how gossip and witchcraft suspicion perpetuate and reinforce the definitions of cooperative and uncooperative behavior.

Concepts of Cooperation

Navajo dictionaries and published analyses of values and ethics, in addition to data from Copper Canyon on actual conversations, indicate that Navajos discuss cooperative behavior in terms of a generalized conception of "help" or "aid." This is expressed by using a form of the verb stem -*ghoł* (to run), which is used in phrases like '*adeeshghoł* (I'll run out of sight). To indicate "helping," Navajos use the phrase *bíká adeeshghoł* (I'll help him, or I'll run after him). Similarly, *shíká 'anájah* means "After me they are running along," or "They are helping me" (Young and Morgan 1943: 84, part 1).

Navajos feel strongly that helping is good, and they live under a diffuse moral obligation to give aid when requested or when it appears to be needed. Another aspect of helping is the importance placed on taking good care of relatives and possessions. This is expressed by the stem -yaał which means "to be aware or alert," or "to take care of," as in baa 'aháshyą́ (Young and Morgan 1943: 232, part 1). Thus one Navajo might criticize another by stating doo hózhǫ́ dibé yaa 'ahályą́da, "He doesn't take very good care of the sheep" (Kluckhohn 1956b: 145), or doo bischíinii yaa 'ahályą́da, "He doesn't take very good care of his parents." In his analysis of Navajo ethics, Ladd has listed eight positive prescriptions that the Navajo say should be followed, several of which deal with "helping" or "taking care of." He has stated these as follows:

1. Take care of your possessions.
2. You ought to take good care of your children.
3. Children should take care of their parents.
4. In general, people ought to help the aged.
5. One ought to help a person who is in dire need.
6. There are other people whom it is particularly important to help; one's wife and her family.
7. In general, you ought to help anybody who needs it or requests it. (Ladd 1957: 253–55)

Although Ladd does not provide the Navajo translations for these statements, they can all be rendered in the native language using forms of "helping" or "running after" and "taking care of."

It is important to emphasize the uncalculated nature of cooperation that is expressed in these native conceptions. A Navajo does not formulate his expectations in specific terms so that he aids a particular person one day with the hope of returned aid at a specific time in the future. Rather, a Navajo is generally obligated to fill the requests made of him, and he expects that he will be able to find someone to fill his own requests. The Navajo notion of cooperation is generalized and diffuse; it is not specific to particular types of situations or to particular kin roles. The specific individual to be asked for aid or the kind of task for which help is expected are both left unspecified.

In contrast to the generalized positive obligation to help and take care of others (i.e., to be cooperative), a number of more specific negative prescriptions indicate that uncooperative behavior is undesirable. Most Navajo behavior prescriptions are negative in form (Ladd 1957: 300–302), and many fit the sentence frames, "One does not do X" or "X is not done" (i.e., "Do not do X"). Examples are: "One does not commit adultery" (doo 'azhdiléeh da); "One does not beat his wife" (doo 'ajiizą́ą́ da); "One does not steal" (doo 'izhni'į́įda); "Lies are not told" (doo hoyochi 'íida); and "Man is not killed" (diné doo biłhéeda) (Haile 1943: 85).

Data from interviews with informants and conversations between Copper Canyon residents indicate that behavior prescriptions that describe uncooperativeness use the Navajo terms for "stingy," "mean," "mad," "jealous," and "lazy." They can be stated as follows:

1. One is not stingy   *doo jichį̱'da*
2. One is not mean   *doo bá' hachį̱'da*
3. One is not mad   *doo bá' hojiłchįįda*
4. One is not envious or jealous   *doo 'ookch'įįda*
  of someone's possessions[2]
5. One is not sexually jealous   *doo le' nizin da*
6. One is not lazy   *doo 'oł hóghéé'da*

I suggest that these statements, taken together, describe the antisocial, uncooperative Navajo, one who is not "helping" or "taking care" of others. Similar notions of uncooperative, "un-Navajo" behavior are part of Navajo beliefs concerning witchcraft. The various kinds of witchcraft have been discussed in detail by Kluckhohn (1944; reprint 1967). The beliefs most relevant to defining uncooperative behavior are those concerning "witchcraft" (*'ańt'į̱*) as practiced by "witches" (*'ádańt'į̱*) and "werewolves" (*yeenaaldloozhii*). Both "witches" and "werewolves" are "inverted" Navajos, or creatures who embody all the characteristics opposite to the cooperative, social individual. Werewolves are said to dress in wolf or coyote skins. They become animal rather than human and travel about at night (hence the name *yeenaaldloozhii*, meaning "one who goes around"). They are night creatures, rather than day creatures like ordinary humans. Werewolves are said to participate in sings in "witchery hoghan" (*'ańt'į̱ bahoghan*)—the opposite of a normal hoghan. They chant the songs from Navajo ceremonials in reverse, feed on corpses, and rob the graves of the dead.[3] "Witches" or "werewolves" practice *bee'iińzįįd* (sorcery). They are believed to cause sickness by taking a portion of a person's clothing or body offal (hair, nails, feces, urine, or body dirt) and chanting over it so that the victim will become ill (Kluckhohn 1944: 31–33; reprint 1967). Instead of practicing curing and concentrating on pleasant conditions (*hózhóníí*), witches and werewolves are concerned with death and ugly conditions (*hóchǫ́ǫ́nii*). Kluckhohn analyzes witchcraft beliefs in terms of their general social and psychological functions rather than in terms of their relation to other cultural concepts. Consequently, the connection between witchcraft and concepts of uncooperative behavior became clear to me only during conversations with members of the Cooper Canyon community. When asked why some Navajos are *yeenaaldloozhii* and would want to practice witchcraft or sorcery, one Copper Canyon man replied:

Maybe that man over there has a big truck and lots of sheep and a good family. Maybe this other fellow over here is jealous (*'ookch'į̱*) of him, so he gets into a skin and goes around at night. Navajos go to the toilet outside and the *yeenaaldloozhii* can get a little piece of it and put it in a grave and the ghost (*ch'į̱dii*) will start working on that man and make him sick.

A young girl gave a similar explanation of her own illness. Her recent headaches and dizziness were diagnosed by a hand trembler[4] as being caused by *bee'iińzįįd*. She explained this sorcery as "somebody wanting to make you sick or wish you were dead," which can be expressed in the Navajo phrase *doo 'akot'éego ntsékees* ("Not all-right, it-being, he is thinking," or "He is wishing harmful or unpleasant conditions").

Witchcraft is associated not only with jealousy and malevolent thoughts directed against the victim but also with "meanness." When visiting one camp, I was told by a young girl riding in the car with me that the wife of the household "looked real mean at us." She maintained that we should be careful or we might get "witch powder" on us. Someone who is designated "mean" or "jealous" on the basis of quarrels or refusal of aid is also likely to be suspected of "thinking against someone" or engaging in witchcraft and sorcery, presumably to enhance his own well-being at the expense of others.

It is important to note that witchcraft is an explanation for illness and is thus part of a post hoc system of causation. As Evans-Pritchard (1937, Chap. 4) has pointed out, witchcraft explains unfortunate events, rather than actual malevolent behavior, which may not have occurred at all but are presumed to have occurred. From the observer's point of view, witchcraft is not practiced by individuals in order to cause illness at some future time. Rather the illness or unfortunate event occurs first and then is explained in terms of presumed witchcraft practiced at some time in the past. The purpose of witchcraft suspicion among the Navajo is not to punish any one individual but to explain the illness and prescribe the correct ceremonial cure which will counteract it. Thus, a living individual need not be accused; a dead relative may be seen as the cause, or no specific person need be named. When a living individual *is* suspected of witchcraft practices, it is not because he has actually engaged in them. Rather, the whispered suspicion that "X is a witch" is offered as an explanation for his "mean" or uncooperative behavior displayed in various social contexts, whether or not his alleged witchcraft is used as an explanation of a particular illness. There are two aspects here: the folk explanation of an illness in terms of witchcraft beliefs and the explanation of antisocial behavior in terms of the same beliefs. The two need not be connected in any one instance; illness can be explained by witchcraft without a specific accusation, and an individual can be labeled a "witch" or "werewolf" in contexts where there is no illness to be explained. On the other hand, as Copper Canyon case material will show, both aspects may be present in a particular incident.

In sum, Navajo conceptions of uncooperative behavior are embodied in negative prescriptions that state that "mean," "jealous," "stingy," and "mad" behavior are disapproved. These same characteristics are part of the cultural definition of "witch" or "werewolf." In other words, all the uncooperative, antisocial attributes of behavior are epitomized in this prototype of the "anti-Navajo": the witch and werewolf.

Concepts of Autonomy and Consensus

One aspect of the Navajo cultural system, which I have discussed, is the generalized obligation to cooperate along with Navajo conceptions of uncooperative behavior. Another dimension of the cultural system concerns concepts that involve (1) an individual's rights over the allocation of goods and services (which stress autonomy), and (2) mechanisms for recruiting joint action (which stress consensus).

The Navajo phrase which fuses both autonomy and consensus conceptions is *t'áá bee bóholníih*, which has been translated as "He is the boss" (Wall and Morgan 1958: 23), but is more accurately rendered by, "It's up to him to decide," "It is his business," or "It's his area of concern." The phrase describes the individual's "right to make a decision" (1) over the use and disposal of his possessions, and (2) over his own actions and the allocation of his time. (In Navajo the third person singular is used for he, she and it; in translating *bi, ba, bee,* I have often used "he," but it should be understood that "he or she" is a more exact translation.)

The use of *t'áá bee bóholníih* to indicate an individual's exclusive rights over possessions is congruent with the fact that most movable property (including livestock, jewelry, medicine pouches, cars, and wagons) is individually owned. Rights with regard to objects are expressed, not through a concept of ownership as in our phrase, "He owns it," but through such phrases as *da dibésh nee hóló̜?* (Do sheep exist by means of you?), or *da tsinabą̜ą̜shish síńtł'á̜'?* (Do you cause a wagon to be at your disposal?) (Haile 1947: 4 and 1954: 24). Ownership also is designated by noun-possession as in "his car" (*bichidí*), "his sheep" (*bidibé*), "his livestock or horse" (*bilį́į́'*).[5] Houses, farm land, and grazing areas are thought of in terms of "use rights" rather than ownership. One can say, "his house" (*baghan*), "his field" (*bidá'ák'eh*), or "his land" (*bikéyah*), but the meaning here is that an individual has the right to use the field and grazing area; if vacated, land can be claimed by other Navajos. Houses are at the disposal of the nuclear family, and in case of divorce the spouse with whose relatives the couple is living retains the right to stay there (Haile 1954: 10–13). Examples of "decision right" over possessions include the following instances taken from interviews with Copper Canyon informants. If someone comes to borrow a shovel or wagon that belongs to the mother of the household, a daughter might say *shimá bóholníih* ("my mother, it's her business), *'éí 'aa diní* ("you ask her"). If the mother is not at home, the individual making the request must return later, since no one except the owner has the right to dispose of the property or to allow others to use it. Likewise, a sheep in the residence group herd cannot be butchered or sold without the owner's consent.

With regard to the allocation of time and energy, an individual has "decision right" and is *t'áá bee bóholníih* over his own actions, insofar as they do not harm others. For instance, if a Navajo wishes to make a trip to the trading post or to visit a relative, the trip is his business and not that of others. Conversely, if an individual's services are desired, he has the right to decide to contribute time and effort; there is no obligation to do so as a consequence of his particular kinship status or the specific situation. A Navajo prefers to wait for a demonstration of generosity (i.e., an offer for help in response to a generalized obligation once the needs of the situation are known), rather than make a more direct request (Aberle 1961: 162). This preserves the "decision-right" of the person being asked and also maintains a general atmosphere of cooperativeness.

Further evidence for the importance of decision-right over one's own actions is provided by Robert Young (1961: 508–11). Sentences such as "I made the horse trot" or "I made my wife sing," can be rendered in Navajo only by "I made the horse trot, even though he did not want to do so," and "Even though she did not want to do so, she sang when I told her to do so." Where the subject is an agent causing an action to be performed by another agent, the latter's will or desire must be considered. One does not make the horse trot because a horse has a will of his own. He may trot even though he does not want to do so, "but he still has the freedom of choice to refuse or decline to trot" (Young 1961: 510).

Similarly, Navajos are reluctant to report the opinions of others or account for their actions. In reply to my questions concerning a kinsman's views on a topic or on his actions in a particular situation, my informants often stated, "I don't know, ask him" (*doo shił bééhózin da, 'éí 'áájí bidiní*), indicating that speculation would infringe on the business or concerns of another.

The first two uses of the phrase *t'áá bee bóholníih* stress autonomy, or the individual as a free agent where his possessions and his own actions are concerned. This autonomy has been cited as a significant aspect of Navajo culture by Ladd (1957: 292) and Leighton and Kluckhohn (1947: 107), and its importance has consequences for the nature of collective action. In a society where the emphasis is on autonomy, joint action is gained by the consent of other free agents. The third use of *t'áá bee bóholníih* indicates this complementary aspect: decisions that imply consensus, the mechanism for mobilizing support from a number of individuals. The ways in which consensus is implied by *t'áá bee bóholníih* (It's up to *him* to decide) or *t'áá 'áájí bídaholníih* (It's up to *them* to decide) are illustrated by examples of marriage negotiations, ceremonial activities, and chapter meetings in Copper Canyon.

First marriages are traditionally arranged by the parents of the couple (Haile 1954: 13–15),[6] but second or third marriages are considered the business of the couple themselves. In such nonarranged marriages, there is no bride-price or traditional ceremony, and the marriage is initiated by the couple coming to live together (Aberle 1961: 123–28); however, as in first marriages, parental support and consent is an important factor. As one young Copper Canyon woman said, in discussing the possibility of a second marriage, "If somebody wants to get married with me, I'd say *shimá bóholníih* or *shizhé'é bóholníih*" (It's up to my mother or my father to decide). Making such a statement implies both the girl's own willingness and the necessity of asking her parents. If she had no interest in the marriage, she would discourage the suitor immediately.

The same elements of making a decision and then asking for consent by stating, "It's up to X to decide," are present in ceremonial cooperation. The following example was given by a Cooper Canyon informant: If a man is asked to be Stick Receiver for an Enemyway ceremony (also known as a Squaw Dance),[7] he might explain to the emissary making the request, *shi doo shóholníih da, 'áájí bídaholníih* (I am not the boss, those over there, it is up to them), referring to other relatives such as his mother, sister, and sister's husband. Another man might refer to his grown children as being *bídaholníih*, if they would be the main relatives to give cooperation during the ceremony. When these individuals agree, the man originally asked agrees to be Stick Receiver. The reference to his relatives already indicates that he is willing to accept the obligations of carrying out the ceremony, but he needs the consent and the assurance of aid from his closest kin. If he had not been willing to expend the time and effort on the ceremony, he would have immediately refused by giving an excuse.

The same pattern (of using the phrase *t'áá bee bóholníih* to indicate an individual whose consent is needed) is evident in chapter affairs. If someone comes to the chapter secretary asking to be placed on a list of workers for the next Tribal Works Project, the secretary may say, *Ńléí bóholníih 'áájí bidiní* (That one, he is the boss, ask him), referring to the chapter president. Upon asking the president, the individual will be given the same answer and sent back to the secretary or to the vice-president. This seems like the proverbial run-around, but if all three officers indicate agreement, the name will be added to the list. In other words, the individual will be sent back and forth until it is clear that none of the officers object and consensus is reached.

In addition to situations involving a small group of kinsmen or chapter officers, consensus is sometimes required of the whole community. In chapter meetings there is an ethic that "it is up to the people to decide." For instance, in speaking about proposals for a Tribal Works Project, a chapter member might say *Jó nihi nihidaholníth* (It is up to us to decide). This calls for consensus in the sense of unanimity, that is, supporting decisions on the part of a group of autonomous individuals.

The relation between autonomy and consensus, which is expressed in the three uses of *t'áá bee bóholníth*, implies authority relations that differ from those in Anglo-American society. Most social scientists conceptualize authority in terms of institutionalized power relationships. Parsons, for instance, first defines power as "the capacity to secure the performance of binding obligations" (1963: 237), and he then describes authority as the legitimate use of power in a system of social roles. "Authority, then, is the aspect of a status in a system of social organization ... by virtue of which the incumbent is put in a position legitimately to make decisions which are binding, not only on himself but on the collectivity as a whole and hence its other member units ... " (1963: 244).

Rather than such hierarchial authority where A's decision is binding on B or a group of B's, Navajo authority is egalitarian. A makes a decision and requests a similar one from B. If B's decision is congruent with A's, it obligates both to participate in joint activities. In contrast to the Parsonian definition, in Navajo society there are relatively few statuses and roles (the parent-child relationship, at times, is the major exception) where a single incumbent has the right to make decisions binding on others. "Bindingness" is, however, achieved through the consensus mechanism. If there is general agreement on an issue or course of action, all those in favor are obligated to "go along" with the joint decision. Those opposed may be persuaded to join also, but there is no notion of "majority rule." An individual who disagrees may always decide not to participate, and this preserves his right of autonomy even in the face of group pressure. As a result of this attempt to reach consensus, action is never taken if there are two opposing factions on a given issue or if near unanimity is lacking.

In sum, the phrase *t'áá bee bóholníth* combines Navajo emphasis on both autonomy and consensus, and it entails egalitarian ratter than hierarchial authority relations. Like the generalized obligation to cooperate, the phrase summarizes conceptions not specific to particular situations and to particular kin roles, but applicable to all adult Navajo in any setting.

Conclusions About Cooperation and Autonomy

The beginning of this chapter describes diffuse positive obligations to "help others" and "take care of others" and contrasts these with a number of negative prescriptions which define "uncooperative behavior." Such an undifferentiated system of obligations fits well with what Marshall Sahlins (1965: 149; 1968: 82), in analyzing varieties of exchange relationships, has called "generalized reciprocity." By this he means "putatively altruistic transactions of assistance given and if possible returned." Examples are "the pure gift," "sharing," "hospitality," "free gift," "help," and "generosity."

In further defining the concept, Sahlins says:

> At the extreme, say voluntary food-sharing among near kinsmen—or for its logical value, one might think of the suckling of children in this context—the expectation of direct material return is unseemly. At best, it is implicit. The material side of the transaction is repressed by the social and is typically left out of account. This is not to say that handing over things in such form, even to "loved ones" generates no counter-obligations. But the counter is not stipulated by time, quality, or quantity; the expectation of reciprocity is indefinite. (1965: 147)

In contrast, "balanced reciprocity" refers to direct exchange where there is a balance between goods given and goods received and the reciprocating transaction is made without delay.

> Balanced reciprocity is less "personal" than generalized reciprocity. From our own vantage point it is "more economic." The parties confront each other as distinct economic and social interests. The material side of the transaction is at least as critical as the social: there is more or less precise reckoning, as the things given must be covered within some short term. (Sahlins 1965: 148)

Sahlins (1965, 1968) and Service (1966) have used the concept of generalized reciprocity to describe kinship relations in both hunter-gatherer and tribal societies. Like generalized reciprocity, Navajo notions of cooperation provide diffuse obligations where the exact nature and timing of requests and counter-requests are not calculated and need not be exactly equivalent. In other words, Navajo ideology of kinship cooperation can be viewed as an instance of a widespread method of interpreting and regulating the exchange of goods and services and the organization of tasks among kinsmen.

Evidence of concepts of autonomy and consensus also has been found in other tribal and band groups, especially in North America. The importance placed on individual autonomy has been recognized in studies of American Indian personality (Lee 1959, Hallowell 1955), especially among Plains and Eastern Woodland groups. Political leadership in many of these same societies was weakly developed, and decision making was based on consensus among equals, often in the context of a council of peace chiefs (as among the Cheyenne, Hoebel 1960) or sachems (as among the Iroquois, Morgan 1851). In other words, the Navajo concepts outlined here are not an isolated instance of combining autonomy with consensus but exemplify a pattern found in other North American societies.

It would seem that an obligation to help others and not be mean, stingy, jealous, or in any way appear uncooperative would conflict with an emphasis on autonomy where individual decision-rights are highly prized. Choices based on an individual's own interests could be construed as legitimate from the point of view of autonomy but considered selfish from the point of view of generosity obligations. There are important ways, however, in which these two sets of concepts, one emphasizing an individual orientation and the other a collective orientation, are mutually compatible. First, the concepts of cooperativeness are highly generalized and this lack of specificity itself preserves individual options. Second, cooperativeness is mainly defined by what is uncooperative. By emphasizing undesirable behavior and by defining the limits on behavior negatively rather than positively, the individual is left with a great number of choices and hence more autonomy.

Furthermore, uses of the phrase t'áá bee bóholníih fuse both individual rights to decide and the necessity of having others agree on the same course of action where collective activity is concerned. This fusion of individual and group interests into the same native phrase leaves room for cooperation while preserving autonomy. The conceptions implicit in such Navajo phrases as shíká 'anájah (they are helping me) and t'áá bee bóholníih (it's up to X to decide) appear on the surface to be distinct and opposing, but in actuality are complementary. Each provides for the possible implementation of the other. In sum, a system which emphasizes generalized reciprocity can also stress individual autonomy, egalitarian authority relations, and consensus decision making. Generalized reciprocity *need not* be associated with an emphasis on autonomy and consensus, but the combination of these elements in the same cultural system has important consequences for the making of requests, as will be discussed in the next chapter.

Public Communication of Cooperation Concepts

Navajos in Copper Canyon continually seek to communicate and define the conceptions of cooperative and uncooperative behavior. This communication and specification take place both in public gatherings and in face-to-face interaction situations involving two Navajos or a small group.

Two important examples of public expression of cooperative concepts are (1) the Navajo girl's puberty ceremony where behavior prescriptions are specifically taught to the young girl, and (2) public speech making at large curing ceremonies, such as the Enemy Way, and nine-night versions of the Night Chant and the Mountain Chant, when cooperative behavior is enjoined and disruption condemned.

Kinaaldá is the name of the four-day ceremony given for a girl at the time of her first menstruation. It culminates in the making of a large cornmeal cake (*'ałkaan*) which is baked overnight in the ground, while songs from the Blessing Way are sung over the girl in the ceremonial hoghan. The following morning the cake is cut and distributed to those who sang and helped. During the four days, the girl must help with corn grinding and other preparations for the cake, and she must adhere to many behavioral prescriptions. Some of these relate to physical attributes, since it is believed that a girl's bones are soft and what she does during those four days will influence her health. The Navajo believe that obeying various prohibitions will provide the girl with positive physical attributes (such as good teeth, straight back, tall build, strong legs, and long hair) (Keith 1964: 32).[8]

Other prescriptions (both positive and negative) are related to cooperation and interpersonal relations, that is, fulfilling the role of a cooperative Navajo. Keith (1964: 32) provides a list of prescriptions, gleaned from interviews with adolescent girls, which I have translated into Navajo (Table 2.1). These are similar to statements by my own informants when describing what a girl is taught at her *kinaaldá*.

TABLE 2.1
Prescriptions for Cooperation and Interpersonal
Relations Among the Navajo (Keith 1964)

Keith's Prescriptions	Navajo Phrase	Translation
Work hard	*doo jił hóghéé da*	One is not lazy
Be generous	*doo 'aa jíchį̨ da*	One is not stingy with something
Don't be mean	*doo hánaha'chííh da*	One is not mean
Don't laugh too loud	*diné (sániida) doo baazhodloh da* (Haile 1954: 32)	One does not laugh about men (and women)
Be helpful	*'aká 'añjilgho'*	One helps someone
Be happy and cheerful	*'ił hózhǫ́ dooleeł*	One will be happy
Be gentle with children	*'áłchíní baa hojílyą́*	One takes care of children
Be dependable	*hojoolíí'*	That someone might depend on someone
Be respectful	*'ách'į̨' hasti'*	Respectability
Be kind	*baa jijoobaah*	One is kind to him

The first four of Keith's prescriptions are negative in form and concern the undesirability of laziness, stinginess, meanness, and ridicule. The remaining six are positive statements which encourage the girl to be helpful and take care of others. These statements are explicitly taught to the *kinaaldá* girl by the women around her, particularly her mother, maternal grandmother, and mother's sisters. Other older women who are present may also lecture the girl on these topics. It is believed that if the young Navajo girl follows these prescriptions during the ceremony, she will have the appropriate social attributes for the rest of her life. As Keith states, "...the girls do not actually learn much that is new. Rather, the *kinaaldá* is a summary, or a way of giving meaning to skills and values learned gradually in childhood. The kind of behavior that will be most important to her as an adult is reviewed in a short space of time; and general rules such as 'Be kind and helpful' are formulated" (1964: 35). In sum, notions of cooperative and uncooperative behavior are communicated, and the ideal of the sociable Navajo is explicitly defined both to the pubescent girl and to those attending the ceremony.

Similar communication is part of the speeches made during the last night of the Mountain Chant (Fire Dance) and the Night Chant (*Yeibichai*). Speeches are also given each night of an Enemyway (Squaw Dance) after the bonfire has been lighted and before dancing begins (Jacobson 1964: 10). The speaker is usually a male relative of the patient, the patient himself, or a chapter officer or Tribal Councilman.[9] Examples taken from the literature and speeches I heard at Copper Canyon ceremonies all follow a common pattern. The speaker usually takes this opportunity to thank everyone for food, for helping with the cooking, and for other contributions; or he may enjoin everyone to "help each other" and "take care of yourselves." There is emphasis on seeing that everything "goes well" and that the ceremony continues smoothly. *Nizhónígo*, which means "pleasant-conditions-being" or "may everything be pleasant," and *yá'át'ééhgo*, meaning "it-is-good-being" or "may everything be good," are the most frequently used phrases which stress the importance of this atmosphere of cooperativeness. Negatively valued behavior is mentioned as undesirable. For example, the speaker may tell those assembled "not to drink" and "not to fight each other" (e.g., the speech recorded in Harmon 1964: 20–26). These public speeches are the most explicit statements of the importance of cooperation where joint activities are carried out with a minimum of disruption and a maximum of mutual aid.

Private Communication of Cooperation Concepts Through Gossip

More frequent than public statements are the communication and definition of Navajo concepts through face-to-face interaction where judgments are made about uncooperative behavior. During visits, when giving rides, while engaged in conversations at the trading post or chapter house, or while participating in a ritual or economic activity, Copper Canyon Navajos communicate the latest news, including events at their own residence group or details about the lives of other Navajos that they have recently heard. Often this news or gossip (*'aseezį́*) deals with troubles (such as an illness, accident, or death) or with disputes. Although gossip may be sympathetic, the speaker often emphasizes negative aspects and communicates his disapproval of any conflict behavior involved.[10] The negative judgment may be made as an explicit statement where a norm describing uncooperative behavior of the form "One is not X" is transformed into a positive statement that "He or she is X" and is attributed to a participant in the incident. Following are some of the most common statements of this kind:

1. He is stingy (about it)	*baa nichį́'*
2. He is mean	*'ayóo bá hachį́'*
3. He is mad	*báhóóchįįd; hashké*
4. He is sexually jealous	*łé' nizin*
5. He is jealous (of someone's possessions)	*'oołch'įį'*
6. He is lazy	*bił hóghéé'*

An additional concept sometimes used to describe undesirable behavior is that of "craziness," expressed by two different phrases: *doo 'áhályá da* and *t'óó diigis*. One Copper Canyon informant explained the differences between the two concepts in the following way: *T'óó diigis* means "You don't know what you are doing, like if you are doing something and you are all shaky; you can't even hold things together." *Doo 'áhályá da* means "half out of his mind." From Kaplan and Johnson's analysis of Navajo psychopathology it is evident that these phrases may be used to describe various forms of mental illness (schizophrenia, epilepsy, the "fits" of violence and "spells" of being out of control associated with moth craziness, ghost sickness, and crazy violence) (1964: 210–11). In Copper Canyon the two terms also are applied to drunks, someone joking at an incorrect time, or other instances of inappropriate behavior. If someone participates in a dispute, becomes angry, and refuses to cooperate, a Navajo, in relating the incident, might say, "He is crazy," thereby labeling the behavior undesirable.

Other phrases used to register the speaker's disapproval are:

1. *doo ya'ashǫ́ǫ́da*:	"I don't like it" or "It's bad"
2. *t'óó baa'ih*:	"It's ugly" or "It's in poor taste"
3. *bąąh yishį*:	"I'm against it"
4. *doo shił 'aaniida*:	"It's not true with me"
5. *doo yá'át'ééh da*:	"It's not good" (more often used to disapprove of objects or a plan of action, than to object to an individual's behavior)

All of the above phrases are not applied to a particular individual at one time. Rather, when A relates to B an incident involving C, he often ends the description with the judgmental statement appropriate to the behavior concerned: "He's just too mean," if there has been an argument; "He's just jealous, I guess," if there are difficulties between a husband and wife; or "He's too stingy," if someone has failed to contribute money or food for a ceremony. If the individual relating a dispute is directly involved, he may make a general statement of his own position by saying, "I don't like it" or "It's too bad" (i.e., the behavior is in poor taste). In addition to situations where behavior is discussed among Navajos, these phrases were used when I posed questions to my informants. "Maybe he's jealous" or, "He's just mad, I guess" were given as explanations of an individual's behavior.

It is important to emphasize that statements that a Navajo is mean, jealous, crazy, or stingy, are rarely face-to-face accusations. They are part of a direct confrontation *only* at the peak of an angry argument between close kin (e.g., parents and children, husband and wife). For instance, the accusation "you're crazy" indicates both that the misdemeanor is a very serious one and that the speaker is directly condemning the behavior of the accused. More typically these statements are used in private to relatives when news is being communicated, and they are formulated as declarative sentences and statements of fact rather than of judgment.

During my first months in Copper Canyon I thought that many of these phrases described individual personality traits. Later I discovered that their use was situational and determined by the relationship between the speaker and the individual to whom he referred rather than to any inherent, stable personality characteristics. In other words, the attribution of meanness, stinginess, or jealousy either (1) points to X's momentary relation with Y and the recent events that had altered a congenial relationship, or (2) indicates the kinship distance between X and Y, where X is more likely to ascribe a negative characteristic to a distant kinsman or nonkinsman than to a parent, child, sibling, or grandchild. Copper Canyon Navajos seem particularly concerned with using terms for emotional states or behavior characteristics to define disapproved or approved behavior, rather than for describing individual personalities or inner feelings.

Judgments about uncooperative or antisocial behavior are often conveyed more indirectly than by using these key words and phrases. At times, none of the phrases I have mentioned are used, and the speaker simply relates an incident without comment; however, the fact that he or she has taken it upon himself or herself to describe a set of events surrounded by conflict and disruption indicates disapproval. Whether or not judgmental phrases are used, disapproval can be subtly suggested through intonation, gesture, and other paralinguistic devices.

Gossip may be sympathetic, but more often it highlights disruption and conveys pejorative judgments about individuals. Engaging in these negative aspects of gossip is undesirable, according to Navajo belief, and is labeled as "talking against someone." The injunction "Don't talk against someone" is often included in a list of Navajo prohibitions. The clearly stated norm not to indulge in derogatory gossip does not, however, explain why Navajos continually break this rule and talk about others with the view of judging their behavior in a negative fashion.

Some suggestive answers can be given by viewing gossip as information management. Drawing on aspects of the exchange between Gluckman (1963, 1968) and Paine (1967) on the analysis of gossip,[11] I find it useful to see Navajo gossip as forwarding an individual's self-interest through impression management with the unintended consequence that Navajo concepts of cooperative behavior are defined and become part of a widely shared cultural system.

Paine's interpretation of the flow and control of information through gossip is readily applicable to the Navajo. Since they live in a dispersed settlement pattern, individuals in one residence group know little about what is happening in other residence groups, particularly those of nonkinsmen. Gossip, then, is an important method of transmitting what is going on. However, the transmitter of gossip may not, in fact, know many of the details of the incident he is reporting, or if he was immediately involved he may only present those details favorable to his own position. It is this latter type of "impression management," in an effort to further self-interest, which Paine stresses. If A is reporting to B his dispute with C, it is in his interest to demonstrate that C was at fault and guilty of mean, jealous, or crazy behavior.

However, in an egalitarian society like the Navajo, with the stress on harmonious social relationships, an individual gains little long-run advantage in boosting his reputation or status at the expense of others.[12] It is important to see that in addition to the component of self-interest which Paine emphasizes, the unintended consequence of gossip is the perpetuation of a cultural system of shared ideas, norms, and conceptions. In other words, through gossip, concepts concerning appropriate and inappropriate behavior are defined. Concrete acts are interpreted as mean, mad, jealous, crazy, or stingy; and in the flow of such interpretations from one Navajo to another, the concepts become part of a shared cultural system.

The details of an incident, therefore, are not as important as the interpretation or judgment which is passed on the alleged behavior of an individual. What matters is not whether an individual actually behaved in a particular way, but that the disapproval of this type of action is communicated. This is especially important among the Navajo where the obligation to cooperate is very general and where individual autonomy is highly valued so that there is a great deal of latitude in acceptable behavior. Like Paine, I view gossip as information management, but this control has two aspects: the pursuit of self-interest through impression management and the communication of what constitutes valued cooperative behavior through the use of judgmental words and phrases.

The dual role of gossip can be more clearly seen in discussing the communication of disputes which surrounded the deaths and funerals of two Copper Canyon Navajos. These two examples were selected since I was able to fully document both cases and since they illustrate aspects of gossip present in other dispute cases not connected with death or funeral arrangements.

CASE A. SILVERSMITH'S DEATH AND FUNERAL

After a long illness, Silversmith died in August 1966 in a Public Health Service Hospital two hundred miles from his home. A burial service was held at the LDS mission (twelve miles from Copper Canyon) by the Copper Canyon LDS elders, with the help of the resident missionaries at the mission.

Silversmith's residence group consisted of his wife, two of her married daughters with children, and two married daughters-in-law with children (see the genealogy in Figure 2.1). One of Silversmith's sisters lived in another residence group with her son, Benally, and his wife. A second sister, Zonnie, lived with clan relatives (Edna and her mother) in a third camp. One of Zonnie's daughters, Betsy, lived in a community fifty miles away with her husband, Edward; another daughter, Mrs. Sage, lived in a fourth residence group with her husband and adult son not far from where Zonnie lived. Mrs. Sage's second son and his wife were visiting from Wyoming at the time of the funeral.

Most of the funeral arrangements were made by Edward (sister's daughter's husband) and Benally (other sister's son). These arrangements included retrieving jewelry from pawn shops in Gallup and purchasing new clothes.

I first heard of a dispute between Edward, Benally, and his mother on one hand, and Silversmith's widow on the other, from Pearl. Pearl's father belonged to the same clan as Benally (making them *bizeedí* or cross-cousins); he had frequent dealings with Benally and his wife during the summer when Pearl used the wife's

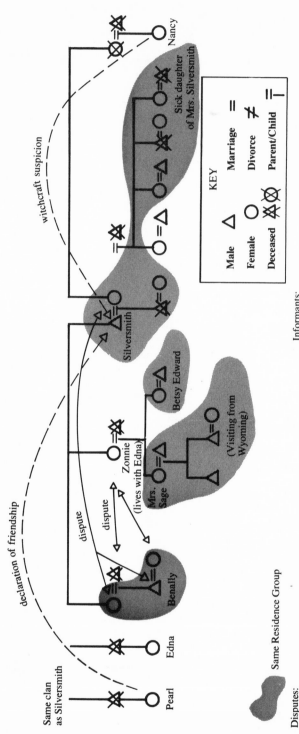

Fig. 2.1 Silversmith's genealogy

KEY

Male	△	Marriage	=
Female	○	Divorce	≠
Deceased	⊗	Parent/Child	⊤

Informants:

1. Pearl: Cross-cousin of Benally (since her father was the same clan as Silversmith): She acted as intermediary in the dispute between Benally, his mother, and Silversmith's wife, and made a declaration of friendship for Silversmith.

2. Edna: Cross-cousin of Benally (since her father was the same clan as Silversmith and Zonnie): Zonnie lived with Edna and her mother. Edna reported the dispute between Zonnie and Benally's mother, and took Zonnie's side.

3. Nancy: Sister's daughter (*bich' é'é*) of Silversmith's wife, who accused Silversmith of sorcery.

Disputes:

1. Silversmith's sister and her son Benally vs. Zonnie (between sisters, and between mother's sister/sister's son).

2. Silversmith's sister and Benally vs. Silversmith's wife (between affines)

Same Residence Group

nieces as sheepherders. Pearl reported to me that she had visited Benally's camp the day before the funeral. They (presumably, Benally and his wife and Edward and his wife, Betsy) had complained that Silversmith's widow would not help buy clothes in which to bury her husband or provide mutton for the mourning period. Pearl, acting as an intermediary, went to the widow's camp and asked her to help. The widow (an old woman of seventy) explained that she was "too sick" and could not do anything. Pearl mimicked the old lady's voice and mannerisms, thereby indicating that she felt this was a feeble excuse. Benally had mentioned the railroad retirement pension that Silversmith's widow would soon be receiving; he threatened that if the widow did not help and come to the funeral, they would have the money cut off. As it turned out, Silversmith's widow did not appear at the funeral, and only one of the stepdaughters attended (although Edward stopped by the camp to offer a ride to any who wanted to come). The widow, however, did provide two sheep for Benally and his mother so that the mourning period could be observed at their camp for two days. Pearl's account is an example of reporting a dispute as statements of fact. Rather than specifically accusing Silversmith's widow of being too stingy or mean, she implied this by hinting that the widow's excuse was not legitimate and by emphasizing the direct sanctions that Benally and his mother threatened.

A second dispute was reported to me by Edna, who provided shelter and occasional help to Zonnie, Silversmith's sister. Edna (who was also *bizeedí* to Benally) reported that Zonnie had been to Benally's camp two days before the funeral. They had asked Zonnie to help with the groceries and provide a sheep to be butchered. Edna said they were "too mean" (*'ayóo báhóóchįįd*), and Zonnie had refused. Zonnie did not want to go to the funeral because of the dispute with her sister and sister's son; she said she would just "stay home and cry and be sorry for her brother." On the day of the funeral she had gone to the camp of her daughter (Mrs. Sage), which was nearby, in order to avoid Benally's mother and wife, who arrived in the car with me to go to the funeral. Edna's report of the dispute lacked many of the details of the conversation between Zonnie and her relatives. Edna clearly took Zonnie's side (as she has done in other disputes between the same individuals), with an overall condemnation that they were "too mean." Presumably, she felt they had made unwarranted demands on Zonnie that were beyond her abilities to meet. This example shows that the details of the argument are not as important as Edna's judgment about the argument itself. The judgment condemned those who presumably started the quarrel and at the same time explained the rift, which resulted in Zonnie avoiding the funeral and not contributing groceries for the mourning period. In sum, Edna's commentary has two aspects: On one hand it exemplifies impression management since her statement was made to justify Zonnie's actions; on the other it defines the kinds of actions which are uncooperative and undesirable.

Similar patterns of communication about disruptive behavior are evident from the events surrounding the suicide and funeral of John Begay.

CASE B.   JOHN BEGAY'S DEATH

John Begay's suicide and the subsequent events were the object of much discussion during July 1966. The family was well known for disputes and drinking. John, his second wife, and her three daughters lived on the edge of the Copper Canyon area with John's daughter, Ruth, by a previous marriage (see the genealogy in

Figure 2.2). Ruth died in January 1966, leaving two small, parentless children in the care of John and his wife. Another of John's daughters, Lucy, had moved out of the residence group in the spring of 1965. She had refused to pay rent for using her brother and sister-in-law's house while they were living in California, feeling that she did not have the money and that they should let her "borrow the house" rent-free. Lucy had argued with Ruth over Ruth's lack of cooperation in fixing the road that led from the residence site to the main road. Lucy also openly criticized her father and stepmother for drinking, and her report to me of a recent ceremony emphasized all the work she had done, in contrast to the fighting and drinking in which her relatives were engaged.

Besides this discordance reported to me by members of John's residence group, a dispute with his neighbors, the Salts, also occurred. The Salts' married daughter reported to me that when members of the residence group were building a new house for her, John came to tell them not to build it, since it was located on "his land," not theirs. This behavior was defined and communicated as "mean" (*bá hachį*). I was told by other nonrelatives that John's mother's brother (*bidá'í*) was the first to settle at John's winter campsite. John later "kicked off" all his brothers and sisters from the land so that he was the only one left. Thus, even before his death, John had gained the reputation of often being drunk, stingy, and quarrelsome.

John was shot in the head with a rifle. After the incident, there was some question as to whether the death was murder or suicide. To some persons, the position of the wounds indicated that they could not have been self-inflicted.

I talked with Mabel, John's stepdaughter, age fourteen, two days after the funeral. She gave me the following details: She said John had gone off with a gun; he often went out shooting, so the rest of the camp did not suspect anything. When John did not return, they went looking for him. The next day, when they had almost given up the search, Nora (John's wife), told Eddie and his wife to look once more; if they did not find John she said they should call the Navajo police. The couple searched again and found John's body near some rocks, where he had fallen. Eddie wanted to bring the body back to the campsite, but Nora told him to call the police from the nearby fire lookout.

The Navajo police arrived to investigate the incident and removed John's body to the hospital several miles away. Mabel commented that the police thought one of the adults in the camp had shot John. That's why they had asked the family so many questions. She claimed there had been twelve policemen on the scene.

Mabel reported that John's sister had come and, "that lady said a lot of mean things." The sister accused the adults of the camp: "You killed my brother." Mabel maintained that the sister wanted all the sheep, but the woman's daughter persuaded her to leave rather than continue the argument. The sister threatened to return for the sheep later, and Mabel indicated that the police had remained all night at the camp partly to protect them from the sister's threatened return.

Mabel also gave an account of a meeting of relatives and chapter officers, which was held two days after the funeral to discuss what should be done with John's property and with the two small children of John's deceased daughter. The meeting was attended by members of the residence group, the widow's brother and mother, and various clan relatives of John, in addition to some of the chapter officers from the community south of Copper Canyon. The sister's claims were not honored, and

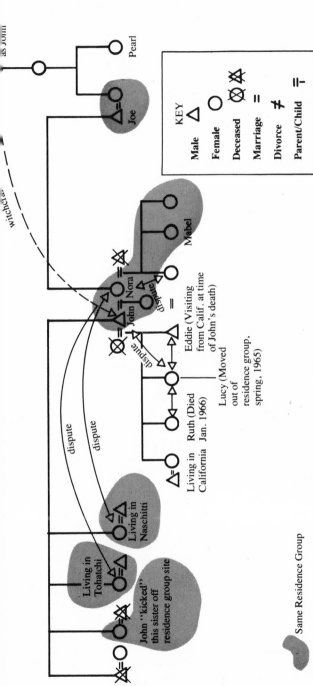

KEY

Male	△
Female	○
Deceased	⊗ ⧖
Marriage	=
Divorce	≠
Parent/Child	=

Disputes:

1. Lucy vs. John and his wife (between daughter and father/stepmother)
2. Lucy vs. Ruth (between sisters)
3. Nora vs. her daughter (between mother and daughter)
4. Lucy vs. Eddie and his wife (between sister and brother/sister-in-law)
5. Nora vs. John's Naschitti sister (between affines)
6. Nora vs. John's Tohatchi sister (between affines)
7. John vs. Salts (between neighbors)

Informants:

1. Mabel: John's stepdaughter: She reported the incidents surrounding John's death and de-emphasized disputes within the residence group and emphasized a dispute with John's sister.
2. Pearl: Same clan as John: She reported her grandmother's story of John's wealth, implying witchcraft.
3. Edna: a nonrelative: She reported John's death as suicide because of jealousy.
4. LDS elders: They reported details of the funeral and the dispute between Nora and John's Tochatchi sister.
5. Lucy: She reported disputes with her father, stepmother, and siblings.

Same Residence Group

John "kicked" this sister off residence group site

Living in Tohatchi

Living in Naschitti

Living in California

Ruth (Died Jan. 1966)

Lucy (Moved out of residence group, spring, 1965)

Eddie (Visiting from Calif. at time of John's death)

John Nora

Mabel

Joe

Pearl

Fig. 2.2 John Begay's genealogy

it was decided that the sheep, field, and other possessions should go to John's widow. Eddie's wife wanted to take the two children to California with her. The little girl, however, said she wanted to stay with her grandmother; when Eddie's wife tried to take the boy, he cried to stay with the grandmother also. According to Mabel, the decision was left to the children rather than to the adults present at the meeting.

Mabel's story de-emphasized any disputes within the camp that may have precipitated John's death or that created dissension at the meeting to dispose of John's property. On the other hand, she stressed the argument with John's sister over the livestock and labeled the woman's behavior as "mean." Mabel never questioned the theory that John had shot himself, while others who reported the incident were more likely to suggest murder or to emphasize sexual jealousy (te' nizin) as a motive for suicide.

For instance, Pearl, who was the granddaughter of a woman in John's clan, thought that the two stepdaughters always wanted to "run off with boys." John did not like this and would not let them go. They had run off to the Squaw Dance on Saturday night, and John got mad at them. Pearl hinted that the girls killed him because he would not let them go off, and that they wanted to get rid of him.

Edna, a nonrelative, had heard from the wife of John's brother's son that they were all drunk. John wanted to marry Mabel. (It had been rumored for several months that he had been giving his wife jewelry for the right to have sex relations with Mabel's older sister.) Mabel was scared and ran away to the Squaw Dance. John got mad; he shot the dog first and the cat next; then he went off by himself with the gun. They found him shot the next day. Edna herself felt that it was suicide because John had been jealous (te' nizin) over his stepdaughter.

I heard about one additional dispute which occurred at the funeral, a graveside service conducted by the LDS elders. There was an argument between John's sister from a distant community and Nora, John's widow. The former noticed that John was being buried with only one turquoise bracelet. She seemed to think that there should be two bracelets, and that Nora was keeping one for herself.

As an outsider, I am inclined to believe the suicide rather than the homicide theory of John's death. However, the actual facts of the case are not as important as ɩ the impression each gossiper wished to communicate in relating either the cause of death or the disputes that surrounded it. Those closest to the incident tended to play down any dissension except that which would justify their own counterclaims. For instance, Nora's brother, who had been present in the camp following the shooting, was unwilling to give any hint of disputes.

Affines, neighbors, clan relatives, and nonrelatives were much more willing to communicate a negative picture of John, his wife, or stepdaughters, both in discussing past disputes in which they had been involved and in theorizing about the shooting. Disputes occurred (1) between two kinsmen (e.g., Lucy and her father and stepmother, Lucy and her sister, and Lucy and Eddy and his wife Nora and her daughter) and (2) between two affines (e.g., Nora and her husbands's two sisters). The manner in which both kinds of disputes were discussed was similar, in that the gossipers put forward the impression that their claims were legitimate and those of the other disputants were not. It is equally important to emphasize that gossip about John and his relatives also was used to communicate concepts of meanness and jealousy. Claims on goods or services that were thought to be illegitimate, such as

John's desire for more land and his sister's claim to the livestock, were considered evidence of meanness. Jealousy was used as an explanation for otherwise unaccountable behavior (suicide).

The two cases demonstrate how the same kin relationships can be the focus either of cooperation or disruption. Both Silversmith and John Begay were old men who died leaving several siblings, a wife, children, and stepchildren. Silversmith's funeral was arranged by his matrilateral kin (sister, sister's son, sister's daughter and her husband). The major disputes were between these kin and another sister on one hand, and the widow on the other. In John Begay's case, the funeral arrangements were made by conjugal kin, that is, wife, children, and step-children, with major disputes between the widow and John's two sisters. A man's ties to his wife, children, siblings, and sibling's children are all potentially important, but among any of these relatives there may be aid or disruption. The sets of kin of Silversmith and John Begay were structurally similar, but the pattern of cooperation was quite different in each case. However, the same notions of cooperative and uncooperative behavior were used to communicate disputes of those who gossiped about various incidents. On a manifest level, these gossipers often look after their own interests, but the unintended consequence of their gossip is the maintenance of aspects of the Navajo cultural system relevant to cooperation. The two cases illustrate both the diversity and variation that is characteristic of actual social relations and the uniformity characteristic of the cultural system used to interpret these relations.

Witchcraft Suspicion and Uncooperative Behavior

Witchcraft suspicion, like the reporting of disputes, is communicated in a face-to-face interaction situation and serves to define uncooperative behavior and, by negative example, to reinforce the commitment to an ethic of cooperation. The Navajo witch or werewolf is the prototype of antisocial, anti-Navajo, and even antihuman behavior, and a clear connection exists between meanness, jealousy, "thinking against someone," and witchcraft practices. Beliefs that describe the practices of werewolves and their role in causing illness are very explicit and widely held, but living persons are rarely accused of engaging in these activities. Navajo are very reluctant to discuss witchcraft (Kluckhohn 1944: 13–20; reprint 1967), but when they do, it is in terms of vague statements, for example, that X's illness was caused by witchcraft or sorcery. Less common are statements that X's illness was caused by Y, or that Y is a werewolf. Even these statements are qualified as hearsay—by using the Navajo phrase *jiní* ("it is said")—so the speaker does not put himself in the position of making a direct accusation.

The vagueness of Navajo witchcraft is related to its function as an explanation for illness, where it is more important to prescribe the appropriate ceremonial cure than to punish a culprit. Likewise, it is more crucial to communicate the notion of a witch or werewolf as the ideal type of social deviant than to punish actual uncooperative antisocial Navajos. In this regard, witchcraft beliefs serve only as indirect sanctions and are more important for the maintenance of a whole system of ideas about cooperation than as a mechanism for directly sanctioning behavior. Examples of ways in which witchcraft suspicion defines uncooperative, mean behavior can be seen by further examining the cases of Silversmith and John Begay.

Silversmith was accused of sorcery (*bee'iińẓịịd*) in a story told to me by Nancy, the niece (sister's daughter, or *bich'é'é*) of Silversmith's wife (see Fig. 2.1). About the time of Silversmith's death, Nancy had performed a divination for a child of Silversmith's stepdaughter, in order to discover the cause of a recent illness. Looking into the glowing coals (*tsííd*), Nancy had seen a stone with markings on it. A search of the area around the family hoghan uncovered a broken piece of metate that Nancy said came from the grave of Silversmith's wife's mother. Carved on one side was a picture of the stepdaughter and her sick child; on the other side was a picture of the father and other children. This stone had been placed there by Silversmith and was causing the child's illness, Nancy maintained. She had discovered this by seeing his face in the coals. Nancy commented that she had seen Silversmith's face in the coals several times when her husband's father was ill, and she labeled as "sorcery" Silversmith's alleged role in causing sickness.

Silversmith's relatives, in contrast to Nancy who was aligned with his affines, had a much more positive picture of the old man. According to Pearl (the classificatory cousin mentioned), he was a good friend. She told me that he used to stop by their house on the way to the trading post and, if he did not have a sack in which to carry his groceries, they would give him a burlap bag. She thought he was "a real nice man." In other words, Silversmith's reputation in the community varied, and the communication of a positive or negative evaluation is primarily determined by the speaker's relation to Silversmith rather than by the old man's actual behavior. In general, the more distant the social relationship the greater the likelihood of witchcraft suspicion. As with disputes, affines and nonkin are more likely to circulate rumors about witchcraft than are kinsmen, although accusations by close kin such as a brother, sister, father mother's brother, or cross-cousin, have been recorded (Kluckhohn 1944: 59–60; reprint 1967).

In Silversmith's case, witchcraft was suspected as an explanation for a particular illness. For John Begay, accusations were much more vague and related to his general reputation for meanness. The stories that circulated after his death concerning past disputes and possible reasons for his suicide contributed to a picture of a quarrelsome, jealous man. My own observations indicate that he and his wife were social isolates, having sporadic and often quarrelsome relations with several close relatives over the past years.

Rumors that John was a werewolf can be related to a story of his wealth as reported by a clan sister* who attended the meeting concerning the disposal of his property. John reportedly had two sealskins, two buffalo skins, two deerskins, two mountain lion skins, several strings of turquoise beads, several bracelets, rings, and many ceremonial fetishes. In addition, he owned many sheep and horses. The report fits the description of a rich Navajo who possessed all the traditional kinds of wealth; it is believed that such wealth is often obtained through stinginess rather than generosity, or by those who transform themselves into werewolves and rob graves. The story is in contrast to the signs of John's poverty which the trader reported and which I had observed while staying at their winter camp during my first months in Copper Canyon.[13] Again, the actual facts of the case are not as crucial as the image communicated. Stories about John Begay combine jealousy, meanness,

---

*Clan sister refers to any woman in ego's clan of his or her generation.

and stinginess with a great amount of traditional wealth. To the Navajo, such accumulation indicates someone who has not been generous and cooperative but who has acted in terms of his own desires rather than those of his kinsmen. While judgment of Silversmith varied, suspicion that John was a witch was more generally believed. He exemplified the social isolate—the epitome of the uncooperative Navajo—and gossip about him defined and communicated the nature of undesirable behavior in its most extreme form.

My interpretation of Navajo witchcraft supports some of the conclusions found in Kluckhohn's classic study (1944; reprint 1967). Kluckhohn emphasized the psychological functions of witchcraft for dealing with aggression and anxiety, but he also pointed out the social functions that witchcraft beliefs have in (1) defining what is "bad," (2) preserving equilibrium in an egalitarian society, and (3) providing a technique of social control (1944: 110–13; reprint 1967). In other words, Kluckhohn recognized the importance of witchcraft beliefs for stating conceptions of undesirable behavior and for exerting pressure for appropriate behavior. However, even though he presented evidence for the indirectness of Navajo witchcraft accusations, he did not recognize the important connection between this indirectness and the system of generalized reciprocity that characterizes Navajo cooperative activities. Furthermore, Kluckhohn did not see the relationship between witchcraft beliefs and statements that "X is mean, mad, jealous, crazy, or stingy," which are part of Navajo gossip and which also define negatively valued, uncooperative behavior.[14] Witchcraft for Kluckhohn was a set of beliefs to be explained in terms of broad, general, psychological and sociological functions. He failed to see Navajo witchcraft as a part of a system of shared ideas relevent to particular situations, especially the organization of concrete cooperative activities through the recruitment of kinsmen.

Navajo phrases presented in this chapter—such as, "I'll help him," or "I'll run after him"; "They are helping me," or "After me they are running along"; "He takes care of him (or it)"; and "It's up to him to decide," or "He's the boss"—and other phrases, along with the contexts in which they are used, express the Navajo view or actors' model of cooperative and uncooperative behavior on one hand, and of individual autonomy and consensus decision making on the other. I have interpreted the use of these concepts and presented an observer's model of the cultural system of cooperation, first by arguing that Navajo ideas concerning help and aid constitute an ethic of generalized reciprocity. This ethic is combined with stress on individual autonomy. Although there are apparent contradictions between these two concepts—since helping everyone would severely limit individual options—the system works out in practice, in part because the notions of cooperativeness are defined in terms of uncooperative behavior. The relative lack of specific obligations to "do X," in contrast to several injunctions such as, "don't do X" or "X is not done," preserves individual autonomy and decision-rights by allowing for an infinite variety of appropriate cooperative actions. Conversely, cooperation is assured by the Navajo phrase that describes autonomy and simultaneously implies the need for consensus and joint effort.

I have shown how Copper Canyon Navajos use the phraseology of cooperation in concrete situations. The positive obligations for helping others and taking care of others, as well as injunctions against uncooperative behavior, are communicated in public statements at various Navajo ceremonies. The attributes of uncooperative behavior—meanness, jealousy, stinginess, laziness, and craziness—along with the attributes of witches and werewolves, who epitomize antisocial Navajos, are continually defined in face-to-face interaction where disputes are reported and witchcraft suspicion is discussed.

This model of the Navajo cultural system of cooperation will be helpful in interpreting the Navajo request situations presented in the next chapter. The model reveals that among the Navajo a system of generalized reciprocity and diffuse obligations to cooperate is counterbalanced with an emphasis on individual autonomy; the interplay of these two sets of ideas has consequences for the specific ways in which Copper Canyon Navajos ask for and receive aid in economic and ritual activities.

Chapter 3

The Etiquette
of Request Making

~~~~~~

Navajo conceptions of cooperation and autonomy provide obligations and expectations for interaction situations in which requests for aid are made. An obligation to cooperate is binding on all adult Navajos, regardless of kinship status or situation. Also, not only is there an expectation that an individual requested to perform a task will do so out of good will and generosity, but there is little or no effort to calculate the "debits" or "credits" resulting from the sum of exchanges between two individuals. On the other hand, an expectation exists that an individual is free to decide for himself whether to honor a request; conversely, the requestor is obligated not to "push his request" and infringe on this autonomy. As a consequence of this paradox that all are generally obligated to cooperate but the individual is free to decide, the request situation is full of ambiguity.

Reasons for this ambiguity are given in Erving Goffman's (1967: 51) analysis of interaction situations. "In general, then, when a rule of conduct is broken we find that two individuals run the risk of becoming discredited: the one with an obligation, who should have governed himself by the rule; the other with an expectation, who should have been treated in a particular way because of this governance. Both actor and recipient are threatened." Among the Navajo, under a generalized obligation to cooperate, the actor requesting help has the expectation of being aided, and the actor who is being asked to provide goods or services has the obligation of filling the request. A refusal discredits both.[1] Moreover, since individual autonomy is important, there are few direct ways in which the person making a request can press his desires; in other words, there are few sanctions within the request situation that he can use in order to achieve compliance. Further pleading or an exaggeration of his difficulties in an effort to avoid refusal or influence a "change of mind" are looked upon as improper. Once a refusal is directly indicated, there is no recourse but to accept it.

The open acknowledgment of a refusal is avoided by the maintenance of ambiguity so that both participants are able to leave the situation without being discredited. Individual autonomy can then be preserved, and a general air of cooperativeness can be retained if it can be said that no direct request was actually made or that a request was never actually refused.

Ambiguity is maintained in two ways. First, requests are indirect; there is a great deal of "feeling out the situation." Oblique hints are made that a favor is desired

[57]

without the individual actually stating his request. Second, refusals are indirect and excuses are made so that the refusal does not actually break the obligation to cooperate.

Request Making

Request situations can be defined as those interaction settings where Navajos ask for goods and services from other Navajos. The Navajo request situation is usually dyadic and involves an individual who needs aid and someone who might be able to oblige his request. The Navajo phrase *t'áá bee bóholníih* (It's up to him to decide) also defines the rules of both the request maker and the individual asked to fill a request.

T'áá bee bóholníih is used to indicate the individual about whom the situation revolves and who is most directly concerned with accomplishing a particular task. The request is his business and should be negotiated by him. He is the individual who needs a ride to the trading post, is owner of most of the sheep to be sheared in a herd, or is the patient or parent of the patient in a ceremony. For complex activities like a ceremony, this individual initiates an activity, allocates his own time and effort to the task, and is the central decision maker in making requests and organizing the aid of others.

The request maker will seek out the individual who is considered *t'áá bee bóholníih* in reference to the goods and services needed. This might be the owner of a car or pickup truck needed for hauling wood or water, the owner of a sheep to be donated for a ceremony, or the tractor owner whose machine and services are to be used in plowing a field. If that person is not at home, the requester will either have to return at a later time or follow him to wherever he is visiting or attending to

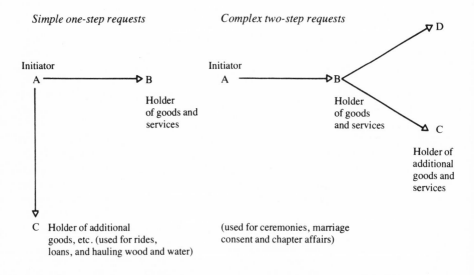

Fig. 3.1   Types of Navajo requests

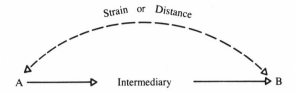

Fig. 3.2   *Two-step request with intermediary*

another task. Because of the distances between Navajo hoghans, several hours may be spent trying to make contact with the correct person, and in the end the request may be delayed until the next day. The requester may have to contact several individuals before finding someone who can perform the desired service or, in the case of a large and complex activity, before recruiting enough manpower to complete the necessary tasks.

There may be other Navajos whose consent and aid are needed before the individual asked to fill a request can consent and say, "It's OK with me" (*Hágoshį́į́*). These additional cooperators are also *t'áá bee bóholníih*, and consultation with them will have the same characteristics as the initial request situation.

In some instances an individual will use an intermediary, which creates another kind of two-step request. Unlike the usual two-step request that (1) allows the initiator to obtain aid from individuals with whom he has no direct connection and (2) permits the person requested to provide aid or support beyond his normal means, the use of an intermediary has a different function. This procedure insures against the embarrassment and discredit to both parties in the event of a refusal. Intermediaries are used in situations where there is an element of strain or distance in the relationship between the initiator and the individual of whom the request is made.

Strain is particularly evident in relations between kin and affines, and intermediaries frequently are used between members of these two categories, even within the extended family residence group (Chapter 4 herein; Aberle 1961: 162). In general, if an affine's consent is needed, ego's kinsman is directly approached, and he or she relays the message to the spouse. When there is a choice between a one-step request of a kinsman or a two-step request involving a kinsman as an intermediary and an affine, Navajos usually will prefer the one-step request. It allows for more rapid feedback and more accurate calculation of the indirect cues concerning possible acceptance or refusal; it also plays on the solidarity inherent in kin relationships, which is lacking in the Navajo definition of affineship. The literature shows that intermediaries sometimes are used in making requests of distant kin, nonkin in the community, and strangers. An important instance concerns the planning of a ceremony, as described by Kluckhohn and Wyman (1940). The sponsor, or *'ook'aahii*, who is usually a close relative of the patient, institutes the ceremony, pays for it, and, in terms of the analysis I have been presenting, is *t'áá bee bóholníih*. This person often sends an intermediary to ask the singer (*hataałii*), who is likely to be a stranger living in a distant community, to perform. The intermediary, called *jish haaghai* (bringing the medicine pouch) makes arrangements to pay the singer and returns with the medicine pouch for the ceremony, which is usually arranged for the next day (Kluckhohn and Wyman 1940: 14).

Whether initiated directly or through an intermediary, the phrasing of a request itself is more bluntly stated in Navajo than in English. We use such forms as "I wonder if I might ask a favor of you"; "I wonder if you would mind doing X for me"; or "If you could do X, I certainly would appreciate it." In contrast, Navajos use various types of imperatives. A Navajo says, "Haul me some water" (*tó sha ní'kaah*); "Herd the sheep out" (*dibé ch'ínínílkaad*); or "We two are going to Gallup," that is, "Take me to Gallup" (*Na'nízhoozhígo diit'ash*).[2] Such requests demand a "yes" or "no" answer in Navajo, rather than something similar to our polite refusals, "I'm very sorry, but I'm afraid I won't be able to do it," or "I wish I could be of some help, but I just won't be able to."

The final and most indirect method of making requests is by "spreading the news" of a coming event that will require the participation of Navajos from more than one residence group. This approach is used particularly in recruiting aid for a large ceremony when the news is circulated several weeks in advance that "X is planning a sing." Kinsmen, neighbors, and clan relatives, in accordance with the ethic of generalized reciprocity, contribute goods and services without being specifically approached by the patient, his spouse, or parents.

In Copper Canyon the phrasing of requests, as well as observance of the *bóholnííh* relationships, is illustrated by the following case:

CASE C. MAKING REQUESTS

Nelly Begay was arranging a puberty ceremony (*kinaaldá*) for her daughter. She appeared at the household where I was staying and asked the husband, Kevin, where his wife, Laura, was (Nelly's deceased husband's sister's daughter). He replied that she was in an adjoining room changing her clothes. Nelly waited until she appeared, as it was clear that she wanted to ask something of the wife, but not the husband. When Laura came in, Nelly said, "Help me" (*shíká 'anájah*) and went on to explain that they were having a puberty ceremony for her daughter that weekend. Laura and Kevin already had heard that the ceremony was planned and probably were not surprised at the request. She explained that she wanted a Navajo skirt and velveteen blouse for her daughter to wear. Laura loaned her the clothes that had been used for her own daughter's ceremony the previous summer. Then Nelly asked about jewelry (*yoo'*: beads). Laura explained that she didn't have any, but that perhaps a neighbor (Sam Grant's mother) would have some.

I drove Nelly and her young son over to Sam Grant's mother's house, and we entered the cabin. Only the daughter and husband were in the room, so Nelly inquired about the mother (*Nimá shą'?*) "Your mother, what about her?" The daughter replied, "She's over there," indicating one of the other dwellings in the residence group. Nelly explained she needed some jewelry, and the daughter left to get her mother. The daughter, of course, could not consent, since it was the mother who owned the jewelry. When the mother returned she asked, "What is it?" (*Ha'át'íí la?*), and Nelly again explained that she wanted some jewelry (*Yoo' ła nisin*: "I want some beads."). Sam's mother hesitated a moment and asked what the beads were needed for. Nelly then explained about the ceremony for her daughter. Sam's mother agreed immediately and produced a bracelet and several strands of turquoise beads for the girl to wear. Nelly thanked Sam's mother, and we left. Later Nelly asked others in the vicinity for jewelry and other kinds of assistance, such as hauling wood and water.

In this example, Nelly, the mother of the *kinaaldá* girl, made the requests of her kin and neighbors, since she was *t'áá bee bóholníih*, or the adult most concerned with the ceremony. She went directly to the person who was *t'áá bee bóholníih*, in the sense of being owner of the clothing or jewelry, and explained, "I need (or want) X." She always stated the purpose of the request and what the object was to be used for; in one instance she prefaced her request with a general plea of "help me." Owners were helpful because of the generalized obligation to fill such direct requests and also because of the high value placed on ceremonial cooperation over other kinds of mutual aid. Other relatives and neighbors not directly contacted by Nelly heard about the ceremony and attended, bringing groceries and contributing their labor to the making of the *ałkaan* (corn cake). (See Chapter 8, Table 8.3, Case 16.)

Precautions Against Refusals

There are several ways in which an individual can infuse the request situation with ambiguity, by dropping some cues that he has a favor to ask, yet withholding the direct demand. At the same time he can probe for the possibility of conflicting obligations or physical disabilities that might lead the other individual to refuse. All these are precautions against a refusal since the requester can "back out" of the situation at any time during these polite preliminaries and neither he nor the other individual will be discredited since no direct question was asked and no clear refusal was made.

One strategy is for a Navajo to phrase the request indirectly in terms of a problem, so that another Navajo can volunteer his services. Aberle (1961: 162) gives the example of a man who wants help and speaks in a general way to a friend about his needs: "We are rounding up the horses and we are having a hard time without enough men around to do the work." If the friend is with his wife, he will consult with her and perhaps help the friend. If the friend cannot or does not want to help, he has the option of talking in a general way about his other pressing obligations. Just as the request was never really made, the refusal is never openly stated. In a similar way, "spreading the news" about a ceremony is a general statement of a problem and plea for aid. Since there is no face-to-face request, those who hear about the ceremony may offer help, but their failure to do so does not discredit them or those who need the help.

Another strategy is to send a message to the person to whom the request is to be made, telling him to come to the requester's camp. For example, the owner of the largest herd in Copper Canyon was sent for by an old lady who was not a relative. The herd owner came to the summer home of his classificatory daughter (*bitsi'*) to ask for a ride, which I provided. We found the old lady on the road herding her sheep, and she made her request when we stopped the car to talk with her. This notification procedure is often used between nonrelatives; it signals that a request is to be made and leaves the other individual the option of not coming. If he never arrives, there is no interaction between the two and no possibility of refusal. If the individual does answer the initial probe by going to the requester's camp, he may not hear the request immediately. More than once I have gone to visit someone after being told that he or she wanted to see me, only to converse for several minutes or an hour with no clue as to the reason for my summons. Then as I would be about to leave, a request would be made.

The delaying of a request until late in the interaction is part of a third strategy. A Navajo avoids talking about the subject of the request until he finds out what the other Navajo is doing that day or the next, and what obligations he has to fulfill in the near future. Only after the requester is fairly sure that the other person is free to say "yes" to his proposal, will he actually make his desires known. After the traditional greeting, most Navajo conversations begin with questions, such as, "Where are you going?" (*Háágóóshą́' díníyá*?) or "What are you doing?" (*Ha'át'íish baa naniná*?). To some extent these are polite phrases equivalent to the Anglo-American "How are you?"; however, they also serve to provide important information on the future activities of an individual of whom a favor might be asked.

In sum, while the phrasing of a request is direct—an imperative statement—the situation surrounding a request is filled with oblique questions and other signs of indirectness. Every attempt is made to insure the acceptance of a request before the actual request is made.

Accepting Requests

If an individual accepts a request, he merely says, *Hágoshį́į* (It's OK with me), or *Táá 'ákot'é* (It's all right with me), and makes the necessary arrangements to carry out the request. In many cases this involves acceptance of payment for services rendered. Formerly, all requests were granted without consideration of cash payment; however, Navajos have increasingly adjusted to a money economy, and there is an expectation that many services (such as, transportation, hauling wood and water, plowing, and sheepshearing) are to be paid for. Payment sometimes is in cash, but more often it is in the form of a credit slip from the trading post, which allows the person giving aid to buy gas or groceries and charge the purchase to the requester's account. This system of payment is related to the recent increase in the use of pickup trucks and automobiles. Upkeep is costly, and it is especially felt that gas should be paid for by the individual being transported or for whom water and wood is being hauled.

The individual making the request should state the amount to be paid for the service, and the offer of a particular sum should be mentioned in the course of asking the favor, for without it consent is unlikely. In accordance with Navajo notions about cooperation, it is the good will and generosity of the requester which is communicated in the price, not the fee of the person providing a service. I once made the mistake of asking a Copper Canyon Navajo how much he "charged" to plow a field and to haul wood or water. He replied, "It's up to the people," indicating the initiator of the request is *t'áá bee bóholnííh* on this matter. He insisted that he does not "charge" people, and that he could only do so if he had a license to haul wood or coal; then he would have them pay so much a load. Fees are associated with the procedures used by Anglos, not with the Navajo way of doing things. There are, however, standard "prices" for services in the sense that people commonly make the same offer for getting the same job done. Most Copper Canyon Navajos pay ten dollars to have a load of wood hauled, though it sometimes costs as little as five dollars or as much as fifteen or twenty dollars. Water is hauled for two to five dollars, and trips to Gallup or Shiprock are usually five to fifteen dollars, plus gas.

If a Navajo does not offer to pay for gas or makes a low offer, the person requested will usually comment, "I don't have any gas" (*Chidí bitó 'ádin*), "I have work to do,'' or some other veiled hint. The requester will then make a more adequate offer, and the second Navajo will agree to the request. Navajos do not bargain to get the best "deal" or the highest payment. An individual will generally accept an offer rather than haggle or refuse, agreeing, for example, to be given a sheep rather than ten dollars for plowing a field. In spite of the money element in request making, the system is one of generalized reciprocity where there is a strong diffuse obligation that one should help if asked. Cash or credit is mainly used to defray gas expenses and is a way of keeping the source of transportation (a pickup or car) available.

Refusing Requests

Navajos identify as extremely awkward those situations in which a refusal is highly likely or openly acknowledged. They apply the concept of shame or bashfulness to describe the actor's uncomfortableness. A person would be characterized as *yaa yánízin* (He is ashamed or bashful about it) if he is making a request with the knowledge that the other person might have a conflicting obligation and might therefore refuse. The phrase also labels behavior in situations where relations are distant and filled with strain. It is particularly appropriate for affine-kin relationships, as exemplified by sons- and daughters-in-law who are. apt to be reticent and circumspect in dealing with members of the residence group into which they are married.

If an individual wishes to refuse a request, there are several alternatives. All are methods of maintaining situational ambiguity, so that it is never explicitly recognized that an individual has failed to live up to the obligation to cooperate. Thus, both the requester and the individual whose goods or services are desired can leave the situation without being discredited and can continue to maintain both a general atmosphere of helpfulness and a mutual expectation for future cooperation.

A blunt negative response is not only improper etiquette but is also subject to strong public disapproval. One Copper Canyon Navajo commented that he was certainly glad his neighbors now had a car. Before they did, he explained, they were constantly coming to him with requests for rides. "Every day we were always on the go, taking someone somewhere." I asked what could be done if he did not want to give someone a ride, and he explained, "You just can't say 'no,' because people will talk about you when your back is turned and say that you are mean."[3]

If an individual does not want to accept a request, it is sometimes possible to remain silent, or at the most, to make some statement that is not a direct answer. In one case, a couple, Iris and Jake, and their daughter, drove up to the camp of the wife's sister where I was helping a group of friends and relatives with the sheepshearing. Iris and her daughter came over from the pickup and explained to those standing near the corral that she and her daughter needed a ride to Shiprock the next day. Since this was being translated into English, I felt the request was aimed at me (either by the wife or reluctant relatives), so I hastily explained that I had to take members of another family to Gallup the following morning. No one else volunteered their services, although three others present owned pickups. One woman made several comments, but she did not offer to provide transportation. After a rather awkward silence, the mother and daughter left. The possibility of such silent refusals increases when requests are made to a group. The confrontation is not as direct, and the focus of refusal does not necessarily fall on any one individual. The situation remains ambiguous, since it is not clear whose obligation it was to accept the request and, consequently, whose reputation as a cooperative Navajo is discredited.

A second way of avoiding a request is to suggest another person who could better provide the service. For instance, one Copper Canyon Navajo, when asked to repair a pickup, sent the requesting couple to his wife's brother, saying that the latter was a mechanic, not he. The same man, however, repairs his own automobiles and occasionally helps others. He could have helped if he had wanted, and may have done so if the requester had been a relative or if he had not been interrupted in another task. The method of suggesting someone else is more acceptable than refusing, though only possible when a case can be made that someone else can more ably perform the same task. This method is not possible in requests for ceremonial cooperation, as all adults are equally capable of helping and there are no requirements for special skills. At worst, the requester can see the strategy of suggesting an alternative as a thinly veiled refusal; at best, he can accept the suggestion as one made out of cooperativeness and with his own best interests in mind.

A third strategy is to offer an excuse; the most legitimate excuses are those of (1) being committed to other obligations, or (2) physical disability, such as sickness or an automotive breakdown. The possibility of such is usually probed for by the requester during an initial questioning period, so that if the individual has given no previous hint of his inability to accept a request, these two kinds of excuses may not be open to him, once the request is made.

From the point of view of the individual asked to provide a service, an excuse communicates willingness but offers an acceptable reason why he cannot help. Previous obligation to others provides a particularly good excuse, since this presents the picture of a cooperative Navajo who aids his kinsman, and the requester leaves the situation with an expectation that one of his future requests might be filled, even though the present request was not. Excuses have their drawbacks, however, since there is always the possibility the requester will not believe the excuse and will condemn the refuser in later conversations with his relatives.

CASE D.   A REFUSAL

When Sarah asked her brother to take her and her mother to Arizona to visit the family of her estranged husband, he kept putting her off. There was a confrontation the day before she wanted to make the trip; the brother said the pickup generator was not working properly, implying that he could not take her. Sarah asked about borrowing his wife's brother's pickup, but the brother replied that he was "ashamed" (*baa yánízin*) to ask since the brother-in-law's family was going to Albuquerque that weekend (i.e., a refusal was fairly certain). In spite of the excuses, the situation was an awkward one, and both siblings left as soon as the refusal was clear. For Navajos there are no ways of pleading for further consideration, no apologies, and no methods for easing a difficult situation.

The next day when we passed the brother on the road, Sarah remarked that the pickup was working well enough for him to haul for another brother-in-law, but not well enough to take her to Arizona. Although made as a statement of fact, Sarah was issuing a condemnation of her brother who should have helped but did not. In the last analysis, no excuse is completely legitimate, and any refusal can be seen as breaking obligations to cooperate.

Implications of Cooperation
and Autonomy Concepts for Request Situations

Chapter 2 introduced Navajo concepts concerning cooperative and uncooperative behavior and those dealing with individual autonomy and consensus. An observer's model of the Navajo cultural system of cooperation showed how these two sets of concepts are complementary and how each allows for implementation of the other. It is thus consistent for the Navajo to maintain a diffuse obligation to help others regardless of kinship status or situation and, at the same time, to retain a high value on individual autonomy.

A model that highlights the complementarity of these two sets of concepts can also be useful in interpreting the recruitment of aid, as shown in this chapter. Cooperation and autonomy concepts provide obligations and expectations for request situations. These are maintained by minimizing direct refusals: The requester only obliquely hints that a request is being made until he is fairly sure of a positive response, and the individual being asked to grant a favor only obliquely hints that he is refusing. In many, many cases requests are granted, but when they are not, both the requester and the refuser can leave the situation without being discredited. They have preserved the atmosphere of good will and generosity and left open the future possibility of cooperation, without damaging the individual autonomy and the right to decide of the two participants. Ambiguity in request situations is a consequence of the continual balancing off of cooperation and autonomy concerns on the part of Navajos.

Part III

SOCIAL
STRUCTURE

Chapter 4

Household and
Residence Group

〰〰〰〰〰〰〰〰〰〰〰〰〰〰〰〰〰〰〰〰〰〰〰〰〰

Parallel to a model of the Navajo cultural system of cooperation, which eluci-dates the expectations and obligations surrounding the making of requests and the giving of aid, are aspects of the social system that can be incorporated in a structural model relevent to analyzing how concrete cooperative activities are organized. Two sets of structural ties will emerge as parts of the model: (1) those that can be analyzed in relation to Navajo domestic groups (the household and residence group), and (2) those that can be treated as ''ego-centered sets,'' which in turn make up a network of ties linking together residence groups throughout the Copper Canyon area.

In dealing with the first part of the structural model, that is, the analysis of the Navajo household and residence group as they are organized in Copper Canyon, it is important to consider and to integrate three aspects. First, I focus on the Navajo actors' viewpoint by analyzing words and phrases that help to define the household and residence group and the kin relationships on which they are based. Second, I utilize anthropological constructs (including the domestic group developmental cycle and a scheme for residence classification), which help to order statistical and demographic data on these units. Finally, I describe patterns of authority and communication which reflect the domestic group cycle and the cultural model of cooperation and show how these are crucial for interpreting the organization of activities.

Concepts Concerning Kin Relations in Domestic Groups

The notion of domestic group as used by anthropologists implies both kinship and locality, that is, a collection of individuals, closely related through cultural defini-tions of kinship and marriage, who are organized into spatially bounded residence units (Goody 1958). Thus, there are two sets of Navajo concepts relevant to the definition of Navajo domestic groups (the household and residence group): (1) concepts describing kinship relations, and (2) concepts dealing with the spatial arrangement of dwellings. I will first discuss kinship concepts dealing with the key pairs of roles that compose the household and residence group: mother-child, father-child, sibling-sibling, and husband-wife relationships.

[69]

The bond between a mother and her children is viewed as strong, enduring, and perhaps the most important tie in Navajo society (Aberle 1961: 166). The relationship between a father and his children, though secondary to the mother-child tie, is also positive and solidary. Gary Witherspoon, in a discussion of Navajo concepts of motherhood and fatherhood, also makes these points.

> The conceptual system of the Navajo makes it clear that the mother-child bond is the strongest. The expression of this bond is found in affection, care, sustenance, and subsistence. The mother is to provide food and care for her growing child both prenatally and postnatally.
> The father's relationship to the mother is one of an outsider coming in. It is a complementary one that makes conception, reproduction, and subsistence possible. He provides those things the mother and children cannot provide for themselves. He is a symbol of strength and leadership. (1970: 59)

The complementarity between motherhood and fatherhood is explicit in Navajo concepts of birth and clanship. A woman bears a child (*'Awéé' yischį́*, "A baby, to it, she gave birth") and simultaneously the baby is "born for" the father (*Hastiin Neez 'awéé' báyizhchį́*, "Tall Man, a baby was born for him"). The child is "born of" the clan of his mother and "born for" the clan of his father. Thus, in identifying himself, a Navajo uses the customary phrase "I am Bitterwater, born for Salt Clan" (*Tódích'íinii nishłį́, 'áshįįhí báshíshchíín*), inserting the names of his own and his father's clans. The mother-child bond is reinforced by common clanship, yet the father-child bond is important in providing a second clan affiliation.

The complementarity of the links between mother and child and those between father and child is retained in Navajo expressions dealing with the nuclear family. The separateness of the mother-child unit within the family is seen in the phrase "Mr. X and his wife and children" (*Hastiin X dóó ba'áłchíní*). The word *ba'áłchíní* (possibly meaning "his born-together," derived from the verb stem *-chį́*), if attached to a man's name, indicates both his wife and his children. The matricentric unit (those belonging to the same clan within the nuclear family) is juxtaposed against the father who belongs to another clan. This distinction of birth is maintained when discussing a woman and her children. If the word *ba'áłchíní* is attached to a woman's name, it indicates only her children (e.g., *Asdzáán X dóó ba'áłchíní*, "Mrs. Long and her children"). In this case, the matricentric unit is split apart because the woman is taken as a point of reference. From her point of view, it is only her children, not the children and her husband, who are "born together" and of the same clan. The phrase "Mr. X and his wife and children" is useful in describing the typical composition of the nuclear family household and the composition of an extended family residence group consisting of the households of an older couple, married daughters, and, occasionally, married sons.

Another important bond is between siblings. For the Navajo, the sibling tie is an extension of the mother-child bond, as shown in the phrase *'áłah hajééh*, which refers to one sibling group of all those born from the same woman's womb (literally, "together, plural objects came up and out"). The phrase groups together siblings of the same mother, even if they have separate fathers, but it does not apply to children of different mothers with the same father. It labels sisters and brothers in distinction to classifactory siblings of the same clan. The phrase is congruent with the birth and clan concepts previously discussed and with actual residential arrangements. Since children tend to stay with the mother if parents are separated, half-siblings with the same mother and different fathers usually reside in the same household or camp, while siblings with the same father and different mothers are normally separated.

A man's siblings can be referred to by the phrase *Hastiin X bił hajééh* (Mr. X, with him plural objects came up and out), or one sibling can be designated by *Hastiin X bił ha'aazh* (Mr. X, with him we two came up and out). Sibling bonds knit together households within the same residence group (in which married brothers and sisters reside) and maintain ties between households of distant residence groups (when siblings have moved through marriage or have established independent camps).

A final dyad of importance is that of husband and wife. The relationship between male and female in the roles of husband and wife is defined both through myth and ritual and through the public expression of the norms governing the relationship.[1] The male-female dichotomy is prominent in Navajo curing ceremonies and is one of the most important dimensions for patterning the use of ritual objects and actions (Lamphere 1969). The Navajo pantheon contains many pairs of male and female supernaturals (e.g., Holy Man and Holy Woman, Holy Boy and Holy Girl). Their exploits are described in Navajo myths, each of which provides a charter for one of the sings. The sexual and procreative aspects of the male-female relationship are the topic of many myth episodes. The breaking of incest taboos and adultery are punished, and marriage relationships are shifting and short-lived (Spencer 1957: 60–63).

In contrast to curing rituals, which stress male-female symbolism, and myth, which treats the sexual aspects of the male-female relationship, domestic aspects are publicly acknowledged as part of the Navajo wedding ceremony. The roles of husband and wife entail certain rights and duties of coresidence and the pooling of goods and services. These obligations are the subject of speeches that follow the wedding feast provided by the bride's relatives.[2]

As one Copper Canyon woman described the content of the speeches, ''They tell the man to take care of the wife, to think of the home—how to build it—and to think about the food and getting wood and water. Later they say he should never take his hand to his wife (i.e., beat her). For the woman, she is told to cook, wash, iron, take care of the house, fix the bed, and keep care of the children.''

Interviews with several Copper Canyon informants indicate the following phrases are typically used by speakers to communicate role obligations:

Navajo Phrase	English Translation
1. *Hazhó' hastiin bits'iiła.* *Hazhó' ba ch'iiyáán ndlį́.*	Cook for the man.
2. *Hazhó' 'esdzáán ba'ahidiilniił.*	Chop wood for the woman.
3. *Tó bá nahikaah.*	Get water for her.
4. *Wóne' nazlaadii 'aha'nahoołnii'.*	Buy furniture (possessions) for each other.
5. *Doo 'oołchį ha'áchį da.*	Don't get mad at each other.
6. *Niha'áłchíní dibé bá shona'ołt'eeh.*	Acquire sheep for your children.
7. *Doo ałda' yájiłti da.*	Don't talk back to each other.
8. *Bá 'ańdli'aa, t'áá 'aniłnii'go.*	Do something for her (or him) when she (or he) tells you to do something.
9. *Yóó'ahołt'e łago.*	Don't divorce each other.
10. *Hazhó' sokee'.*	Stay together nicely.

The last two statements stress the importance of a stable marriage, while other injunctions emphasize the establishment of a common household and the division of labor between a man and his wife. A woman's chores (cooking for the husband) are juxtaposed against those of a man (hauling wood and water, building a house, etc.). Two injunctions stress the avoidance of behavior that is undesirable for all Navajo, no matter which role is being followed: getting angry and "talking back."

Despite norms prescribing stability, marital bonds are weak (Aberle 1961: 165), and divorce is common during the initial years of a marriage. Kluckhohn's comments on Rimrock marriage were also true for Copper Canyon during the post-World War II years. "It was very unlikely that any man would reach old age without having been married to at least two different women. A great many would have had three wives and a considerable number four or more. A fair number of women would have only a single husband by the age of 60, but many would also have had two, three, or more. Most fertile men and women who lived to the age of 60 would have had children from at least two different spouses" (1966: 353). In other words, the facts of married life are more congruent with the view of shifting relations expressed in myth than with the norms stated at Navajo weddings.

In sum, the Navajo husband-wife relationship is unstable, yet the obligations of this relationship are the only rights and duties attached to particular roles that are publicly acknowledged on a ritual occasion. The tie between a mother and her children is seen as strong and enduring, while the tie of a father to his children is positive but more distant. Sibling ties are an outgrowth of the mother-child bond and remain strong even after adulthood. There is no one term for the nuclear family that suggests it is an undifferentiated unit, or contrasts it with the extended family. The phrase "Mr. X and his wife and children" describes the nuclear family but indicates that the mother-child unit is a distinct subgroup separated from the father. The phrase, since it is based on notions of common birth and clanship, is flexible in its application to particular collections of kin. It can refer to a nuclear family of a young couple and children, or to an older couple, their married children, and (by inference) their grandchildren.

Concepts Concerning Spatial Relations

In addition to concepts that describe kin relations, in defining domestic groups it is also important to examine concepts that relate to locality. Among the Navajo, this would necessarily entail a discussion of the *hoghan* as a social space, and the ways of describing spatial relations within and between clusters of hoghans. *Hoghan* is the Navajo term for dwelling; the prefix *ho* refers to space and *-ghan* means "live-in," so that a literal translation of the term is "a space which is lived in." The six-to-eight-sided log dwelling with a cribbed log roof and dirt covering is called *hoghan nímazi* (round house) by Copper Canyon people, to differentiate it from the one- or two-room log cabins that became popular in the 1950s. A common Navajo question refers to both the dwelling and the area of residence rather than to the group who inhabit the hoghan. Thus, "Where do you live?" (*Háadish nighan?*) is the same as asking, "Where is your house?", since *nighan* (you living) is a verbal element that can sometimes be treated like a nominal one, such as in *nighan* (your house) in the phrase *Nighanish hólǫ́?*, "Do you have a house?", or literally, "Your house, does it exist?".

The floor plan of the *hoghan nímazi*, as it is used during a curing ceremony, is divided into male and female halves. The men always sit on the south side and the women on the north. There is a four-fold direction and color scheme that patterns the use of actions and objects during a ritual. Female objects are often associated with west and north, male objects with south and east. The east, in turn, is associated with the "sacred" (*diyin*), and the north is associated with its opposite— ugly conditions" (*hóchǫ*) (Lamphere 1969).

The same sex associations have been preserved in the arrangements of belongings in a hoghan or cabin when it is not being used for a ritual. Belongings associated with the woman's role (cupboards, dishes, food, etc.) are on the north side; the man's workbench for silversmithing may be placed on the south side. The stove occupies a central position, and the bed and clothing (stored in suitcases) are in the rear. A loom is usually placed on the south side, even though it is associated with women, probably because there is little room for it on the north side, already crowded with shelves, tables, and benches. Thus the hoghan itself reflects the importance of the husband-wife relationship, both in the symbolic associations made during rituals, and in the spatial arrangement of objects in it. The hoghan structure is a spatial reminder of the role of the male and female in the establishment and maintenance of the household.

Typically, several hoghans or cabins are clustered together and occupied by members of related households. In addition to several hoghans, this cluster may contain a sheep corral, a horse corral, one or more storage sheds or a cellar, one or more woodpiles, and barrels for water storage. At Copper Canyon, winter clusters are more elaborate, with more storage area, a more permanent corral, and larger houses, which often have tar paper roofing and cement stucco outer walls to provide better insulation. Hoghans, or plain log cabins with dirt roofing, are the rule in summer clusters. Several families put up tents to provide extra sleeping room, and many have summer "shades" (*chaha'oh*) for cooking and eating. All the above items are not necessary, since an isolated individual without livestock may live in a single hoghan or cabin without any of the additional accoutrements.

While living in Copper Canyon, I investigated, both through formal eliciting procedures and through informal observation of Navajo conversation and interaction, the ways in which Navajos discuss the spatial arrangements of dwellings. I discovered that there is no Navajo term that designates clusters of hoghans, whether composed of one or several dwellings. Even the question "With whom do you live?" is ambiguous. To the query *Háish yił dabighan?* (Who, with-you, plural they-live?), the same informants could answer either *Sha'áłchíní t'eiyá* (My children only), referring to the nuclear family in one hoghan, or *Shimá, shizhé'é, shádí, shideezí, sha'áłchíní, dóó shił dabighan* (My mother, my father, my older sister, my younger sister, my children, also, I live with), enumerating members of a residence group and implying that they live in separate hoghans. Using even more general terms, the same informant might state *Shik'éí shił dabigan* (I live with my relatives). It is understood that not all of the relatives, only some, live in the same place. This answer would probably only refer to a cluster of hoghans, not just to a single nuclear family dwelling.

To a member of the Copper Canyon community the reference of each of the three statements would be clear, since his knowledge of the speaker's residence group and kin affiliations would supply the correct context. As an outsider lacking sufficient knowledge to solve the inherent ambiguity in an informant's answers, I could clarify the situation by asking who lives "in the same hoghan" (*t'ááła'í hoghan*), and who lives "in different or separate hoghans" (*t'áá 'ał'ąą hoghan*). I could also discuss with my informants how closely hoghans are grouped together. Dwellings which are "side by side" are *bííghahgóó*, and those which are "rather close" are *binaagóó*, while those which are "far away" are *t'áá nízaadi*. The first two terms delineate hoghans in the same cluster, while the third term describes houses in neighboring clusters. Use of these spatial terms for isolating clusters is not always possible, however. In areas of fairly dense settlement (especially in parts of Copper Canyon), people who live *binaagóó* might be classed in two different clusters rather than one, if kinship affiliation and amount of daily cooperation are considered in addition to sheer distance between houses.

In sum, when speaking in Navajo, it is feasible for the anthropologist to find out who lives in a cluster of hoghans, how they are related to each other, and which individuals occupy which hoghan. Informants are also skilled in drawing sketch-maps of clusters, giving the spatial relationship of hoghans and their occupants. In contrast to the anthropologist, the Navajo stranger to a community is not as inquisitive, since this would be a form of rudeness. He is more likely, when visiting a residence cluster, to observe who goes in and out of which hoghan and make inferences from what he is told. His hosts, if the visit is a long one, will probably tell him who the members of the residence group are and what their kinship statuses are. However, there are no formal introductions, as this would be extremely impolite. The children of the camp disappear immediately when a stranger arrives; they return only after the visitor has been there for some time and after they have become accustomed to his presence. Adults act in a similar manner, especially affines in the camp, such as sons-in-law and daughters-in-law.

It is also possible to ask where someone lives (*Hastiin Neez, háadish bighan?*, Mr. Long, where he-lives?), and get directions to the residence group site. However, as in the case of most Navajo discourse, the reference is to an individual, not to a group. One cannot ask, "Where is his household?" or "Where is his residence group?", but asks, "Where does he live?" (*Háadish bighan?*). Likewise, a Navajo cannot refer to "my household" or "my residence group," although he can refer to "my house" (*shighan*, meaning the dwelling), or to "my children" (*sha'áłchíní*), or he can enumerate the relatives with whom he lives. Even terms like "my relatives" (*shik'éí*), or "my clan relatives" (*shití'ízini*), are of little help since these refer to classes of people more inclusive than those who dwell in a single hoghan or a cluster of hoghans.[3] In sum, the Navajo language does not provide labels for the household and residence group, though the native language can be used to discuss spatial arrangement of residences.

Household Structure and Composition

Despite the brittleness of marriage, Navajos place importance on the husband-wife relationship both in the public expression of norms governing these roles and in the spatial organization of the hoghan. Mother-child, father-child, and sibling-sibling bonds are all positive and strong. On the basis of the evidence, and even though a Navajo label is lacking, I suggest that the nuclear family household is the smallest domestic unit and that the hoghan is the dwelling which defines its spatial boundaries.

Not all hoghans in Copper Canyon, however, contain nuclear families. Due to death, divorce, and bachelorhood, there may be a variety of other combinations of kin living under the same roof: widowed or divorced women and their children, widowed or divorced men and their children, isolated bachelors, or a grandmother and grandchild. There may also be some "doubling up" with portions of two nuclear families in the same hoghan: a grandmother, her married daughter, husband, and children, or a young married couple and either the husband's or wife's parents and unmarried siblings.

Conversely, a nuclear family may occupy two adjacent hoghans. For example, the parents and some children may sleep in one dwelling, and older children may share a cabin attached to the main room or located a few feet away. Although spatial units and kinship groups may not always coincide, Navajos recognize a cluster of people "who cook and eat together," expressed in the phrase *'ałahji' ch'iiyáán dił'į dóó 'ałahjí da'ííyą́ą́* (together food is prepared, and together they eat). Interaction concerning these activities usually stabilizes around a nuclear family in a single hoghan. Table 4.1 classifies data on the size and composition of households in Copper Canyon, using the criteria of commensality as the basis for defining the household.[4]

TABLE 4.1
Households in Copper Canyon

	Number of Households	Population	Percent
A. Nuclear households (man, wife, and children)	109	626	75.69
B. Women and children (widowed or divorced)	14	77	9.72
C. Women alone (widowed or divorced)	8	8	5.56
D. Women, children, and grandchildren; women and grandchildren	6	21	4.16
E. Men and children (widowed or divorced)	4	17	2.79
F. Isolated men	3	3	2.08
	144	752	100.00
Nonresident nuclear families	48	197	
Nonresident mothers and children	5	21	
Nonresident individual adults	45	45	
Totals	242	1015	

These statistics also are compared with data available from other communities: Rimrock, Shonto, Klagetoh, and Navajo Mountain (see Appendix 1). The data from Copper Canyon are remarkably similar to those from other areas despite the fact that Navajo Mountain and Klagetoh were studied initially in 1938 (Collier 1966), Rimrock in 1950 (Kluckhohn 1966: 368), and Shonto in 1956 (Adams 1963: 56). In general, 60–75 percent of the households are composed of nuclear families, about 10–15 percent contain widows and children, and the remainder include grandmothers and grandchildren, isolated males, or nuclear families with additional relatives.

Classification of the Copper Canyon data was problematic in some cases, due to the doubling up of parts of nuclear families, as previously mentioned. For example, when a couple is first married, they sometimes spend the first months or year of their marriage in the house of either the boy's or the girl's parents. In such cases they share food and utensils with the older couple and the unmarried children. The younger couple contributes to the food supply and the daughter or daughter-in-law helps with the cooking, while the son or son-in-law chops wood, hauls water, and helps with other household chores. Until a new house or hoghan has been constructed for the younger couple, and until separate arrangements for food, water, and wood are made, both couples are classed, along with unmarried children, as one household. In a few cases, a girl remains with her mother while the husband returns to his parents; this happens when the marriage is breaking apart, and before it is clear that the couple will be separated permanently. The girl, even if she has young children, cooks and eats with her mother; I have classified her and any children as part of the parental household.

On the other hand, several old women stay in the same house with a daughter or other relative. They have their own food supply (purchased from welfare income) and their own utensils. If they cook and eat separately from the rest of the family, they are counted as a distinct household, despite the sharing that takes place between such a "grandmother" and her relatives. These women maintain a fair amount of independence and, for example, may not move up on the Mountain when the rest of the household does, or may stay with other relatives for several days at a time.

In sum, although the Navajo do not distinguish in verbal discourse a unit equivalent to the nuclear family household, there is both cultural and social evidence that allows the investigator to isolate this domestic group. Bonds between nuclear family members are viewed as positive and strong, and the nuclear family shares food and sleeping arrangements in the same dwelling. Moreover, Copper Canyon census data lend themselves to classification in terms of nuclear family households. Exceptional cases are those where death or marital separation has broken up a nuclear family or where old age or the economic circumstances of a newly married couple has produced a situation where additional relatives are temporarily living in the same hoghan with a nuclear family. Census material from other communities (summarized in Appendix 1) also shows the importance of the nuclear family as a residential unit, even though the data were gathered by different investigators at different points in time in widely separated areas of the reservation. The theoretical predilections of individual anthropologists and differences in population density, economic adaptation, or acculturation seem to have had little effect in creating differences and variations at this level of social structure at least. Data are remarkably similar, supporting my analysis that the nuclear family household is the smallest unit of Navajo social structure. The definition of the next largest unit of social integration—the camp or residence group—is much more complex and necessitates a discussion of the developmental cycle of domestic groups as well as the use of Navajo concepts already described.

Developmental Cycle of Domestic Groups

In order to define and classify data on a second important Navajo social unit—the residence group—it is helpful to introduce an anthropological construct: the developmental cycle of domestic groups. The notion was introduced by Fortes (1949: 63) and utilized by Goody and others (1958) to conceptualize shifts in the composition of housekeeping units due to biological maturation of individuals involved and to replacement of every generation by the next through death and birth (Goody 1958: 1). "The domestic group goes through a cycle of development analogous to the growth cycle of a living organism. The group as a unit retains the same form, but its members, and the activities that unite them, go through a regular sequence of changes during the cycle that culminates in the dissolution of the original unit and its replacement by one or more units of the same kind'' (Goody 1958:2). The processes of formation, expansion, fission, and replacement characterize these changes and mark the stages or phases of the developmental cycle.

Conceptualization of the Navajo developmental cycle will focus on the phrase *Hastiin X dóó ba'áłchíní* (a man, his wife, and children) and describe changes in the composition of this unit as the nuclear family grows and becomes an extended family. As noted earlier, the Navajo phrase applies equally well to the members of a nuclear family living in one hoghan (a household) or to an extended family living in a cluster of hoghans (several households).

In the first phase of the cycle, a newly married young couple resides with either the husband's or wife's relatives and establishes a household within the parental camp. Navajos usually agree that a young couple should live with the wife's mother (uxorilocally). There are circumstances, however, under which this is neither possible nor desirable. Virilocality results when the wife has no mother with whom to live, when a young husband cannot get along with his in-laws, or when a job or the requests of a man's parents (for help in herding or farming) make it desirable for him to stay with them. Very often a son and his wife will stay with his widowed mother, especially when there is no daughter and son-in-law to give aid. Young couples at Copper Canyon also are likely to take wage jobs and settle in other reservation communities or in cities in western United States. The trend in the 1960s has been for many to return, between jobs or after a period of a few years, to live in the extended camp of either husband or wife. Whether younger couples will continue to return to the reservation or whether they will begin to settle in the cities and remain there through middle age is not yet clear, but Aberle's 1967 data suggest that the latter will be the trend.

A couple may share the same hoghan as the parents, but soon a new dwelling is constructed, and independent cooking and eating arrangements are maintained. One or more brothers or sisters may marry and live in the same camp in separate dwellings.

The second phase involves the fission of the residence group. One or more of the younger couples move off to found new camps as couples become economically self-sufficient. The new residences are usually located within a few miles of the parent camp and often within its previous grazing territory. During this period, one or both parents may die, and one or two of the children with their families may remain at the parent camp area to retain control of the land and other resources. While the Navajo often abandon or destroy dwellings after the death of inhabitants, they usually do not abandon the area the family controls for grazing. New units produced by the moving off of middle-aged couples and their children are camps reduced to their smallest proportions: the nuclear family household.

In the third period of the cycle, new camps are expanded as children marry and form new households. These, in turn, eventually repeat the process of fission and growth.

As shown earlier, there are no Navajo concepts corresponding to the household or residence group, and no close fit between Navajo phrases describing the spatial relation of hoghans, or those describing groups of kin. However, using the Navajo concept of *Hastiin X dóó ba'áłchíní* (a man, his wife, and children) in combination with the notion of a developmental cycle of domestic groups, it is possible to define a residence group as either a nuclear family living in an isolated hoghan, or an extended family living in a cluster of hoghans. In the former case, the residence group is composed of one household of those who cook and eat together; its focus is a middle-aged couple in the second state of the developmental cycle. In the latter case, the residence group is composed of several households; it contains young couples in the first phases of the cycle, and an older couple or widow in the third stage of the cycle. The internal composition of an extended family residence group varies depending on the postmarital residence affiliation of the younger couples, that is, whether they are residing uxorilocally or virilocally. The utility of this definition will become clear after examining variations in residence patterns, problems in the classification of residence groups, and patterns of authority and communication within the residence group.

Residence Patterns and the Domestic Group Cycle

The data on residence patterns reveal two facets of the developmental cycle of the residence groups: (1) the degree to which couples move off to found new camps and (2) the strength of uxorilocality as compared to virilocality in postmarital residence.

If the residence affiliation of couples in Copper Canyon is examined in relation to age, the process of becoming residentially independent can be illustrated. In Table 4.2 a couple is classed as residing uxorilocally if they are living in the same residence group as the wife's relatives. They are living virilocally if they are in the same residence group as the husband's relatives. Independent means that a couple have established a household and are heads of a residence group some distance from, but still within the neighborhood of, parents or other relatives. Neolocal is differentiated from independent so as not to confuse acculturative influences (where young couples take jobs away from the residence group of parents) with the developmental process described in the domestic cycle. The difference is between nonkinship and kinship considerations in residence choice. The residence of one Copper Canyon couple is determined by the husband's job at the trading post and is classed as neolocal. Neolocal figures in parentheses indicate couples who have moved out of Copper Canyon and have taken jobs in other reservation communities or off the reservation. They are part of the nonresident population (263 members) as contrasted with the resident population (752 members).

TABLE 4.2
Residence of Copper Canyon Couples, 1966

Age	Type of Residence				
	Uxorilocal (no.)	Virilocal (no.)	Independent (no.)	Neolocal* (no.)	Total† (no.)
To 35	16	14	3	1 (29)	34 (63)
36–55	22	7	19	(16)	48 (64)
Over 55	1	1	22	(3)	24 (27)
Total (no.)	39	22	44	1	106 (154)
Total (%)	36.8	20.8	41.5	.9	100

*Numbers in parentheses indicate couples who had moved away from Copper Canyon and were living in reservation towns or off-reservation urban areas.

†Numbers in parentheses are totals of preceding figure and parenthetical figure of preceding column.

TABLE 4.3
Residence of Rimrock Couples, 1963

Age	Type of Residence				
	Uxorilocal (no.)	Virilocal (no.)	Independent (no.)	Neolocal (no.)	Total (no.)
To 35	30	18*	4	12	64
36–55	11†	10	24	6	51
Over 55			21		21
Total (no.)	41	28	49	18	136
Total (%)	30	21	36	13	100

*Includes 3 fratrilocal couples, one with his brother's exwife.
†Includes 2 sororilocal couples.

Younger couples, if they choose to reside in the community, tend to live in the camps of either the husband's or wife's relatives. As a couple becomes older, one or more of the parents die, or the couple moves off to found a new camp; hence, an increasing number of independent residence choices exist among older Navajos.

Data from Rimrock, New Mexico, show how the rate of moving off can vary from community to community depending on demographic variation in local populations and differences in the availability of land.

In Rimrock, couples tend to become residentially independent and heads of their own residence groups at an earlier age than at Copper Canyon, and there is less movement of younger couples to other reservation communities and to off-reservation cities to take wage jobs. Wage work, in Rimrock, is available in a nearby town and at the BIA boarding school. Thus, the meaning of the category neolocal (residence that is not kin determined) is much different in Rimrock than at Copper Canyon. Eleven younger and middle-aged couples have moved in or near the town to take wage jobs, and they are classed as neolocal although they are only five to twenty miles from their relatives. A smaller number of neolocals (seven couples) have moved to more distant towns and cities for jobs. This is in marked contrast to Copper Canyon where there are few local wage opportunities so that twenty-nine younger couples (45 percent) have taken jobs and moved out of the community to places fifty to one thousand miles from their families. Independence also differs in the two communities. There is greater population dispersion due to the availability of more land in Rimrock, and couples are able to move off from relatives earlier in the life cycle. Thus 60 percent of the middle-aged Copper Canyon couples are living uxorilocally or virilocally, while only 40 percent of the Rimrock couples are doing so.

In sum, young Rimrock couples are more likely to live in their parents' residence group, while Copper Canyon couples are just as likely to move out of the community as to establish a household uxorilocally or virilocally. Due to a broader land base, middle-aged Rimrock couples are more likely than Copper Canyon couples to become independent during this period of their life. It is more typical at Copper Canyon for a couple to become independent when either the wife's or husband's parents die, or when one parent dies and the other goes to live with one of the other married children. Some middle-aged couples (mostly those in their late thirties and early forties) still reside away from Copper Canyon.

TABLE 4.4
Residence Patterns of Household Heads, According to Neighborhood

Pattern	Neighborhood	Household Heads (no.)	(%)
Matrilocal	Single adult near matrilineal relatives	14	10
Uxorilocal	Same camp as wife's relatives	43	30
Uxorilocal	Same area as wife's relatives	33	22
(Subtotal)		(90)	(62)
Virilocal	Same camp as husband's relatives	24	16
Virilocal	Same area as husband's relatives	14	10
Virilocal	Same area as deceased husband's relatives	6	4
(Subtotal)		(44)	(30)
Independent	Not related to anyone in same area	11	8
(Subtotal)		(11)	(8)
Total		145	100

Though data from both communities illustrate the process of fission and formation of new residence groups, the characteristics of the domestic group cycle are more clearly seen in the Rimrock statistics. Figures from Copper Canyon reflect movement out of the community and less moving off of middle-aged couples due to the smaller land base and the slightly more dense settlement pattern of the community.

Residence data are useful in determining the strength of ties with the wife's relatives in comparison to those with the husband's relatives. Table 4.2 indicates that younger couples, if they remain in Copper Canyon, are equally likely to reside uxorilocally as virilocally (47 percent compared to 41 percent). However, examination of the residence of all couples shows that only 37.7 percent are residing uxorilocally and 19.0 percent virilocally. This apparent low rate of uxorilocality is due to the use of a classification scheme designed to reveal the process of moving off.

If the data are reclassified to show which couples, in moving off to found new camps or in continuing the camps of deceased parents, still remain near the wife's relatives, the strength of uxorilocal ties can be more accurately indicated. In Table 4.4 the distinction between residence in the same camp and residence in the same neighborhood is maintained, but it is still possible to determine whether the couple lives closer to the wife's or the husband's relatives; the table summarizes the residence patterns of household heads, and is based on the male member of the 106 resident couples listed in Table 4.2 and thirty-nine single adults, including both males and females. Data on nonresident couples have been omitted.

These data indicate the strength of uxorilocality over two generations and suggest that ties among married females of the same matriline are similar to those of other communities. Fifty-two percent of residence choices are uxorilocal in Copper Canyon and Shonto, as compared to 48.3 percent in Many Farms and Rimrock (Richards 1963:29). On the other hand, matrilineal ties of married males (virilocality: 30 percent) seem intermediate between Many Farms (20.7 percent) and Rimrock (28 percent) on one hand, and Shonto (42 percent) on the other.

The Navajo themselves say that a married couple should live "with his or her mother''; the wife's mother is preferable, but the husband's mother is a reasonable alternative, especially if the wife's mother is deceased or remarried. It is important, then, to stress that these are ties of matrifiliation, not matrilineal descent. It is the mother-child bond, particularly the mother-daughter bond that is important, not membership in a corporate matrilineal group.

In sum, an analysis of residence patterns supports the usefulness of the concept of a domestic group cycle. The cycle includes (1) the establishment of a household of young married couples in an existing camp, (2) the moving off of middle-aged couples to found new camps, and (3) the maintenance of the old residence site by one of the middle-aged couples after the death of parents. In addition, residence patterns demonstrate the importance of uxorilocality, with virilocality as an accepted and frequent alternative. This is true for the residence choices of young couples within extended family camps and for older couples within a larger local area or neighborhood. I have suggested that these residence ties are ones of matrifiliation, not matriliny. As indicated by both cultural concepts and residence choices, the bonds between a woman and her married daughters are strong. If, however, these are broken by death, a couple is likely to reside near the husband's mother or married siblings. Couples are also likely to live virilocally (rather than uxorilocally) for economic reasons or due to a long history of disputes with the wife's parents or siblings.

Composition of Residence Groups

The concept of a domestic group developmental cycle leads us to expect at any one point in time that the composition and size of residence groups within a community will vary from nuclear family camps (in the middle phase of the cycle) to extended family camps (with couples in the first and third phases of the cycle). In turn, due to the factors just discussed, the composition of an extended family camp will vary according to whether the residence choices of sons and daughters have been virilocal or uxorilocal. Variation in the composition of Copper Canyon residence groups is shown in Table 4.5.

TABLE 4.5
Classification of Copper Canyon Residence Groups

Type of Residence Group	Number	Percentage
Nuclear Camps		
Husband, wife, and children	28	
Woman and children	3	
Man and children	2	
(Subtotal)	(33)	42.3
Isolated individuals	5	6.4
(Subtotal)	(5)	
Extended camps		
Uxorilocal	22	
Virilocal	6	
Mixed	12	
(Subtotal)	(40)	51.3
Total	78	100.0

In classifying the data, I have used the following considerations derived from Navajo conceptions related to kinship and the spatial arrangement of dwellings:

1. Kinship: How closely does the cluster conform to the notion of an expanding nuclear family (*Hastiin X dóó ba'áłchíní* or *Asdzáán X dóó ba'áłchíní*)? A residence group is thus made up of a man, his wife, and children. If the camp is an extended one, some of the children have married and built their own houses.
2. Space: How closely are the houses clustered? Are they "side by side" (*bííghahgóó*) or "rather close" (*binaagóó*), rather than "far away" (*t'áá nízaadi*)? In the anthropological literature this spatial clustering has been described as hoghans "within shouting distance" of each other (Levy 1962).

A camp is uxorilocal-extended when only married daughters reside there; it is considered virilocal-extended if only married sons have remained, and mixed-extended if married sons and daughters live with one or both parents.

Appendix 2 gives a complete list of Copper Canyon residence groups, their composition, and number of residents, in addition to maps showing summer and winter locations. Appendix 3 compares data on residence group composition with statistics from other Navajo communities.

Thus far I have combined Navajo concepts relating to familial roles and spatial relationships between dwellings with the anthropological notion of a developmental cycle to propose a structural model of Navajo domestic groups; and I have developed criteria for reclassifying residence patterns and for determining the composition of residence groups. These criteria follow Navajo concepts as far as possible and are explicitly stated, whereas the classification systems built into data analysis from other Navajo communities are not (Adams 1958, Kluckhohn 1966, Richards 1963). This approach has the following advantages: (1) It provides a dynamic model which better accounts for the variation in residence patterns and residence group composition within one community than a static model. (2) It allows the comparison of data from several different communities.

As an example, my discussion of the differences between residence patterns in Copper Canyon and Rimrock brought out the effects of population density, a broader land base, and the nearness of wage jobs on residence choice. Also, Appendix 3 shows that residence groups in more sparsely settled western Navajo communities are larger and further apart, while residence group composition in Copper Canyon seems similar to that of Rimrock (an off-reservation community) and to that on the reservation as a whole.

I have written as if both the household and the residence group were easily identifiable, bounded groups, with a stable constellation of roles where members of the group manage a joint estate and are obligated to each other in terms of specific rights and duties. Navajo households exhibit these characteristics to a greater extent than do residence groups, which lack corporateness for several important reasons.

Although there are ways of discussing residential arrangements, there are no Navajo terms which might indicate that the Navajo themselves conceptualize those living in a hoghan cluster as a bounded unit. Even using relevant Navajo concepts concerning genealogical and spatial relationships, it is often difficult for the investigator to decide whether these kinsmen constitute one, two, or even three residence groups. The separation of parents and married children or of several siblings and their spouses may be gradual. The residence group cycle lacks major discontinuities, so that, at any one point in time, siblings may be at the beginning of a period of fission where cooperation is becoming more occasional but where spatial separation is not entirely complete.

Finally, the residence group (if it can be called a group) does not own property collectively. Livestock is individually owned and jointly managed, and fields are jointly used. Rights to use the land on which the residence group is located are controlled by those living in the residence group, particularly the older couple. This involves concepts of "use rights" rather than ownership, so that grazing territory is vaguely defined and constantly shifting. Members of unrelated extended families often move between camps of extended families already located in an area, either without consulting the "older" families or by claiming rights to the area through a relative in the previous generation who had resided there. In general, grazing and residence rights are always changing and are not perpetuated from one generation to the next, making them poor criteria for establishing the corporateness of the residence group.

Division of Labor, Authority, and Communication in Household and Residence Group

Daily patterns of cooperation, authority, and communication, however, make the household and residence group more easily identifiable than larger collections of relatives. There is a rough division of labor in the household, with the wife performing the cooking, housecleaning, weaving, washing and ironing, and the primary care of children. The husband usually carries out the heavier tasks, such as housebuilding and repair, water and wood hauling, and wood chopping. As already noted, these tasks are mentioned specifically in speeches made at the traditional Navajo wedding ceremony when the bride and groom are morally counseled as to the duties of their new roles. Many other activities are shared, however, and on numerous occasions one partner takes over a task usually delegated to the opposite sex when the other spouse is absent. For example, almost every Navajo male can cook; when his wife is away, he can prepare mutton stew, boil coffee, and make fried bread or flour tortillas. Similarly, a woman often carries water from a nearby spring, or if she drives a pickup truck, she may haul it from a distant well; she often chops wood for the cookstove and frequently makes repairs. The flexible division of labor is clearly related to the existence of households containing a widowed or divorced man or woman, a bachelor, or a grandmother. Most household tasks can be performed by one adult of either sex as long as there are other adult relatives within the same residence group who can aid in tasks requiring two or more people.

Joint activities within the residence group concern the care of the sheep herd and the cultivation of fields. The specific organization of tasks will be analyzed in Chapter 6, but general patterns of authority and communication, which are relevant to the organization of all tasks, can be outlined here. The major characteristics of communication in the residence group have been described by Aberle (1961). In an extended family camp the parents or widowed mother are the focus of communication and of organizing cooperation. Requests for aid are made directly between parents and children, though a father may use the mother as an intermediary with his daughters. Siblings communicate directly, or (especially with cross-sex siblings) use the mother as an intermediary. In-married affines are in a peripheral position. For instance, in the uxorilocal extended camp, a young man seeks help only through his wife and is solicited for assistance only through her. The wife communicates freely with all members of the group except her sister's husband, and uses her sister as an intermediary there (Aberle 1961: 161). For the young daughter-in-law who resides virilocally with her husband's parents and siblings, the husband is at first an intermediary between his kin and his wife. Then more direct communication develops between the wife, the mother-in-law, and sisters-in-law. The husband, and even the mother-in-law, becomes the intermediary only for requests involving the father-in-law and other males in the camp.

In general, the older couple is *t'áá bee bóholníih* for most situations and is in the position of making requests for aid of their children and spouses, especially in matters concerning livestock, fields, and transportation. The younger couples are most often in the position of giving aid or asking for loans or help with a ceremony.

As a couple becomes older, their position in relation to others in terms of authority and communication changes, as might be expected from discussion of the development cycle of domestic groups. During the early years of marriage when a couple resides in an extended family camp, the spouse who is a kinsman, especially a daughter, is closely tied to the parents and siblings. The in-married son-in-law is always being asked to help his in-laws with whom he has respectful but distant relationships. In turn, he still has important obligations to his own parents and siblings that take him away from his wife's camp. The wife and husband do not form a team who mutually consult on their daily affairs; rather the wife is a communicator and buffer between the parents and the son-in-law.

By the second phase of the residence group cycle, the couple has growing children and are more concerned with their household. There are advantages for the son-in-law if he wishes to move off to establish a new camp. He and his wife, if they have become a smoothly working team, can handle by themselves their own growing number of livestock and the cultivation of a field. If the son-in-law is a wage earner in or near the community, there is even less reason to remain with his wife's relatives.[5] In an independent camp he will be more free to run his daily affairs without being "at the beck and call" of in-laws with whom he has uneasy relations. By moving off, a son-in-law (in joint consultation with his wife) becomes *t'áá bee bóholníih* in a wider range of situations. The same advantages are available to a son living virilocally if he establishes his own camp. However, since his relationship with his parents is smoother, it is also to his advantage to remain in the home camp, gradually taking over decisions as the parental couple get older.

Also, as the parental couple increase in age, and after their death, tensions between siblings and their spouses, within the younger generation, increase. Brothers and sisters quarrel over livestock; accusations are made that one sibling has not contributed enough goods or labor to a ceremony. The magnitude of these arguments lessens with distance; by moving apart, tensions decrease and daily cooperation changes to more occasional visiting and requests (see Downs 1965 for a case example).

During the third phase of the residence group cycle when the couple (now older) is head of their own residence group containing married children, there are still important ties with siblings of the husband or wife. These ties are crucial in ceremonial cooperation where more individuals than those living in the residence group are needed to carry out a ceremony.

In sum, the vagueness of Navajo terminology, the lack of major discontinuities in the fission of the residence group, and the absence of a joint estate—all these factors qualify the notion of "residence group" and "household" as "groups." On the other hand, the primary kin (parents and married children) who live within shouting distance and who are in daily cooperation, especially for livestock and agricultural activities, and who jointly make use of the same area of land, form a regular pattern of communication and cooperative effort. Specifiable patterns of authority indicate that the older couple in an extended family residence group are the main requesters who organize herding and cultivating activities. In a nuclear family residence group (a couple in the second phase of the domestic group cycle), the husband and wife jointly consult on these matters and are *t'áá bee bóholnííh*. These considerations make it clear that this localized and tightly cooperating number of primary kin are more easily identifiable as "groups" than are larger collections of relatives.

Chapter 5

Clanship and the
Wider Network of Kin

~~~~~~

This study proposes a structural model of Copper Canyon Navajo domestic groups and uses that model to interpret kin ties and authority relationships within the household and residence group. It also carefully qualifies the definition of both domestic units, emphasizing that they are not corporate groups but units based on kinship and coresidence within which stable cooperation patterns exist. Before a model of the structural regularities that extend beyond Navajo domestic groups is proposed, an examination of Navajo concepts related to clanship and middle-sized kin groups, and anthropological analyses of these, will be presented. Two issues will be important in assessing previous studies: (1) the extent to which there are persisting "groups" beyond the domestic group level; and (2) the relative importance of genealogical versus clan ties in structuring cooperation.

In this chapter it is necessary to be more critical of previous studies than was the case in reassessing the nature of the household and residence group. I suggest here an alternative model that radically departs from those put forward by other anthropologists, using the constructs of "set" and "network" to analyze cooperation between kinsmen and clan relatives who are not coresident. This scheme goes beyond Navajo terminology for clanship, kin grouping, and neighborhood, but is consistent with the cultural model of cooperation discussed in Chapters 2 and 3 and, as I will show later, it is useful in analyzing actual cooperative behavior. This chapter also presents data on the spatial distribution of members of three Copper Canyon clans and their dispersal in various neighborhoods, showing how the segmentation of clans lends itself to the analysis of cooperation in terms of overlapping "sets," which link together residence groups in a "network of ties."

Navajo Concepts

Navajo concepts relevant to defining social relationships beyond those found in the household and residence group include (1) concepts of birth and kinship that define clan relationships; (2) concepts describing genealogical kin in addition to those in the nuclear or extended family; and (3) concepts based on locality rather than kinship.

As indicated earlier, a Navajo communicates his social identity to a Navajo stranger by stating his clan affiliations rather than his name. Clan membership is grounded in the Navajo concept of birth (indicated by the verb stem *-chííł*): Just as an individual is "born of" his mother and "born for" his father, he is "born of" his mother's clan and "born for" his father's clan. All those connected to ego through birth (a concept which includes both clan affiliation and actual biological ties) are "his relatives" (*bik'éí*). "My relatives" (*shik'éí*) refers to a large number of people, including members of my clan, my father's clan, those "born for" my father's and "born for" my clan, in addition to father's father (FF), mother's father (MF), son's son (SS), and mother's brother's son's son (MBSS), genealogical kin who are not affiliated by clan but who are labeled with kin terms also applied to clan relatives.

Clanship connects an individual to four sets of relatives, as seen in the following native phrases: (1) he is "on the side of" his clan (*-ńlíjí*, "he is-side," or "he is of this side"); (2) he is "born for" his father's clan, as expressed in the phrase *báshíshchíín* ("I am born for him or it"); (3) those who are "born for" his clan are children of males in his clan, which is expressed by the phrase *sháshchíín* ("he or she is born for me"); (4) those who are "born for" his father's clan (i.e., children of males in father's clan) are *'ahidiilchíín* ("we started out together in birth," i.e., our fathers are of the same clan). (Again I have used the pronoun "he" to translate third person verb and pronoun forms which actually mean he/she/it.) Using the example of someone whose mother is Bitterwater Clan and whose father is Salt Clan, the four relationships are:[1]

báshíshchíín:	*ńlíjí:*	*sháshchíín:*	*'ahidiilchíín:*
anyone who is Salt Clan (*Áshįįhí ńlį́*)	anyone who is Bitterwater (*Tódích'íi'nii nlį́*)	anyone born for Bitterwater (*Tódích'íi'nii yáshchíín*)	anyone who is born for Salt Clan (*'Áshįįhí yashchíín*)

A Navajo should not[2] marry anyone in any of these categories, as they are all "related to each other" (*'ałk'éí*) (*'ałk'éí jílíígo doo 'ahazhdoogeehda*, "related to each other, they being, do not marry each other").

The Navajo consider everyone of the same clan to be *t'ááłá'í dine'é* (one people), and those of different clans to be *t'áá'ał'ąą dine'é* (different people). Some clans are considered "related to each other" (*da bik'éí'it'é*: "they are relatives").[3] Members of related clans refer to each other by kin terms and may not intermarry. Such clans have been called "clan groups" or "phratries." There is no universal agreement on which clans should be classed together; however, the government survey—by consulting the available ethnographic sources and several informants—named nine clan groups and eight unassigned clans (where there was no consensus on affiliation or where it was agreed the clan did not belong to any group). Clan groups range in size from two to six clans, usually with one very large clan and several small ones (Aberle 1961: 183).

All members of every Navajo community can be categorized by clan, since members of the same clan and related clans see themselves as related to each other, address each other by kin terms, and do not intermarry. Potentially these kinsmen, who may be scattered in many residence groups throughout the community, could constitute groups that cooperate on particular occasions. On the other hand, cooperation should be based on recognized genealogical ties, which are emphasized so as to include a wider range of kin than those living in the same household or residence group.

Several Navajo phrases describe such genealogical, as contrasted with clan, relatives. The term *'átah hajééh*, as previously noted, designates one sibling group of "all those born from the same woman's womb" in connection with relationships within the nuclear family. The solidarity of the sibling group is strong and continues after brothers and sisters have ceased to live in the same household or residence group. As couples move off from the parent's camp, they maintain cooperation with the natal camp, as these are the "nearest" relatives (both spatially and genealogically). After the parents have died and the children are heads of their own family camps, married brothers or sisters are still an important source of help for ceremonies and other activities where a larger number of people are needed. Thus, the cooperation of elderly siblings spans several residence groups, and the term *'átah hajééh* may be appropriately applied to a sibling group at this stage in its life cycle, but technically it does not include the children and grandchildren of these siblings, who would also take a significant part in ceremonial activities. Another set of phrases does incorporate these relatives: a couple, their children, and their grandchildren. Taking the point of view of the grandparental couple, *Hastiin X ba'átchíní da'ahiilchííhígíí* means, "Mr. X, his wife and children, and their children, or the ones who bear after them." *Asdzáán X ba'átchíní da'ahiilchííhígíí*[4] means, "Mrs. X, her children, and their children." These two phrases could be taken as indication of a "group" of kin similar to a matrilineage, but including the son's children and, as mentioned in the first phrase, the male as well as the female founder. These phrases, however, are not found in daily conversation, and my informants have used them only when pressed to give a description of kinship relationships in Navajo.

Finally, there are two Navajo phrases that refer to locality rather than kinship as an organizing principle. The terms *kéédahat'ínii* or *kéédahat'ínígíí* mean "neighbors" or "those who dwell nearby."[5] In a broad sense, either phrase can be used to refer to a whole neighborhood or subsection of a community; for example, *kindahizhini kéédahat'ínígíí* (Black-house area, the people who live, they being) refers to all the people who live in the area of Black Mesa (the English name for the Navajo place located several miles north of the Copper Canyon trading post, which is called *kindahizhini*). As used in Copper Canyon, these terms may or may not refer to a group of relatives who occasionally cooperate. If, as in the case of Black Mesa, several siblings have established continuous residence groups, cooperation and kinship will coincide with the term "neighbors." In other areas of Copper Canyon, several sets of kin may occupy a named area, or only one residence group may exist on a place name site, with camps of other relatives at either another named place or in an area with no name. Thus, place names do not always coincide with collections of kin who are also "neighbors," and the term "neighbors" often can be appropriately applied to those living in unrelated camps whose residents do not cooperate even though they live close by.

In sum, Navajo concepts of clanship are important in establishing the social identity of the individual and in providing a set of social categories that delineate relatives (those included in ego's clan and phratry or in one of the three additional clans to which ego is related through his father, men in his own clan, and men in his father's clan) and nonrelatives (those in other clans who are marriageable). The question remains open as to whether the clan or a subsegment of the clan constitutes a cooperating group of kinsmen. Navajo concepts relating to genealogical kinship and locality are also inconclusive. There seems to be no term that unambiguously points to a stable group of cooperating kin beyond the residence group. It is important, then, to discuss the constructs that various anthropologists have proposed to describe groups based on either clanship, genealogical kinship, or locality.

Clan and Local Clan Element

Navajo clans are dispersed and nonlocalized; neither historical nor contemporary evidence exists to show that an entire clan constitutes a social group. Aberle describes the clan as "...a matrilineal exogamic category, membership in which is stipulated. It is egalitarian in character, lacks authoritative functions, and holds no property; it is unorganized. Clans are not ranked with respect to each other. They are variable in size and degree of localization" (1961: 111). The clan's main function is to regulate marriage and hospitality.

The government survey of the early 1930s (reported in Aberle 1961: 181) shows forty-five clans among 85–90 percent of the population. Allowing for clans that may have been overlooked, Aberle estimates the number of clans at about fifty. When the survey was conducted, the Navajo population was only thirty-five thousand and the size of clans ranged from thirty-six hundred to one. Four clans made up 39 percent of the population and were found in many parts of the reservation; other clans were found in only one area.

It is apparent, then, that an entire clan does not engage in collective action, since members of the clan, especially if it is large, may be spread over several hundred miles. Aberle has therefore used the term Local Clan Element (LCE) to designate members of one clan who live in a particular community.[6] Clan names once may have referred to people from a particular area (e.g., those from a place called House-in-the-Rocks, or *kiyaa'áanii*). With the growth and dispersal of the Navajo population over the last few centuries, the correlation between clan and place has broken down: instead, communities are made up of subpopulations from clans whose total population may be widely dispersed.

Aberle suggests, historically at least, that LCE operated in dispute settlement, provided mutual aid, and monopolized, but did not own, land:

> ... the LCE, although not highly organized, operated as the major unit of aid outside the extended family, bore the major responsibility for the person's derelictions, and served as the major agent for an individual in disputes which could not be handled on an interpersonal basis. In all these respects, it can be assumed that the first recourse was a person's own LCE, the second his father's and the third the LCEs of his clan group. (1961, pp. 117–18)

Since members of the same LCE are dispersed into several clusters, and since an LCE does not own land, it seems equally possible that only segments of an LCE or, more likely, genealogical kin, especially if they reside in the same local area or neighborhood, perform the functions Aberle describes. Although it is possible to categorize Navajos within a community according to clan, the Navajos themselves do not distinguish linguistically or behaviorally between members of the clan as a whole and members of its local contingent, the LCE. A Navajo will not differentiate between a man or woman who is "House-in-the-Rocks" (*kiyaa'áanii*) at Copper Canyon and one who is "House-in-the-Rocks" from another part of the reservation. Both are addressed by the same kin terms and are subject to the same marriage prohibitions and hospitality obligations—the two major social concomitants of common clanship. This suggests that the Navajo do not think in terms of a group which acts jointly, as Aberle implies, and indicates that the LCE is the construct of the observer rather than the natives.

Outfit and Other Middle-range Groups

Rather than emphasizing clanship as a basis for group structure, many anthropologists have posited a group larger than the household or residence group that is composed of genealogical kinsmen who cooperate in ritual and economic activities. The most commonly used label for this group is "outfit," a term proposed by Clyde Kluckhohn. He defines the outfit as follows:

> This Western term is used to designate a group of relatives (larger than the extended family) who regularly cooperate for certain purposes. Two or more extended families, or one or more extended families linked with one or more independent biological families, may habitually pool their resources on some occasions—say, planting and harvesting, and the giving of any major ceremonial for an individual member. (Kluckhohn and Leighton 1946: 62)

Kluckhohn stresses that an outfit may be scattered over a good many square miles, that cooperative work is not absolutely regular, and that membership is fluid. According to Kluckhohn, there is usually a male who is recognized as a leader and who has prestige through age, ceremonial knowledge, and wealth. The Navajo will constantly attach the name of this individual to the aggregate of kin they have in mind.

Terms similar to "outfit" have been proposed by other students of Navajo social organization. Kimball and Provinse (1942) suggest "land use community." Malcolm Carr Collier uses the term "cooperating unit" to describe groups at Navajo Mountain and Klagetoh (1966); William Adams (1963) suggests the concept of "resident lineage" to describe these groups at Shonto. It is not clear whether these are exactly equivalent to Kluckhohn's outfit, since few authors, including Kluckhohn, publish both hoghan maps and genealogical data describing the exact composition and residential placement of members in a community. The major exception is Collier's thesis, based on 1928 field data and published in 1966. Using maps, genealogies, and case material, she shows that at Klagetoh cooperating units are composed of two or more camps of either married siblings or a parental couple and married children who pool livestock and farming resources. At Navajo Mountain, in contrast, these activities are performed by members of a single residence group, or camp. Whether the cooperating units at Klagetoh are equivalent to, or smaller than, the outfits described by Kluckhohn is impossible to decide.

There also is no agreement about the equivalence of outfit, land-use community, and resident lineage. Kluckhohn states that outfits are not always land-use communities (Kluckhohn and Leighton, 1946; 1962 ed: 110). Adams (1963: 59) suggests that resident lineages are not functional—that is, they do not cooperate together—and hence are not the same as outfits. Some of this disagreement relates to the importance locality plays in the investigator's definition of a particular concept. The resident lineage and the land-use community are defined as localized groups of kin occupying adjacent land, while the outfit and the cooperating unit need not be.

Anthropologists who have published since Kluckhohn's initial definition include William Ross (1955), Jerrold Levy (1962), and James Downs (1965)[7] and Gary Witherspoon (1975); these authors have continued to use the term outfit in analyzing social organization in Fruitland, Tuba City, Piñon, and Rough Rock-Black Mountain. Kluckhohn (1966), in his final statement on the Rimrock community, still discusses the outfit as an important group, and his definition and description remain unchanged.

In sum, disagreement concerning the outfit and similar middle-range cooperating groups seems to revolve around: (1) size and composition of such a group; (2) its existence on all parts of the reservation; and (3) localization of the group, that is, whether it occupies continuous territory or whether its members are dispersed.

In a joint article with two other participants in the Harvard-Columbia National Science Foundation Field School, I attempted to clarify these definitional problems and proposed a precise genealogical definition of the outfit so that three generations of kin could be delineated whether or not they resided in the same neighborhood. I used this definition to describe the relation of outfits to local areas and their formation and fission throughout Rimrock's history (Reynolds,. Lamphere, and Cook 1967). Additional fieldwork, however, has convinced me that the term *outfit* does not correspond to any group that the Navajo recognize, either in terms of their own concepts or in terms of their cooperative activities.

I am also unpersuaded by Witherspoon's analysis that members of camps descended from a female head constitute a "group," i.e. a unit which is corporate, exists through time, and wherein individuals are bound by a set of rights and duties with regard to each other. It may be that in Ramah and Rough Rock between 1900 and 1950 cooperation was more closely focused on a collection of related camps where older males or females were easily identified as "leaders" or "heads." However, as these individuals died, a new leadership generation has not been so readily identifiable, and cooperation has taken a more ego-centered focus. However, in the present-day context, Witherspoon's data are not detailed enough to substantiate his assertion that "outfits" are viable groups. If the major functions of the outfit are "cooperation in performing major ceremonies; arbitration and resolution of local disputes . . . and mutual economic assistance in times of great scarcity and dire need" (1975: 108), then case material needs to be presented to show who came together in these situations, who focused the activity, and who was not involved. We need to know in what contexts various members of the "outfits" cooperate, in which they do not, and at which times members outside the "outfit" are drawn into a helping situation. I would argue that the kind of analysis presented in this book presents a better observer's model than one based on the assertion of the importance of groups like the "outfit." Before proposing an alternative analysis, however, it is important to discuss one other middle-range group, the matrilineage, as an anthropological construct for describing Navajo groups.

Mary Shepardson and Blodwen Hammond, in a restudy of Navajo Mountain, have suggested that the concept of lineage is "functionally useful for the analysis of settlement, residence patterns, cooperation, and locus of frequent interaction in Navajo society" (1970: 49). They offer the following definitions:

A lineage, perhaps best referred to as a *maximal lineage* consists of all the members alive or dead who trace actual descent unilinearly from a common ancestor. In the Navajo case this is a matrilineage, that is, the descendants of a common ancestor through females. A lineage group, to use Radcliffe-Brown's phrase, is composed of all members of a lineage who are alive at one time (1952: 14–15). A *localized matrilineage* includes those members of a matrilineage who live in one community, and a *minimal matrilineage* embraces the children of one mother. (1970: 49)

Shepardson and Hammond have presented evidence of the importance of the maximal matrilineage in inheritance of land use rights and monopoly over water resources. They also cite instances of ceremonial cooperation among members of a lineage group.

An Alternative Analysis: Set and Network

Rather than redefine the outfit or other middle-range groups, and instead of using the concept of a matrilineage, I will present an alternative model stressing the importance of networks. There are several reasons for rejecting the usefulness of constructs based on the notion of a social group with fixed membership criteria, joint economic or ritual activities, or a clearly definable set of rights and duties between members participating in various roles. I would argue that the notion of a group, defined in terms of one or more of these attributes, and used as an analytical tool, does not adequately characterize the ways in which the Navajo conceptualize social relations or organize activities.

The Navajo terms described earlier do not seem to fit with concepts proposed by anthropologists; for instance, the phrase "Mr. X, his wife and children, and their children" (*Hastiin X ba'áłchíní da'ahiilchííhígíí*) can be used to denote the range of kin covered by the outfit and cooperating unit, but it says nothing about occasional cooperation, an aspect important to the definition of both anthropological constructs. *Kéédahat'ínii* refers to those living in a local area, as do the concepts of land-use community and resident lineage, but the Navajo phrase does not indicate that these individuals are genealogically related as the anthropological concepts imply.

During the course of fieldwork, as I attempted to elicit Navajo phrases that might be equivalent to outfit, I became less and less convinced that the Navajo discuss cooperative activities in terms of this or a similar group. The difficulties my informants expressed in answering questions about the phrases that I thought might describe middle-range groups indicated that I was trying to validate a preconceived anthropological concept quite different from the Navajo interpretation of social relationships. Furthermore, questions about who should or does cooperate in a particular activity were answered vaguely by phrases like "my relatives" or "everyone helps."[8] If pressed, an informant would give a list of particular kinsmen who cooperated on a given occasion. Daily conversation did not reveal references to groups but to individual kinsmen who might be asked to provide aid.

I have even greater reservations about the concept of matrilineage. As with outfit, there is no congruence between native concepts and such anthropological notions as maximal lineage, lineage group, or localized matrilineage. Copper Canyon Navajos do not have a way of specifying or labeling a matrilineage of any depth except for the minimal lineage, that is, the children of one mother or those who are *áłah hajééh.*

Aberle has suggested that "Mrs. X, her children, and their children" (*Asdzáán X dóó ba'áłchíní da'ahiilchííhígíí*) refers to a matrilineage, but this is not its usage in Copper Canyon. Linguistic evidence alone suggests that use of the term lineage or lineage group would amount to confusing the development of a matrilineal descent group with the strong ties between a mother and her children and the tendency for matrifiliation to produce stable uxorilocal residence patterns over two or three generations.

Furthermore, anthropological analysis of the lineage system was developed in the study of societies (mainly in Africa and Oceania) where lineality regulates much of the jural-political sphere.[9] In contrast to such societies, the Navajo do not place importance on genealogy in reckoning descent and in ordering political relations between groups. Where African lineage groups or localized lineages are often corporate, land-holding units, those Navajo who trace descent to the same genetrix, do not hold joint rights in a common enterprise nor are they bound by a common set of jural rules distinct from those applicable to all members of the society. To use the concept of lineage in reference to Navajo social organization implies more rigidity than is the case and also ignores the strong ties an individual has through his father to his father's genealogical kin. These are not ties to the father's matrilineage (or corporate descent group) but are ties of filiation that stem from the definition of the father-child relationship and that are potentially important in defining residence, access to grazing or farm land, and the use of water sources.[10] In sum, I feel Shepardson and Hammond's data can be readily conceptualized using other concepts and without relying on the notion of lineage.[11]

Navajo terms for clanship, kinship, and neighborhood, which describe relations outside the domestic group, are part of the actors' model of their social world. They serve to classify individuals as relatives, as members of a particular clan, as one of a group of siblings, as the direct descendant of a man or woman, or as a resident in a local area. Relatives, both genealogical and clan kin, are in turn classified by particular kin terms depending on generation, sex, sex of connecting relative, and sex of speaker (Aberle 1961). I have argued that this actors' view of social relationships does not correspond to group-based constructs proposed by anthropologists such as outfit, cooperating group, LCE, and matrilineage. However, neither does Navajo terminology give a systematic or highly structured classification of the ties to matrilateral and patrilateral kin, relations between neighboring residence groups, and patterns of recruitment of aid that emerge as important aspects of the anthropologist's data on everyday Navajo activities. It is necessary to go beyond Navajo concepts, but without imposing a group-based construct where no groups seem to exist. A model is needed that will preserve the matrilateral bias of the Navajo system, including strong ties betwen a mother and her children, the prevalence of uxorilocal residence, and ties to the individual's matrilineal clan. The clan system also involves ties to the father's matrilineal clan, those "born for" ego's clan and those who are "born for" the same clan as ego. It is important to account for these and other patterns that are part of Navajo social organization, for example, the existence of virilocal and neolocal residence patterns and the importance of ties to the father and his genealogical kin.

Both the matrilateral bias of Navajo social organization and the presence of alternative patterns can be described using the concepts of set and network and focusing on the recruitment of aid in particular situations. The major activities involving kinsmen from several residence groups are ceremonial occasions, such as

Navajo chants, girls' puberty rites, peyote meetings, and funerals. These cooperative situations have an ego-centered focus. There is always an individual or pair of individuals, such as the patient in a sing or peyote meeting, or the parents of the patient, who are the primary organizers of cooperation. It is necessary, then, to utilize concepts appropriate to the analysis of shifting ego-centered activities.

Anthropologists, who have discussed kinship in societies with bilateral kindreds or cognatic descent groups, make analytic distinctions relevant to the ego-centered nature of Navajo cooperation (Freeman 1958, 1960; Pehrson 1954; Mitchell 1963; Keesing 1966; Appell 1966, 1967). Both Freeman (1960: 203) and Keesing (1966: 347) find it necessary to distinguish between the kindred as a category of kin and as a group that participates in joint activities. Freeman states that the kindred as a category is not bounded, but rather there is a shading off as degrees of relationship increase in distance (1960: 210). This category of kin gives the individual a wide range of optative relationships. Among the Iban, "a man's kindred represents a field in which he is able to move largely at will" (1960: 211), and, like the Lapp kindred, it provides him with a wide range of alternative courses of action (Pehrson 1954). In addition to the optative nature of recruitment, Freeman finds that many kindred-based groups are "action groups," which are temporary, recruited for a particular purpose, and formed about an individual (1960: 213). Among the Iban, there is no compulsion for an individual to associate with any particular member of his or her kindred, and there is an extensive network of interlocking kindreds that has importance for political affairs.

The literature on kindreds has relevance for the Navajo, not because of the notion of bilaterality, but because of other qualities of kindreds: the presence of a social field rather than a bounded group, optative relationships within this field, ego-centered recruitment, and a network of relationships. I do not maintain that Navajo social organization is bilateral or cognatic in orientation, but that its matrilineal bias and the presence of alternative patterns can be described in terms of the same characteristics as can bilateral kindreds. These same characteristics also have been used in studies of networks (Barnes 1954; Bott 1957; Epstein 1961; Mayer 1966). Since the concepts of set and network have been defined to include the above properties, and since they are more neutral than are the notions of bilateral kindred or cognatic descent groups in specifying which kinship links are necessarily important, I have found them useful in interpreting Navajo cooperation.

The ego-centered set is distinguished from the socio-centered concept of network. The network is an "unbounded system of relationships between pairs of people making up a field of activity" (A.C. Mayer 1966: 102). Some individuals are directly in touch with others, and these, in turn, are linked to additional individuals. Such linkages can indirectly connect many persons, although no particular individual necessarily has a relationship with all or even a significant number of the others in the network (see Barnes 1954 for the initial definition of network). In contrast, the set is a finite number of linkages initiated by an ego that forms part of such a network (A.C. Mayer 1966: 102).

Using the Copper Canyon data, I was unable to resolve satisfactorily the difficulties in isolating and describing sets and networks that anthropologists have only recently confronted (see the articles in Mitchell 1969). First, ties between members of different categories of kin and between other relationships cannot be assumed to be similar and should be treated differentially. This is one of·the critical deficiencies of Bott's analysis (1957). She treats kin, neighbor, and friend ties as if they were equivalent in determining the connectedness of networks among working-class Londoners. To avoid this particular error, I have used the concept of set only for ties among genealogical kin and have treated clan relatives and neighbors separately. This is based on evidence that Navajos interact more frequently with genealogical kin than with clan relatives or neighbors, even though genealogical kin and clan kin are not distinguished terminologically. However, as I will show in Chapters 7 and 8, for those Navajos who have few genealogical kin, clan relatives and neighbors are important. Unfortunately, I have not yet devised a way of incorporating them into the analysis of ego's set to show how they can substitite for genealogical relatives.

Second, in describing ties of the same type—for example, between ego and two kinsmen or between ego and two neighbors—a method of measuring the strength of these ties, either in terms of content, frequency of contact, or value, is necessary. The most well-developed scheme is that used by Kapferer (1969) in his study of a work-room dispute among East African townsmen. He was able to determine the relative strength of a dyadic tie by differentiating between several types of exchanges that had or had not taken place between two individuals. Since I became aware of network analysis only after my fieldwork was completed, I did not collect the data necessary to work out an equivalent scheme for comparing the content and frequency of Navajo cooperative exchanges in order to measure the strength of ties. Thus I have differentiated only between those who contributed goods and services on a particular occasion and those who did not. These two drawbacks—the inability to compare genealogical kin, clan, and neighbor ties within a set and the lack of a scheme to measure the strength of ties—have limited the precision of my analysis but not the broad conclusions. As the data in Chapters 7 and 8 will show, I have been able to use set and network in a rather loose heuristic sense and have been able to isolate the principles that account for the recruitment of actual cooperators from sets of kin.

In applying the concept of set, I will assume that each ego has a number of living genealogical kin who form a set of ideal, or potential cooperators. Like a bilateral kindred, the composition of this potential set shifts from one ego to another as one moves within the same genealogical space. Like Freeman's category of kindred, the boundaries of this potential set shade off with increased genealogical distance from ego. Unlike the kindred, an ego's potential set may be significantly skewed in the direction of matrilateral relatives, especially if ego is residing near them. In other words, although both patrilateral and matrilateral relatives have been considered in calculating sets, the probability that matrilateral relatives will actually give aid may be greater.

The range in terms of genealogical distance and number of living kin within a set of potential cooperators varies greatly from individual to individual. For a Navajo, the important kin are usually all those within a three-generation range, and the number of these living at one time can vary from one or two to fifty or sixty. In the calculation of potential cooperators, only adults within one or two genealogical links have been counted, as this includes all the important adults within a three-generation range on whom an individual is likely to call. The potential set is distinguished from actual cooperators who participate in particular activities.

Using this model, we can see that there is a shift in ego's potential set throughout

TABLE 5.1
Clan Membership at Copper Canyon

Clan Members*	Deceased	Nonresident	Resident	Total†
I. *Clans With Membership Greater Than 12*				
A. House-in-the-Rocks people *kiyaa'áanii*	19	39	165	223
B. Within-His-Cover people *bit'ahnii*	12	30	99	141
C. He-Walks-Around-One people *honágháahnii*	8	14	57	79
D. Mountain-Recess people *dziłtł'ahnii*	6	3	59	68
E. Red-House people *kinłichíí'nii*	4	4	123	131
F. Red-Running-Into-the-Water people *táchii'nii*	3	3	79	85
G. Salt people *'áshįįhi*	11	5	19	35
H. Water's-Edge people *tábąąhá*	3	2	27	32
I. Red-Bottom people *tł'ááshł'í*	5	10	16	31
J. Bitter-Water people *tódích'íi'nii*	3	5	22	28
K. Mud people *hashtł'ishnii*	2	0	26	28
II. *Clan Unknown, or With Membership Less Than 12*				
In-married males, clan unknown; or individuals from clans less than 12	40	32	27	99
In-married females, and children, clan unknown; or individuals from clans less than 12	7	92	70	169
Errors and Omissions				17
Total Membership of I & II	123	239	789	1168

*Translations of clan names are taken from Young and Morgan, 1951: 444–45. The letters -i, -ni, or -nii at the end of a name mean "those being," or "ones who are."

†Membership includes all people on my genealogies, that is, deceased ancestors, residents of the community, and nonresidents.

his lifetime. As a child, the most relevant ties are through his parents: a contrast between two sets of consanguines of own and ascending generations. On the maternal side, this includes the mother, her parents, her siblings and their children, and possibly the siblings of maternal grandparents. On the paternal side are the father, his parents, his siblings, and their children. Which of the two collections of relatives is more important depends on if the parents are living uxorilocally or virilocally.

TABLE 5.1
Clan Membership at Copper Canyon

Clan Members*	Resident	
	(No.)	(%)
III. *Linked Clans–Resident Members*		
Within-His-Cover and Mud people (B & K)	125	
He-Walks-Around-One and Mountain-Recess people (C & D)	116	
Red-House and Red-Bottom people (E & I)	139	
IV. *Proportions of Total Resident Population*		
A, B, & E	387	49
A, B, E, & F	466	59
A, (E & I)	304	38.4
A, (B & K), (E & I)	429	54.4
A, (B & K), (C & D), (E & I)	545	69.1

After marriage, and as the grandparents and older relatives die, ties shift to a contrast between consanguines and affines. On one hand, are parents, married and unmarried siblings, and children. On the other hand, are the spouse's parents, siblings, and children. As a couple becomes older, their children, children's spouses, and grandchildren emerge as important, with their own siblings and siblings' children thrust into a secondary position. The locus of support begins to shift to consanguines and affines of descending generations.

To recapitulate, I suggest the use of the concepts "set" and "network" in analyzing social relationships that extend beyond the household and residence group, rather than relying on previously used concepts based on the structure and function of groups, such as the outfit, cooperating unit, or matrilineage. Although this model is not isomorphic with Navajo categories of kinship and locality, it is consistent with the ideology of request making described in Chapter 2, and it seems to allow for the wide variety of kin actually recruited, as will be described in Chapter 7.

Clanship and the Network of Residence Groups

The appropriateness of an analysis based on sets of overlapping kin that create a network of interrelated residence groups is supported by data on the spatial distribution of various clusters of genealogical kin within the same clan and the history of residence choices made by clan members.

Table 5.1 summarizes information on Copper Canyon clanship. The eleven clans, or Local Clan Elements, listed in the table have more than a dozen resident members. A large number of men and women who are married to a member of the community come from neighboring areas or other parts of the reservation. The number of clans represented, therefore, is greater than eleven, but membership in these additional clans is small.

Maps 5.1 and 5.2 show the winter and summer areas within the Copper Canyon community that are dominated by members of the eleven LCEs. Because virilocal and independent residence choices are important variants to the uxorilocal residence rule, a considerable number of nonclansmen may be living in camps within an area designated by the name of one clan. Furthermore, several dispersed

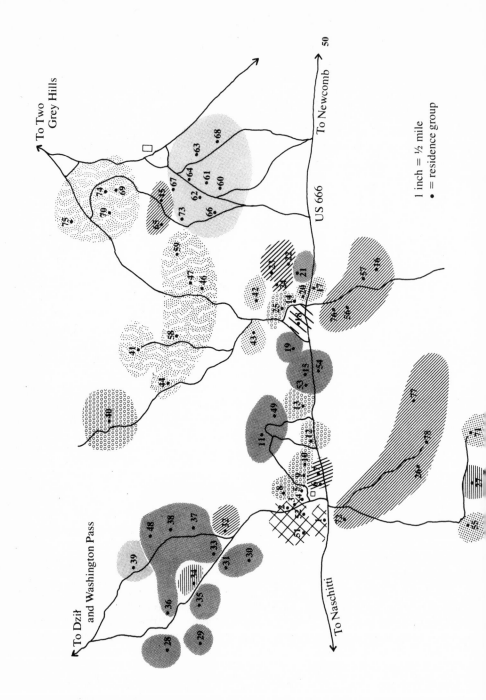

To Two Grey Hills

To Dzit and Washington Pass

To Newcomb

50

US 666

To Naschitti

1 inch = ½ mile
• = residence group

KEY

House-in-the-Rocks people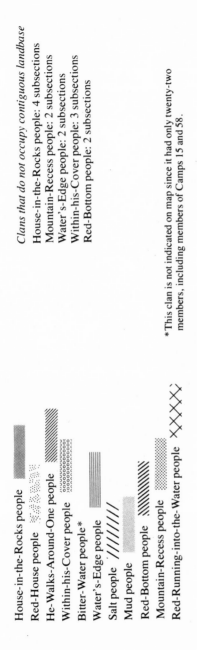

Red-House people

He-Walks-Around-One people

Within-his-Cover people

Bitter-Water people*

Water's-Edge people

Salt people

Mud people

Red-Bottom people

Mountain-Recess people

Red-Running-into-the-Water people

Clans that do not occupy contiguous landbase

House-in-the-Rocks people: 4 subsections

Mountain-Recess people: 2 subsections

Water's-Edge people: 2 subsections

Within-his-Cover people: 3 subsections

Red-Bottom people: 2 subsections

*This clan is not indicated on map since it had only twenty-two members, including members of Camps 15 and 58.

Map 5.1   Location of clans in winter residence area

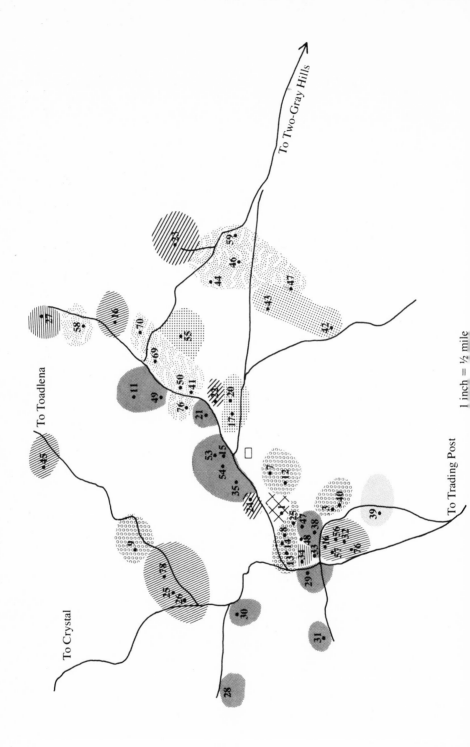

To Two-Gray Hills

To Toadlena

To Crystal

To Trading Post

1 inch = ½ mile

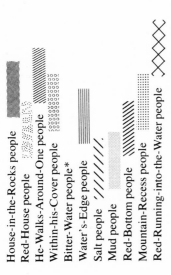

House-in-the-Rocks people

Red-House people

He-Walks-Around-One people

Within-his-Cover people

Bitter-Water people *

Water's-Edge people

Salt people

Mud people

Red-Bottom people

Mountain-Recess people

Red-Running-into-the-Water people

*This clan is not indicated on map since it had only twenty-two members, including members of Camps 15 and 58.

Map 5.2 *Location of clans in summer residence area*

areas, rather than one compact area, may be occupied by members of the same clan. Examples are the dispersal of Mountain-Recess people (*dziłtł'ahnii*), House-in-the-Rocks people (*kiyaa'áanii*), and He-Walks-Around-One people (*honághááhnii*), both in summer and winter locations. These dispersed locations coincide with segments of the clan that are not related genealogically.

Reasons for this dispersal can be seen more clearly by examining the settlement pattern within three clans: Within-his-Cover people (*bit'ahnii*), House-in-the-Rocks people (*kiyaa'áanii*), and Mountain-Recess people (*dziłtł'ahnii*). These three LCEs were selected because they represent contrasts in size and internal genealogical composition. Within-his-Cover people and House-in-the-Rocks people are the two largest LCEs in Copper Canyon, with living population of 129 and 204, respectively. They are good examples of how large numbers of Navajo are related both by matrilineal genealogy and by clan. Mountain-Recess people, the third example, is a smaller clan with only fifty-seven living members. All the Within-his-Cover people in Copper Canyon belong to the same matrilineal segment five generations in depth, while the other two LCEs are internally differentiated; House-in-the-Rocks people is composed of three different genealogical segments and Mountain-Recess people has four distinct genealogical units.

The Within-his-Cover people genealogy (Appendix 4) shows that all members are descendants of two sisters who are said to have moved from the region east of the wash into the Copper Canyon area around the turn of the twentieth century. These sisters and their children utilized the land near the present Copper Canyon trading post in winter and moved to Cottonwood Pass during the summer months. This residential clustering can still be seen on present-day maps of winter and summer residences (Maps 5.1 and 5.2).

An examination of the moves away from the two original neighborhoods made by six descendants of the two Within-his-Cover women shows that clan localization has been broken up by the nonuxorilocal residence choices of second and third generation women and their husbands. (See Appendix 4 for a summary of these moves.) The most common option has been for a Within-his-Cover woman and her husband to live near his relatives or their fields, eventually founding an independent camp in that area. However, in one case a Within-his-Cover woman and married children founded a camp in previously unclaimed territory. This variation in residence choice is congruent with present-day patterns, since fourth generation Within-his-Cover people, most of whom have not yet reached middle age, are living both uxorilocally and virilocally, while some have taken wage jobs off the reservation. Presumably some of the women living virilocally will remain in the area of their husband's kin even after his death. As their children grow up and marry, those residing in their camps will create small clusters of Within-his-Cover people within neighborhoods occupied by members of other clans.

The House-in-the-Rocks people of Copper Canyon illustrate a slightly different pattern of settlement and residential expansion. They constitute the largest LCE in Copper Canyon, but they include three distinct genealogical segments, each of which settled in the Copper Canyon area at different times and in different places. Appendix 4 shows the genealogical relationships among members of these three segments, along with maps of their winter and summer residences. In the winter there is a large cluster of House-in-the-Rocks people in the Gray Area so that it appears as if one segment had settled and expanded in this area. However, a close inspection of the genealogical ties and residence histories of these clansmen demonstrates that the clustering is due to both the expansion of segment 2 and the independent settlement of members of segments 1 and 3 in the area. The other two winter neighborhoods in which House-in-the-Rocks people reside appear to be occupied because two women and their spouses settled in these locations previously unclaimed by others. (One couple was clearly moving away from the woman's own siblings but not near the husband's relatives.) In the summer, House-in-the-Rocks people are dispersed in several neighborhoods. Three clusters that are predominantly House-in-the-Rocks people coincide with the three oldest living House-in-the-Rocks women (from segments 1 and 2), their married children, and a few married grandchildren. Other locations are those of House-in-the-Rocks men (in segments 1 and 2) and their children (who belong to different clans).

The four Mountain-Recess segments are genealogically shallow in comparison to the House-in-the-Rocks segments and to the Within-his-Cover matrilineage, since each unites only two or three generations of married couples. In the oldest living Mountain-Recess generation are the remnants of four siblings groups that coincide with the four segments. Two segments have a long history of close cooperation since the founder of segment 1 raised the two oldest women in segment 2 (Desba and her sister) as well as her own children. Members of these two segments plus members of segment 3 all live in the same neighborhood (Blue Mesa), while segment 4 is located ten miles away near the wash. In the summer, Mountain-Recess people live in four distinct neighborhoods that coincide with residence options made by individual extended families, rather than by a whole segment.

Comparison of all three LCEs shows that the Within-his-Cover people are more localized both in terms of summer and winter settlement patterns than are the House-in-the-Rocks and Mountain-Recess people. In other words, residence groups composed mainly of Within-his-Cover people are predominantly clustered in one summer and one winter neighborhood, while House-in-the-Rocks and Mountain-Recess residence groups are found in several neighborhoods. The movement of Within-his-Cover people away from the original settlement sites illustrates the expansion and spread of residence groups in accordance with the developmental cycle of domestic groups as it operates over several generations. The pattern has been described for Rimrock, where the territorial outlines of the outfits isolated by Kluckhohn were broken up by the marriage and dispersion of third and fourth generation sibling groups (Reynolds, Lamphere, and Cook 1967).

In personal communication, Jerrold Levy suggested that his data from the Kaibito-White Mesa area can be seen in terms of clusters of genealogically related kin who, prior to 1930, occupied large tracts of land separated from tracts used by neighboring groups. Since the early 1960s, Levy has observed considerable shifts in cooperative patterns among these blocks of kin, which indicates that they are breaking into smaller segments. The low population density and recent settlement of the western reservation have undoubtedly allowed investigators to isolate localized groups of kin that are no longer discernible in the eastern reservation. The data from Rimrock, which are of considerable historical depth, and the example of the Within-his-Cover people in Copper Canyon, support Levy's suggestion. Two or three generations of kin, when initially settling in an area, may utilize an undivided block of land, but succeeding generations marry and move to other neighborhoods, thus breaking the residential continuity of genealogically related kin and dispersing segments of a clan to several parts of a community.

The developmental cycle of domestic groups, along with virilocal and independent residence choices, also accounts for the settlement pattern of the House-in-the-Rocks and Mountain-Recess people. Women who were the founders of each segment within a clan have settled with their husbands in the Copper Canyon area at different locations and different times. Their children have often expanded into the surrounding area creating a cluster of genealogical as well as clan relatives. Some women have moved with their husbands near the husbands' relatives or to an independent location, creating a cluster of clansmen away from the original site. Even when residence choices of members of several segments converge in the same area (e.g., the House-in-the-Rocks people in the Gray Area) this is due to the independent developmental cycles of several extended families, not to the importance of clan ties per se.

Despite differences in genealogical composition and settlement pattern, patterns of cooperation are similar in all three LCEs. Three generation segments of Within-his-Cover people are no more likely to cooperate with each other even though they are genealogically related than are three generation segments of House-in-the-Rocks people, which have only ties of clanship with each other. In both cases the LCE does not seem to provide the basis for cooperation regardless of whether it is composed of members of one large matrilineage or several matrilineages.

In contrast, three segments of Mountain-Recess people live in the same neighborhood and cooperate often. It would appear that, in this instance, the LCE is a social unit. I would argue, however, that the apparent unity of Mountain-Recess people is a function of the clan's small size and the spatial proximity of many members. Extended families of Mountain-Recess people have few genealogical relatives on whom to call, making nearby clan relatives the most appropriate substitutes. The interaction between the three segments in Blue Mesa and the segment living near the wash ten miles away is minimal, indicating that clanship and locality, rather than clanship per se, play a greater role in organizing cooperation.

In sum, data on the internal composition and residential location of Copper Canyon clans indicate that settlement patterns can be best accounted for in terms of the expansion and fission of domestic groups. Uxorilocal residence, in combination with some virilocal and independent choices, has produced both homogeneous neighborhoods dominated by one sibling group and heterogeneous neighborhoods containing segments of several sibling groups or several unrelated couples and their married children. This suggests that less attention should be paid to matrilineality and clanship and more to the ties between genealogical kin, both those who are clustered in the same neighborhood and those who have moved away. The situation is best conceptualized, I would argue, in terms of ego-centered sets of kin and their spouses that create pools of potential cooperators. Over a period of time the activation of ties by numerous adults creates a network of residence groups that binds together, and even extends beyond, the Copper Canyon community.

This model is also appropriate for describing social structure in other communities as it allows comparison between areas where there are differences in length of settlement, population density, and size of land base. I have already suggested that the groups called "outfits" in Rimrock and on the Kaibito Plateau are localized groups of kinsmen under conditions where there has been a relatively low population density and where there have been only three or four generations of the growth and fission of residence groups, since these communities were settled following Fort Sumner in the last decades of the nineteenth century. Similar conclusions could probably be drawn about cooperating groups at Klagetoh and resident lineages at Shonto. Neighborhood segments of matrilineages or Local Clan Elements would appear to be present where there has also been a three to four generation cycle of residence group fission, but where there has been little virilocal residence on the part of in-marrying males and little outmigration of females to other neighborhoods in the same community. I do not view changes in the former situation as a break-down of outfits, cooperating groups, and resident lineages, or the latter as a disin-tegration of matrilineages or Local Clan Elements. Rather, both situations reflect a particular phase in the settlement of an area of the reservation, and their alteration is part of a process reflecting population expansion and variations in residence choice that have been part of Navajo social structure for a long period of time, certainly since the establishment of the Navajo Reservation.

Even changes in settlement patterns and cooperation between residence groups directly traceable to the impact of American technology and institutions—for example, use of the automobile, the decline of the pastoral economy, and migration to urban areas—should be viewed as bringing out tendencies already part of Navajo social organization, which has always been extremely flexible and where variant patterns have long been apparent. Rather than argue that Navajo groups are chang-ing (e.g., that outfits or matrilineages are disappearing), it seems more appropriate to argue that these groups never existed *as groups* and that the Navajo are using the same kinds of ties in differing ways in new sets of circumstances.

In the next chapters I will concentrate on the organizational, rather than the structural, features of Navajo life; by examining a wide variety of activities, I will show how individuals use conceptions described in the cultural model and social relationships described in the structural model (of domestic groups, sets, and net-works), to accomplish particular tasks.

Part IV

COOPERATIVE
ACTIVITIES

Chapter 6

Livestock
and Agriculture

~~~~~~

I have outlined a model of the cultural system of cooperation as it operates in Copper Canyon, and I proposed a model of the social structure that has two components: (1) the domestic groupings that consist of households, which are in turn combined into residence groups, and (2) the individual's set of genealogical kin from which he can recruit aid within and beyond the residence group. The next chapters examine cooperation in two ways: first, through a cross-sectional analysis of different tasks as organized in all residence groups, and, second, through an in-depth analysis of activities (especially ceremonial activities) engaged in by a cluster of kinsmen.

The cross-sectional analysis initially focuses on those activities that center around the residence group and illustrate its importance. Later, I turn to activities in which individuals utilize both ties within the residence group and ties with members of sets of potential cooperating kin who live outside the residence group. Case material is presented wherever possible (1) to show how the cultural system of cooperation is used to recruit aid and (2) to reveal particular strategies that account for the actual kin recruited.

In this chapter, pastoral and agricultural activities are analyzed in cross-sectional terms, since these tasks best illustrate the ways in which members of Copper Canyon residence groups cooperate. As indicated in the discussion of the developmental cycle of domestic groups, some residence groups are composed of nuclear families at the second stage of the cycle, while other residence groups contain extended families with an older couple or widow at the third stage of the cycle, and one or more married children and their spouses at the first stage of the cycle. These differences in residence group composition shape and constrain the handling of activities so that the same task will be organized differently in residence groups of varying size and composition. The contrast between nuclear and extended family camps will be a continuing one throughout the following discussion.

Pastoral Activities

In Chapter 4 I defined the residence group in terms of genealogical and spatial criteria. These units are highly correlated with the pooling of sheep. A nuclear family residence group or an extended family cluster of hoghans usually contains a sheep corral, and the owners of sheep kept in the corrals are primarily adults (but sometimes children) living in the nearby hoghan or hoghans.[1] In some cases the herd contains a few sheep of a son, daughter, or sibling who resides in another camp and does not have enough sheep to pool with a spouse to form a separate herd. Significantly, no range of kin who fit the definition of "Mr. X, his wife, and children" (*Hastiin X dóó ba'áłchíní*), and who live in adjacent hoghans, have more than one herd of sheep.

In 1966 income from sheep contributed only 12 percent of the total community income, but forty-four of the seventy-eight residence groups (or two-thirds of the population) had herds of sheep. Although many herds were quite small, herding, shearing, dipping, and other activities which surround the care of the herd are nevertheless important if stockraising is continued even in a minimal way. Cattle were owned by members of a few extended families; since cattle graze unattended and do not have to be sheared or dipped, little cooperative effort was needed to maintain them.

The small size of sheep herds and their relatively low contribution to community income reflect the impact of the stock reduction program and changes in the Navajo economy over the past thirty years and probably effect cooperative patterns at Copper Canyon. Aberle characterizes the effect of stock reduction as follows: "The median sheep holding in 1915 was less than 50 sheep; in 1940 the median remained somewhere in that range; in 1958, the median figure was *no* sheep units. One third of the population had more than 100 sheep in 1915, more than 60 sheep in 1940, and more than 24 sheep units in 1958" (1966: 83).

Apparently some areas of the reservation were more severely reduced than others, and in some communities permit limitations have been ignored. For instance, average herd size at Navajo Mountain (Shepardson and Hammond 1964: 1035) and at Rimrock (1964 field data) is around two hundred sheep per camp, while at Copper Canyon it is about half that size. On the other hand, data on the contribution of livestock to tribal income as early as 1958 indicate that the situation at Copper Canyon is similar to that on the reservation as a whole (Kluckhohn and Leighton 1962: 62). Residence groups with large herds, typical in some communities and a tiny minority in others, may handle livestock activities differently than at Copper Canyon, but as livestock and agricultural production continue to decline, the patterns found at Copper Canyon will become more and more typical.

Four important tasks are related to the care of sheep and goats: herding, lambing, shearing, and dipping. These tasks were performed by members of the residence group (whether a nuclear or extended camp) where the herd was located. The major exceptions were: (1) instances of herding done by someone outside the residence group (usually a temporary measure); (2) situations in which members of other residence groups helped with shearing; and (3) circumstances when two residence groups combined herds for sheepdipping.

A summary of the work groups involved in livestock activities is presented in Table 6.1.

Of the forty-four camps with sheep, seventeen (41 percent) were nuclear

TABLE 6.1
Ownership of Sheep in Copper Canyon Camps

Camps	With Sheep (no.)	Without Sheep (no.)
Nuclear Camps and Isolated Individuals	17	19
Extended Camps		
2 households	16	8
3 households	7	3
4 households	2	1
5 households	2	2
Totals	44	33
Grand Total	77	

families, widowers and children, or isolated individuals. Extended family residence groups held the remainder of the sheep; 34 percent were camps with two households, 20 percent were those with three households, 4.5 percent with four households, and 4.5 percent with five households. The most usual situation was for members of one or two households to care for the herd.[2]

Since World War II, with the reduction of herds and the growth of population, sheep have become the concern of the older generation (those fifty to seventy years of age). By the 1960s, most of the sheep were cared for by these older Navajos, if not owned by them. Only five herds were maintained by nuclear family residence groups where the couple was middle-aged rather than older; and two middle-aged bachelors had herds. In all of these cases, the parents of the individual who had inherited the sheep were deceased so that care and ownership had necessarily devolved on an individual at middle age rather than being retained by older Navajos. Children, who formerly did much of the herding, were in school nine months of the year and could be herders only during the summer. Many middle-aged and younger men worked on the railroad, or had temporary jobs, and were only occasionally able to participate in livestock activities. Thus, as the following detailed analysis of pastoral activities shows, an older couple or an older individual, either in a nuclear or extended residence group, were the primary caretakers of the herd. The couple or individual were the focus for organizing such activities as herding and shearing, and they communicated requests for cooperation to other members of the residence group. Technically each owner was *t'áá bee bóholnííh* for his own sheep, but in practice one or two older adults were *t'áá bee bóholnííh* in the sense of loosely managing how and when a task was to be completed.

Herding

As Downs (1964: 32–34) points out, the general pattern is for Navajos to keep the sheep in a corral (*dibé bighan*) during the night and the middle of the day. Sheep are driven out and allowed to graze twice daily, usually between mid-morning and noon and during the late afternoon until sunset. During one of these periods they are watered at a natural dam or a trough attached to a windmill or improved spring. This pattern overgrazes the land near the camp and near the water supply. Water sources remain fixed, but the residence group may move to areas where the grass is more plentiful. Areas near hoghans and springs sometimes are overgrazed in Copper Canyon, but the amount of moving is limited due to the proximity of other residence groups. I know of only one residence group that moved its winter camp in the early 1960s because of the sheep herd, and this was much to the displeasure of the new neighbors, who felt that their territory was being infringed upon.

The location of water is of crucial importance for reasons stated by Downs: "In general, five miles is the maximum radius which will permit midday penning at the homestead and still provide adequate grazing time for the flock. A ten-mile radius will require that the herder remain on the range in midday, and a radius greater than ten miles will require that the flock be moved" (1965: 1394). In Copper Canyon, water is within two or three miles of each residence group, even on the Flats where water resources are fewer and spaced further apart.[3] The great number of springs on the Mountain and the Top means that water is usually one-half mile or less from the camp site.

Differences in the summer and winter terrain, rather than the location of water, produce differences in herding requirements. The winter areas (the Flats and the Gray Area) are treeless and relatively flat. Thus it is possible to let the sheep graze by themselves for several hours and to chase them back into the corral at noon or sunset. In the summer (on the Mountain or the Top), the terrain is forested, and a herd can easily become lost if not closely watched. Moreover, distances between residence groups are smaller, and sheep must be kept out of neighbors' cornfields and away from others' grazing ranges. Fortunately, children are home from school, and the job of herding can be left to them or rotated between both children and adults.

One individual can easily look after a herd of sheep, whether the herd contains twenty or two hundred and fifty sheep. With a large flock, the herder needs to be on horseback to retain full control of the situation. While it is possible to let a herd of fifty sheep graze by themselves on the Flats, this is not possible for a herd of two hundred. This many sheep must be watched so that the herd does not scatter and sheep become lost. Such a large herd can be managed by one person, but there are constant demands on his time; he is not as free to make trips to the store and to ceremonies as he would be if the herd were smaller, or if there were others with whom the herding could be shared.

In Copper Canyon, the most typical pattern, therefore, was to rotate herding duties among two or more people, which allowed more freedom of activity. There may have been one individual in the camp who did most of the herding, but others were often requested to help when that person had something else to do. Also, during the summer months, in terrain where sheep must be carefully watched, the added herders (children home from school) gave more freedom to the adults who usually did the herding during the remainder of the year.

Ways in which this system of rotation was accomplished varied with the genealogical composition of the residence group. For the seventeen nuclear camps, herding was handled by one, two, or at most three adults.[4] In most instances it was a husband and wife who jointly shared the herding responsibilities, although in two cases an unmarried adult son helped. At times one spouse did more herding than the other; a woman did the herding while her husband was away for wage work, and a man herded because most of the sheep belonged to him and not to his wife. If the couple had young unmarried children, they were used for herding during the summer. The following case material illustrates how herding was arranged in a nuclear family (Camp 49).

CASE E. HERDING IN A NUCLEAR FAMILY CAMP

The forty sheep and goats in the herd primarily belonged to Thomas, the husband; he did most of the herding. Stella, the wife, herded when Thomas wanted to go somewhere. If sheep were lost, both went looking for them. In the winter, the sheep were let out to wander in the morning and afternoon; Thomas usually chased them in at sunset, though Stella performed the chore occasionally. This left them both free much of the day and allowed for trips to Gallup and Shiprock. In the summer, the two younger children were home from school. The other two children had graduated from high school and were away from the reservation in job-training programs; when the daughter was home on vacation she helped with the herding, although this was for only a few days a year.

Sheep must be closely watched in the morning and afternoon. If both parents wanted to go somewhere, the children were left with the sheep. If the whole family was to be away, the sheep were often herded out to graze very early in the morning and then penned for most of the day while the family was gone. They were herded again at sunset when the household returned. Several times during the summer, children from neighboring camps were asked to look after the sheep. These included children from Camp 11 (who normally lived in Gallup and were visiting their mother's sister, who was also Stella's mother's sister); children from Camp 23 (children of the brother of the wife in Camp 24, who stayed with their father's sister in the summer, since their own parents were divorced); and a son or daughter of the wife in Camp 75, who were summer neighbors of Stella and Thomas. Herders outside the household were not used in the winter, but in summer were an adaptation to the requirement of having to watch the sheep closely so they did not wander off through the wooded hillsides.

Extended camps with two households (a total of sixteen in Copper Canyon) usually had the following composition: one household contained an older couple (or widow) who were the parents of a son or daughter who lived with a spouse and children in the second or junior household.[5] The widow or older couple had prime responsibility for herding the sheep. She, or they, called on one or both of the adults in the junior household in order to rotate the herding among more individuals. Herding was always done by at least two individuals, and sometimes three or four were recruited from two different households.[6]

Within such two-household residence groups, the particular combination of adults who did the herding varied. In one case it was a widow and her son (Camp 7). In another it was an older couple and the son-in-law (Camp 8). In a third instance, herding was shared by the older couple, a daughter, and the son-in-law (Camp 44). Various methods of rotating the herding were worked out, involving members of both households.

The pattern of using members of two households to do the herding also held true for camps of three, four, and five households (eleven extended camps). The parental couple, or widow, still had prime responsibility for the herd and did most of the herding. As in the case of two-household camps, they (or she) were *t'áá bee bóholníih*. They (or she) called regularly on a couple in one of the other households, rather than calling equally on all the remaining households (whether they were two, three, or four in number). In other words, one of the junior couples would help with the herding while others would not. This might have been the household of a son and daughter-in-law or a daughter and son-in-law. Some specific arrangements are illustrated by the following case.

CASE F.   HERDING IN A LARGE EXTENDED FAMILY CAMP

Nancy was sixty years old and had seven adult children from three different marriages. She was currently living with her fourth husband, Johnny, in an extended family camp with three married sons and one married daughter, a total of five households. (A second married daughter lived in a distant community; and a third daughter, Laura, lived with her husband, Kevin, near Nancy's previous residence site, Camp 13.) The herd of about forty or fifty animals contained sheep that belonged to Nancy, her fourth husband, and several of the children, including Laura. The coresident son-in-law, Willie, owned a few sheep and goats which presumably were part of the herd. In the winter, when the family was on the Flats, the sheep needed little attention and could be let out in the morning and late afternoon to wander; Johnny often took on the task of chasing them back into the corral.

During the summer, when the family was on the Mountain, the sheep needed close watching. Often two or three of the sons and their families did not move up, and most of the herding was managed by Nancy, her husband, and the coresident daughter and son-in-law, with some help from Laura's children who lived close by in the summer. In 1965, Nancy hired the young daughter of her parallel cousin (*bideezhí*) (who lived in Camp 40, adjacent to Nancy's summer camp) to do the herding for most of the summer.

In 1966, Nancy asked her daughter and Willie to take the herd up on the Mountain early in June, before other households in the camp were able to move up. After Nancy and Johnny moved to the summer camp, Nancy shared the herding with her son-in-law while Johnny was working; she often sent for Laura's children to take over the herding chores on days when she had other things to do. The children were not always reliable; on one occasion, two of the children left the sheep to wander through the trees, and Nancy had to round them up and bring them back to the corral. In early July, when there was a lack of green grass near the summer camp, the two men, Johnny and Willie, with help from Nancy and her daughter, built a corral further up the Mountain. In response to Nancy's request, the younger couple camped temporarily by the new corral and cared for the sheep until the summer rains brought improved grazing conditions.

Nancy was the focus of organizing herding activities. She made requests to her husband (who was young and often treated like a son) and to her son-in-law, Willie, through her daughter. She is the one who asked Laura to send her children to herd during the summer.

This matricentered management of the herd was found in other extended families (e.g., Camp 35); it was the usual pattern when a widow lived with married coresident children (e.g., Camps 20 and 23). However, it was not the only pattern found in Copper Canyon. As a widow became old and less able to engage in strenuous physical activity, either a younger couple (either a son or daughter and spouse) took over management of the herd jointly, as was also done in nuclear family camps (e.g., Camps 46 and 11), or the son alone took primary responsibility with only a little aid from his wife and mother (e.g., Camp 7). Often when both members of an older couple were alive, both consulted and organized herding, and either one or both made the arrangements with the younger couple. They undoubtedly communicated with a young in-law through the coresident son or daughter, and requests could have been initiated by either the mother or the father (e.g., Camp 44).

In sum, the pattern of sharing herding between two households applied for large extended families as well as small ones. This, of course, could be characteristic of Copper Canyon and not of communities where herds are larger. Since Copper Canyon herds were small and the herding requirements minimal, especially in winter when the sheep grazed unattended, a small work group of three or four adults was adequate. Under other conditions—with large herds or during a drought when water resources were distant from the residence site—members of *all* households of large residence groups might have participated in the herding (see Downs 1965: 1403–4 for a concrete example). Greater responsibilities would tend to be shared more broadly.

It is possible, of course, for an isolated bachelor to herd his sheep by himself; and this pattern did occur in Copper Canyon. It was much more typical, however, for herding duties to be shared by a couple in a nuclear family residence group, or by adults in two households in extended family residence groups, whether they were composed of two, three, four, or five households.

Lambing and Shearing

Tasks during the lambing season include watching the ewes during the birth of the lambs and caring for the lambs, especially during bad weather (See Downs 1964: 36). Since most herds in Copper Canyon were small, and since lambs were born over a two- or three-month period (February through April), the demands made on the residence group members were not large.

In contrast, shearing takes place in a relatively short time and usually represents a burst of activity for the residence group. Shearing occurs in the spring (between April 20 and May 10 in 1966), and in most residence groups it was done before the family moved to the summer camp.[7] In Copper Canyon, hand clippers were used for shearing, and removal of the pelt usually required twenty to thirty minutes, though an accomplished shearer could work more quickly. The length of time needed to shear an entire herd obviously depends on the size of the herd and the number of Navajos working. The largest two herds in the community (200–250 sheep) were sheared in two days, with six to nine people working. According to one informant, a group of six adults sheared 108 sheep in one day. On the second day of shearing the same herd, eighty sheep were sheared by nine people between early morning and noon. Another group worked more slowly, shearing only fifty sheep each day for two days with five adults working.

Unlike herding, the organization of cooperation for shearing depends on the size of the herd rather than the composition and size of the residence group. The

TABLE 6.2
Distribution of Sheep in Copper Canyon Residence Groups

Herds	Nuclear Camps	Extended Camps	Total
Under 75 adult animals	9	24	33
Over 75 adult animals	7*	4	11
Total camps	16	28	44

*Includes one herd operated jointly by two nuclear camps.

relationship between the type of residence group (nuclear or extended) and the size of the herd can be seen in Table 6.2

Few herds in the community were larger than seventy-five animals (only 25 percent of all the herds); a herd of this size was slightly more likely to be controlled by a nuclear residence group than by an extended one.

For small herds there was a general assumption that each individual should shear his or her own sheep. In practice, members of a residence group who owned sheep in the herd usually did the shearing at the same time, and everyone pitched in rather than each selecting his own sheep. If several adults were working they might do all the shearing in one morning. If only one couple were working, they might stretch out the process over several days.

In a nuclear camp the husband and wife usually shared shearing responsibility.[8] In extended camps, those who sheared were also the ones who herded, plus anyone in the camp who owned some of the sheep. In several cases a son or daughter who lived at another camp, but who had sheep in the herd, came over to participate.

In shearing herds of over seventy-five sheep, participants usually came from outside the residence group (whether it was a nuclear camp or an extended camp of two households).[9] A herd this size seemed to mark the boundary between getting help and not doing so. One woman and her fourteen-year-old son sheared a herd of seventy-five without help from other relatives. Her mother herded the sheep but was too old to do more strenuous work, such as shearing; the woman's husband was employed off-reservation on the railroad, so she and her son sheared a few sheep each morning until the whole herd was completed. This was an unusual case, however. Other nuclear and extended residence groups with herds of the same size received outside help. Workers were paid twenty or twenty-five cents for each pelt, and were also fed a customary meal of mutton stew, bread, and coffee at midday or at the end of the shearing.

Eleven herds in Copper Canyon numbered over seventy-five animals. Navajos from outside the residence group assisted in shearing at least seven of these herds. (Data were unavailable for two others where outside help was probably forthcoming.) Table 6.3 lists those who cooperated in each instance. The same couples helped in several different cases, but the combination of those present was never quite the same. Those helping were usually classificatory relatives; in other words, they were distant genealogical kin or clan relatives, but not the nonresident close kin of those owning the herd (e.g., adult siblings and sibling children).

Recruitment of shearers followed the etiquette of request making outlined in Chapter 3. Requests were made indirectly, often by spreading the news that a particular camp was shearing on a particular day. What appeared to be a simple

TABLE 6.3
Shearing Groups for Herds of More Than Seventy-five Adult Sheep

Camp Number	Adult Residents	Adults Who Helped With Shearing*	Close Genealogical Relatives Not Present at Shearing
Camp 7	Older widow: son & wife	*Bizeedí* of wife (FZD), Camp 11; *bideezhí* of wife (clan sister: MMMZD), Camp 14; *bizeedí* of wife (FZDD) and her husband, Camp 32; *bizeedí* of wife (FZDD), Camp 31; *bideezhí* of wife (MZD), Camp 6. (Shearing group was composed mainly of Pentecostals, possibly a basis for recruitment, although all members were related to wife.)	Other sisters and brothers of wife; other parallel cousins (besides the woman in Camp 6); a brother of the husband; husband's sister's son
Camp 9	Bachelor (brother of wife in camp 7)	Same group as for Camp 7. (Shearing took place the next day.)	Other sisters and brothers; other parallel cousins (besides the woman in Camp 6)
Camp 44	Older husband & wife; daughter & son-in-law	*Bitsí* of husband (clan relative, Camp 49), and husband who was *biyáázh* of wife (ZSS); *bizeedí* of wife ("born for" wife's clan: Camp 11); *bimá yázhí* of husband (younger woman in his clan) and husband in Camp 27; wife and two adult children of man in older husband's clan (Camp 39)	Wife's siblings and siblings' children (though many lived in nearby camps)
Camp 42	Husband & wife	Wife, adult son, and daughter (Camp 39); *bádí* of wife (MZD), Camp 20. (Wife in Camp 42 and wife in Camp 39 were *bádí/bideezhí*, older sister/ younger sister, to each other.)	——
Camps 26 & 78	Husband & wife (26); wife's mother (78)	*Bidá'í* of husband (ZS or MMZS), Camp 49, and wife; *bínaaí* of wife (same clan, Camp 27) and his wife; daughter and son-in-law, Camp 27; *bínaaí* of wife (same clan), and his wife, Camp 32; unrelated woman, Camp 19	Wife's brothers and sisters, many of whom lived outside community
Camp 59	Older husband & wife; unmarried son	No data	No data
Camp 45	Older husband & wife	No data	No data
Camp 77	Older husband & wife (both ill)	Shearing may have been done by children living outside the community	——
Camp 8	Older husband & wife; daughter & son-in-law	These four resident adults did the shearing, possibly with help of nonresident daughter	——
Camp 21	Older widow; daughter & son-in-law	The daughter and her 14-year-old son	Sister's daughters in Camps 32 and 49; brother in Camp 5; nonlocal siblings. (Local relatives probably would have helped if asked, but daughter chose to do it by herself.)
Camp 30	Older widower & unmarried children	No data. Possibly clan relatives from neighboring area	——

*Kin terms have been prefaced by *bi-* rather than *shi-*. Thus, *bizeedí* means "his cross-cousin," as contrasted with *shizeedí*, "my cross-cousin."

reporting of fact was also a statement that the herd owners were in need of help. Navajos expect that kinsmen, in response to a description of need, will volunteer their services in congruence with the ideology of cooperativeness and generalized reciprocity. In some cases the couple, or male head of the residence group, directly notified relatives of the shearing. For instance, the older man in Camp 44 went to his clan daughter in Camp 49 (*bitsi'*, "born for his clan") and asked her and her husband to take him around to notify relatives about shearing. This follows the pattern of visiting and making requests by stating specific needs, as described in detail in Chapter 3. Most camps where they stopped were ones in which a clan relative lived, although they also visited camps where members of the daughter's clan lived. Only a few of these relatives actually came, but it was enough to shear the herd of 250 in two days.

Those who came tended to be distant relatives without herds of their own or with small herds. Several couples (in Camps 49, 27, 35) sheared in at least two residence groups. The groups selected were those in which there was a clan tie through either the husband or wife. I have the general impression that a Navajo would not go if he or she were not asked or did not have a remote kinship tie. I asked Laura, the wife in Camp 14, why she had not gone to shear for Camps 26 and 78 (who had a combined herd), although she had helped at Camp 7. These camps were several miles from her own home and I was unaware of any kinship link. Laura replied that members of Camps 26 and 78 had not asked her. Then I learned that she was not related to either the husband or wife in Camp 26, but she was a clan sister (*bideezhi*) of the wife in Camp 7. The most significant pattern in shearing recruitment is that helping relatives were not brothers, sisters, or sister's children of those who organized shearing. Often such close relatives lived nearby, and they would have been the logical kin on whom to call. However, these siblings, in many cases, had herds of their own to shear, while more distant relatives (clan cousins, clan siblings) with few or no sheep were more likely to have the time and want to earn the extra cash involved in helping with shearing at another camp.

In the three shearing groups in which I participated, the patterns of authority and communication were as follows: The oldest male connected with the herd (a bachelor who had his own herd; an older son who lived with his wife and widowed mother; a father in a camp which included his wife, married daughter, and son-in-law) oversaw the shearing. He did little shearing himself, and he did not give direct instructions or commands to those who came to help. Instead, he tended to take over the small tasks, such as letting unsheared sheep into the shearing corral, tying the bags of wool and loading them into a pickup, and sharpening the shears. He indirectly and unobtrusively watched the progress of the shearing, which usually proceeded smoothly, with both male and female shearers working individually. The son-in-law, in one camp, worked along with the nonresident shearers, though he performed a few of the coordinating activities, such as sharpening the shears.

The women of the residence group (the sister, wife, or wife and married daughter) butchered and prepared a meal of mutton stew, fried bread, and coffee for the shearers either at midday or at the end of the shearing. When the herd was completely sheared, the husband paid the workers. In one instance, the husband paid the single males and some of the couples by handing money to the men; but the wife gave money to a woman of one of the other couples for them to divide among themselves. The indirect method of payment, from husband to wife and from wife to husband, is related to kinship ties. The two men were not kinsmen, but the younger wife was related by clan to the older husband. Since relatives of opposite sex practice mild avoidance, the transaction was best handled with the older wife as an intermediary. In these cases, the oldest male of the camp was *t'áá bee bóholnííh* and the major organizer, with the females taking over the hospitality-oriented tasks involved with feeding the shearers. In camps with a slightly different composition, an older widow might oversee the shearing. However, in Copper Canyon, all the camps with large herds, where shearers were recruited from outside the residence group, fit a male-oriented communication pattern rather than one focused on a female.

Sheepdipping

Sheep are dipped yearly on the reservation in a program administered by grazing committees in each Land Management District.[10] They are herded through a specially constructed trough containing a chemical solution to control the spread of skin diseases, ticks, and other external pests. In 1966, dipping took place at Copper Canyon in July on two days decided upon at a chapter meeting. Thirty-three herds were dipped during these two days. (Other herds were dipped with sheep from two different nearby communities at other times during the summer.) Vaccination of lambs and ewes for soremouth and blue tongue (two common sheep diseases) took place later in the summer.

Each residence group brings its herd to the dipping vats near the summer chapter house. At any one time several herds are usually located separately in the area around the vats awaiting their turn. Eight steps are required in seeing that the sheep are dipped:

1. Herding the sheep into the first holding pen;
2. Separating the lambs and kids from the adult animals, and putting the adult animals into the narrow runways leading into the dipping vats;
3. Pushing and pulling the animals through the runways until they are near the vats;
4. Throwing the animals into the vats;
5. Pushing the swimming sheep and goats through the long vats with a long-handled, forked stick;
6. Counting the sheep as they emerge and letting them into a holding pen;
7. Herding the animals out of the holding pen and back to the residence group;
8. Paying the dipping fee to the grazing committee members, chapter president, or treasurer, and having the number of sheep on the grazing permit compared with the number of sheep dipped.

Dipping is an occasion when all the households in the residence group participate. Members of residence groups arrive in a pickup truck or car and park near the dipping vats. Those with larger herds butcher a sheep and cook the noon meal over an open fire. One or two of these serve anyone who has been working on the dipping and who comes over to eat.

A rough division of labor exists in the dipping activities. The children often do the herding and look after the sheep while waiting their turn to enter the holding pen. Both men and women aid in separating the lambs and kids from the sheep and goats and in pushing the animals through the runways. Men and teen-age boys throw the animals into the vat. Women and children push them through, although some of the old men help. Young men do the counting and herding of the animals into the holding pens after they clamber out of the troughs. There is joint effort on the part of everyone. Some of the men and teen-age boys work most of the day lifting sheep into the vats, even after their own herd has been dipped. Both men and women help with the animals in herds that precede and follow their own.

It is the responsibility of the residence group, however, to see that their own sheep are put through the vats. Thus the personnel engaged in each task is constantly changing, and the number of people helping varies depending on the size of the residence group. Larger residence groups have a full cadre of helpers, including many children. Nuclear camps and isolated individuals are able to put the sheep through by themselves, but some receive aid from close relatives who reside in other camps.

Ten camps combined in groups of two to dip their herds. One or both of the combining herds were small, and it seemed more efficient to pool resources. Four of the five combined herds were based on close genealogical ties. Only one group was composed of two unrelated camps (2 and 48). In this case both camps had small flocks, and there were no herds among the respective kin with which to combine. The kin ties utilized to put together the other four herds included a mother and adult son (Camps 16 and 57); a brother and sister (Camps 15 and 35); a father's brother and brother's daughter (Camps 69 and 70); and a mother's sister and sister's daughter (Camps 11 and 32). Only the last case does not follow the rule that if those with small herds agree to combine they do so with the herd of the closest genealogical kinsmen who both own a herd and live nearby. The combining of herds in Camps 11 and 32 for dipping is the exception for the following reasons, which illustrate how the principles of authority and request making outlined in Chapters 2 and 3 operate in a concrete instance.

CASE G. COMBINING HERDS FOR DIPPING

Camp 32 consisted of a widow, Betsy, and her adult granddaughter in one household, who did most of the herding, and a married son, Andrew, and daughter-in-law, Rebecca, in another household. Genealogical kin who had sheep herds are indicated in Figure 6.1.

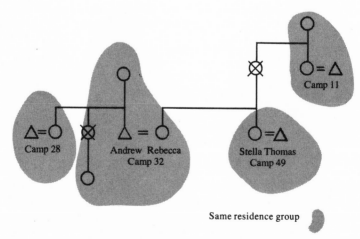

Fig 6.1   Rebecca and Andrew's kin

Dipping the sheep with the herd in Camp 28 was not possible for two reasons. Andrew's sister and brother-in-law (John Begay) lived just across the district fence-line; they had dipped their flock with Navajos from the adjacent grazing district. Also, the sheep belonged to John and not to Andrew's sister. Since he was *t'áá bee bóholníih* for the herd, a request would have had to be made from Andrew to his sister and then to the brother-in-law. This would be an awkward and very indirect request, and the brother-in-law's reputation as a ''mean'' Navajo, and probably a ''werewolf'' (see Case A, Chapter 2), made the possibility of cooperation even more unlikely. Likewise the herd in Rebecca's sister's camp belonged mainly to the husband, Thomas (of Case C). A request would have to go from Rebecca to Sarah, the sister, and then to Thomas. The only request that could be made to kinsmen who controlled the herd was to Rebecca's mother's sister (and grandmother) in Camp 11. This was, in fact, the herd with which Camp 32 combined.

The two days of intense interaction that characterize dipping actually reveal the importance of the residence group as a unit of cooperation. Unlike herding, dipping is apt to bring the participation of the entire residence group. Rather than a system of rotation, it calls for the concerted effort of adults and children in all households for part of a day. In only a few instances—where two small herds are combined into one—is help recruited from outside the residence group. In these situations, requests are most often made by someone in a camp with a small herd to a close relative who is *t'áá bee bóholníih* for another herd.

Dipping is also a community occasion where there is a spirit of mutual aid, regardless of kinship ties. Members of the residence group are responsible for their own herd, but men and younger boys help for the greater part of a day by throwing the sheep into the vats and counting the dipped animals. As a participant-observer, I could see changes in personnel as each herd was dipped and as a new residence group took over the work. But there were constancies in the cooperation that depended neither on particular kinship relations nor on political roles (such as chapter office or grazing committee membership). On one hand, the occasion illustrates a community-wide event where the norms of generalized reciprocity (described in Chapter 2) are operative and where individuals help because it is a good thing. On the other hand, concrete ties within the residence group are important and supply the aid needed to see that each herd is dipped. Dipping is one of the activities that most clearly demonstrates the importance of the residence group as a unit of cooperation.

Cultivation of Fields

Fields planted by members of the Copper Canyon community are located in four areas. Fields are found on the Flats at Crumbled House Mesa (*kináázhoozhi*), Black House Mesa (*kindałizhini*), and Blue Mesa (*bis dooł'izi si'ą*). They are also scattered throughout the Mountain near summer residence sites.

Since the 1940s, those who cultivate a field have been required to obtain a permit from the Land Operations Office of the Bureau of Indian Affairs Sub-agency at Shiprock. Permits are held by both men and women and sometimes by a couple.[11] In a few cases, an adult son or daughter had recently acquired a field relinquished by an aging parent. Whether the field is in the husband's or wife's name usually depends on whether the couple is living in the use-area of the husband's or the wife's parents. Presumably the rights to the field have been obtained through parents of the spouse whose name is on the permit. Of course there are exceptions, and some husbands have their names on permits for fields located near the wife's relatives. Size and exact location of the field are estimated when the permit is given; thus, these data are not as accurate as if the land had been surveyed. Fields range from three to twenty acres, with the average being ten acres.

The name on a permit is largely a formality to meet government requirements, and it does not always indicate who cultivates the field. The field is at the disposal of the residence group, that is, a couple and their married children who live near them.

In Copper Canyon, of the seventy-seven residence groups, twenty-one had no fields; another five groups had permits for fields but did not cultivate them in 1966. The remaining fifty-one camps had fields which were planted. Fourteen of these camps had two fields but planted only one of them. The unused fields were mostly in Blue Mesa. This area seems to be planted less and less each year because of the small amount of water for irrigation and the fact that some camps have access to other fields on the Mountain close to their summer homes. The holders of Blue Mesa fields, who seemed to be abandoning them, lived several miles away and had a second field.

There are five important agricultural tasks: (1) clearing the field and cleaning the irrigation ditches (for fields on the Flats, which are irrigated), (2) irrigation (only in the Flats fields), (3) plowing and planting, (4) weeding (once or twice during the summer), and (5) harvesting.

These tasks usually are performed by men, though women help with the planting, weeding, and harvesting. During the summer of 1965, high school boys on the Tribal Summer Program weeded several fields, especially those of the chapter officers and their relatives. One household in the residence group takes the lead in agricultural activities. Often this is the parental couple, but it may also be one of the junior couples. The latter is most often the case when parents are aging and prefer to leave cultivation to the younger generation.

Fields are irrigated in the spring only on the Flats. Water running down the main arroyos from the spring melt is diverted into the field for two or three days until the ground is soaked. Customarily, those living furthest to the east use the water first; only later is the water allowed to flow into fields closer to the mountains. Thus, when the runoff begins to slow down, the camps furthest from the source already will have been irrigated.

Sometimes a neighbor may cut off the water to divert it to his fields while it is running in the fields of another family. In one instance, the latter family went to the neighboring camp and explained the situation; the water was then diverted back into the ditch and allowed to run back into the first field. Often someone complains that another is using the water too long, or is wasting it, but rarely does open conflict occur over irrigation. Interestingly, there is no mutual cooperation between camps to clean ditches or further organize irrigation.

Plowing is most often done by tractor. Only four or five residence groups used a plow and team of horses. Since only five men in the Copper Canyon area had access to tractors, these men usually were paid to plow the fields. Residents of Black House Mesa and Crumbled House Mesa hired men from the neighboring area to do the plowing.

When the plowing is done, members of the residence group are on hand to cast the seed (corn, squash, or melons) into the ground after a furrow has been made. These are covered over when the tractor makes the next furrow. In this way, plowing and planting are accomplished simultaneously.

The choice of someone to plow the field with a tractor depends more on proximity and availability than on kinship ties. The individual in the household who is *t'áá bee bóholníih*, or most concerned with cultivation (husband or wife in the senior couple, son or daughter in the junior couple), makes arrangements with the owner of the tractor and offers to pay for the plowing. Such arrangements can be made at a public place like the trading post or the chapter house, or by going to the individual's camp. The husband in Camp 14 plowed fields mainly in the Blue Mesa area (near his own camp), while the son-in-law in Camp 35 (who had borrowed a tractor from his relatives in Crystal), plowed fields on the Mountain near Cottonwood Pass where his residence group had their summer cabins. He was extremely busy plowing several fields within one week; when he did not appear on the scheduled day or the day after, one family made arrangements with the son in Camp 46 to do the plowing.

Harvesting is a casual operation, with corn and melons being taken from the field as soon as they are ripe. The produce belongs to those who plant it, though it is widely distributed among other members of the residence group and other relatives. Produce is purchased from nonrelatives, and Copper Canyon residents often go to Black House Mesa at the end of the summer to buy corn, melons, or peaches from the residents there who have much larger fields. As is the case with other Navajo requests, the price is set by the requester and accepted by those giving the food. If, however, a family loads a pickup full of melons, squash, or corn, and goes from camp to camp with the produce, they are considered vendors; it is appropriate to ask how much an item costs, and they reply with an asking price.

In sum, fields, though they may be held in the name of one individual or couple, are at the disposal of the residence group. For the nuclear residence group, the husband takes the lead in cultivation, though the wife helps with some tasks. This is true even if the field has been acquired through the wife's relatives (i.e., obtained through her mother or father). For extended families, one household usually is responsible for planting and taking care of the field. Usually this is the parental couple; however, as they become older, either a married son or daughter living in the camp will take over cultivation. It is unlikely that a field will be placed in the name of a son-in-law while the wife's parents are still living in the camp. The older couple or widow will be consulted if the junior couple wishes to plant. The field will remain in the mother or father's name, even though the junior couple have become the actual cultivators. Likewise, a nonresident son or daughter or granddaughter may ask to plant in the parent's field, especially if members of the residence group have not been using it. Produce is given to other households in the residence group, though the household doing most of the cultivation keeps the bulk for itself.

A male who is not a member of the residence group, but who owns a tractor, is asked to do the plowing. Accessibility rather than kinship ties determine choice, in contrast to shearing activities where clan kin ties are relied upon. As with pastoral activities, the organization of cooperation varies depending on the size and composition of the residence group. Rather than a rotation system between two households, as in herding, one household in an extended camp takes more responsibility than the others.

Conclusions

Comparison of these cooperative patterns with those in other communities is difficult because detailed information on who does the herding, shearing, dipping, planting, and harvesting is not available for a range of residence groups in one community, much less across several different communities. One exception is Malcolm Carr Collier's 1938 study of Navajo Mountain and Klagetoh (1966). She shows that agricultural and pastoral activities were performed by residence groups at Navajo Mountain and by several residence groups related by ties of kinship and marriage (a cooperating group in her terms) at Klagetoh. However, she does not give a detailed analysis of how various livestock activities are handled within a residence group or between residence groups depending on the number and relationship of household members involved, the size of the herd, and the demands of a particular task.

On the basis of the Copper Canyon data, my knowledge of the Rimrock community, and the scant data from other communities, I tentatively suggest the following generalizations:

1. Under present-day conditions, agricultural and pastoral activities are handled by the residence group in a wide variety of communities throughout the reservation (Copper Canyon, Rimrock, Navajo Mountain, Piñon).

2. This pattern has undoubtedly existed since the post-Fort Sumner period, though it may have increased since the 1940s. At least the data from Rimrock, which go back to the 1870s, suggest that nuclear and extended families settled in the area in dispersed hoghan clusters and may have planted and herded separately.

3. In the past when herds were larger and more fields were planted, there was probably a tendency for *occasional* cooperation in pastoral and agricultural activities among siblings and their spouses or among married children and their parents who lived in different hoghan clusters. I would not call these "outfits" or "cooperating groups" for reasons listed in Chapter 5. Instead, I see cooperation related to the developmental cycle of domestic groups, with recruitment of aid following the patterns illustrated in Cases F and G.

4. As herding and agricultural activities have declined, these tasks continue to be coordinated with the residence group, but there has been a growing tendency to involve only one or two households in an extended family camp, especially where herds and fields are small and little manpower is needed. For the minority of families who have large herds, there would be a tendency for adult members of all households to be involved in herding, shearing, dipping, or in the cultivation of fields. If help is needed for a task like shearing, it may be increasingly the pattern to recruit distant relatives—rather than siblings and adult children—and to pay them for their labor.

In sum, I would argue that there has always been a great deal of variation in residence patterns and residence group composition within Navajo communities, between communities, and at various points in time. It is also likely that there have been variations in the way in which members of residence groups handled agricultural and pastoral activities, though several trends can be related to recent changes in the Navajo economic base. The content of Copper Canyon patterns may not be prevalent elsewhere, but the cultural model of cooperation presented in Chapters 2 and 3, and the structural model of domestic group development and fission outlined in Chapter 4, can be used to interpret both present-day patterns in a variety of communities and to suggest an analysis of Navajo social organization as it existed in previous periods.

To summarize, in this chapter I have analyzed pastoral and agricultural activities in terms of cross-sectional data on all the herds and fields held by Copper Canyon residents in 1965–66. Herding, shearing, dipping, and the cultivation of fields are all activities that demonstrate the importance of the residence group. The patterns of cooperation that emerge differ for each of these pursuits, but the residence group is still the arena in which tasks are coordinated. One or two households may share most of the responsibility for carrying out some tasks, such as herding and planting, but sheepdipping involves the full participation of the residence group, including the households that do not help with herding. Nonresidents join residence group members for shearing large herds and for plowing. For shearing, they are distant relatives rather than close genealogical kin (nonresident siblings and siblings' children); for plowing, they are men who have access to a tractor.

I have utilized case material to illustrate the way in which the organization of tasks reflects the concepts of authority and the ethic of generalized reciprocity outlined in Chapter 2, and the strategies of request making discussed in Chapter 3. Requests generally follow the lines of communication and authority within the residence group. In other words, the older couple or widow is *t'áá bee bóholníih*. They (or she) ask a son or daughter to help, or make the same request of an in-married affine through the coresident child.

Chapter 7

The Transportation Problem

In Chapter 6 I examined the organization of agricultural and pastoral activities which, though still highly valued, play a smaller part in the Copper Canyon economy than they played in the 1930s. In contrast, the car and pickup truck have increased in importance. The impact of the use of motor vehicles by the Navajo should not be underestimated. Trucks and automobiles have made it easier to haul wood and water from distances of several miles; they have shortened the amount of time it takes to move household possessions to seasonal residences; and they have given Navajos increased access to trading posts, stores, hospitals, and schools.

The domestic group model discussed in Chapter 4 proved to be a useful analytic tool for isolating patterns of cooperation in pastoral and agricultural tasks that are focused in the domestic sphere. Domestic groups—the household and the residence group—may have been the units for coordination of transportation in the past when Navajos depended on the horse and wagon for hauling and transport. However, the advent of the car and pickup has "opened out" cooperative patterns to include kin ties beyond those within domestic groups and, in addition, has created a greater demand for transportation (especially rides to and from trading posts and towns), although not every adult has direct access to a car or pickup. The household and residence group are still important in recruiting aid, but it is necessary to use the model of ego-centered sets of kin in order to understand how Copper Canyon Navajos obtain transportation.

Activities that require transportation include: getting rides, hauling wood and water, and moving to summer or winter residence sites. Again, using cross-sectional data, I will discuss the ways in which these activities are managed, presenting case material to illustrate particular instances of request making. The use of kin ties within the residence group is influenced by two factors: first, the composition of the residence group in which the adults of a household live, and, second, the presence or absence of transportation in that residence group. Outside the residence group, the particular composition of an adult's set provides the pool of primary and secondary relatives on which he or she may call. When transportation from ego's residence group or kin set is unavailable, clan or neighborhood ties are utilized.

Giving and Getting Rides

There are many times when a Copper Canyon Navajo needs to get from one place to another. The most frequent occasions include: (1) trips to the trading post for groceries; (2) trips to off-reservation towns to shop, make payments on pawned jewelry, sell piñon nuts, or buy hay; (3) trips to one of the two nearest hospitals, each fifty miles away; (4) trips to boarding schools to pick up children on vacation; and (5) trips to county, state, BIA, or tribal government offices to obtain various services.

The problem of getting a ride is best conceptualized using a model of ego-centered sets. In other words, individuals utilize kin ties in a "set" of potential cooperators, some of whom live in the same residence group and some of whom live in other residence groups in Copper Canyon. As outlined in Chapter 5, a "set" is defined as those adults within one or two genealogical links of any particular ego. This includes all the important adult kinsmen within a three-generation range on whom an individual is likely to call. The potential set is distinguished from actual cooperators who agree to provide transportation after being approached by the relative in need. Neighborhood and clan ties will also be discussed as they relate to getting rides.

The individual who owns the car or pickup is *t'áá bee bóholnííh*, that is, the person who is asked when transportation is needed. Within a household the spouse and children of the car owner have primary access to transportation in the vehicle, and, therefore, it is easiest for them to get rides. For those who do not own a car or pickup and whose spouse does not own one, a ride is obtained by asking a car owner in the same or another residence group, or by hitchhiking. A man often hitchhikes or drives alone, but a woman is more likely to take her husband, older children, mother, or sister with her. Giving and getting rides is one of the most constant and random activities of cooperation; since there are so many situational variables, clear patterns are difficult to find. The element of randomness is due to three factors.

First, the ownership of cars and pickups was not evenly distributed over the Copper Canyon population. Cars were usually owned by men and were driven by the owners, though some wives and teenage children also drove. Of seventy-eight camps, forty-four had at least one motor vehicle (a car, pickup, or tractor).[1] Nine camps had only wagons and seventeen had no transportation; the transportation available to seven camps is unknown. From another point of view, of the 145 households, only forty-eight owned a pickup or car. Thus, 52 percent of the residence groups had access to a car or pickup, but only 34 percent of the households owned one. It was not likely that a particular couple had a vehicle; it was more likely that there was a vehicle in the camp. Pickups and cars were owned by Navajos who were middle-aged or younger since these were the only ones who had the income and skills to own and operate them. With such an uneven distribution of vehicles (so that a few residence groups had two or three cars or pickups and others had none), one cannot expect the patterns of transportation to be the same in all segments of the community.

Second, the segment of the population that owns vehicles is always in flux. Those who have access to a car or pickup one month may not have it the next because it is in need of repairs, has been repossessed by the auto agency for lack of payments, or has been wrecked in an accident. There may be a lapse of several months before an individual or couple can get enough money to pay for parts and repairs or for the payments on another car. Many of those who have a car at any given time have been without a vehicle at some time in the recent past.

Third, since a ride is a much more immediate problem than many other cooperative activities, a Navajo is likely to make a request of someone near at hand. If there is no transportation in the individual's own household or residence group, he may walk to a neighbor's house, ask someone when he is at a public gathering place (such as the chapter house or trading post), or make a request of a visitor to his own residence group. These patterns are more likely than walking five or six miles to make the request of someone in his set of primary and secondary relatives (e.g., sibling, adult child, or sibling's child). This would be a last resort only if several other possibilities had already failed. Transportation is an activity where the proximity of someone with a car is equally, if not more, important than kinship considerations.

From the point of view of an adult who does not have transportation and whose spouse does not own a car in working order, there are five possible ways of getting a ride:

1. Arranging a ride with a relative or spouse in the same residence group who owns a car. (If an in-married affine is the car owner, the request is made indirectly through the connecting relative.)
2. Arranging a ride with a close genealogical relative, that is, someone in an individual's set of primary or secondary kin. (A member of a spouse's set may be called upon, using the spouse as an intermediary.)
3. Arranging a ride with a more distant genealogical relative, a nonrelative, or a clan relative.
4. Hitchhiking: Starting out for the destination and catching a ride with someone who comes along.
5. Requesting a ride from someone who comes to visit or whom one sees at a public gathering place. This is likely to be someone included in items 2 or 3 above.

The strategy used by most Navajos is to begin with the first possibility and work through the list. Possibilities within the residence group are tried first before ties within a set of genealogical kin are utilized or before more distant or nonrelatives are asked. This method of working from close kin, both genealogically and spatially, to more distant and nonkin is best illustrated by a specific case.

CASE H. REQUESTING TRANSPORTATION

Children attending BIA boarding schools were to come home for Christmas vacation, and Edna (Camp 20) had arranged to have me pick up her daughter from a school near Gallup. The roads were icy, however, and I suggested she make other arrangements. She first talked to her sister-in-law (wife of a deceased brother who lived in Camp 17). This woman, Amy, also had children in the same school and had asked the daughter-in-law in a third residence group to pick up her children. (This was Camp 18 where a clan brother, his two wives, and children lived. The camp pickup, which was to be used, belonged to the younger wife but was driven by the daughter-in-law.) Edna and Amy decided that if Edna's daughter was to come also, some of the children would have to ride in the back of the pickup, which would be too cold. Instead, they would ask Lucy (Camp 14), who had a car and who was a clan sister of Edna's husband. Lucy agreed, but first had to make a trip to another boarding school to pick up her own daughter. Another woman (who lived in Camp 43 nearby and was Edna's clan sister) had asked to go along. Unfortunately, Lucy's car broke down on the muddy roads; the woman from Camp 43 hitched a ride, and Edna was forced to look for another means of transportation.

All the possibilities among Edna's and Amy's set of genealogical kin had already been tried or were known to be unavailable. Edna's sister's husband (Camp 17, also) had taken his car to Gallup where he was at work. Amy's son-in-law (Camp 6) was working in the trading post and could not take time off to pick up the students. Another son-in-law (coresident with Amy) was working on the railroad; hence his car was unavailable. Edna and her husband owned two cars, but since he was working for the railroad in Nebraska and Edna could not drive, they were useless. The next possibility was to ask someone more distantly related. Amy and Edna decided to ask Lester (son of Amy's clan brother in Camp 18). He was married to Lucy's mother and they lived in Camp 13. (Lucy's mother was also Edna's husband's clan and distantly related genealogically.) Lester, after some hesitation due to his wife's suggestion to refuse the request, finally agreed to go when Edna offered him five dollars to pay for the gas. Figure 7.1 illustrates important genealogical and spatial relationships.

It is most important to emphasize the order in which requests were made. Cars in Amy's residence group (Camp 17) and Edna's residence group (Camp 20) were unavailable for various reasons. Another close choice, Amy's son-in-law (Camp 6), was also eliminated. Then Amy went to her clan brother's residence group (Camp 18) where Edna had no relatives. When this possibility seemed unworkable, Edna suggested that she aproach Lucy, who was related to her husand but not to Amy. Each woman used her own kinship connections and acted as negotiator in making the request of the car owner, even when the request included the other woman and her children. They finally settled on someone who was more distantly related to both of them and who was outside their respective residence groups and sets of genealogical kin.

The kinship base of the request-making strategy creates definite transportation patterns in the Copper Canyon community as a whole. As indicated by the case of Edna and Amy, the choices made by adults in various households in either getting or giving transportation are partly determined by the composition of their residence group. Some households are nuclear residence groups in the second stage of the residence cycle. Other households (of younger or older couples) are embedded in extended family residence groups of two to five households. The presence or absence of a car or pickup in the residence group is a second and equally important factor. The combination of residence group structure and transportation produces four possible arrangements: (1) nuclear residence groups with transportation;[2] (2) nuclear residence groups without transportation; (3) extended family residence groups with transportation; and (4) extended family residence groups without transportation. Thus, there are four characteristic solutions, one for each situation. Adults (usually a couple) in a nuclear residence group where there is a motor vehicle will provide transportation for themselves and their children and, possibly, for relatives in other residence groups whose members are in the kin set of the husband or wife of the household.

The nuclear residence group without transportation has to depend on other residence groups where there are relatives in either the husband's or wife's set. In an extended family residence group the household that has a car will provide transportation primarily for themselves and for those in other households in the residence

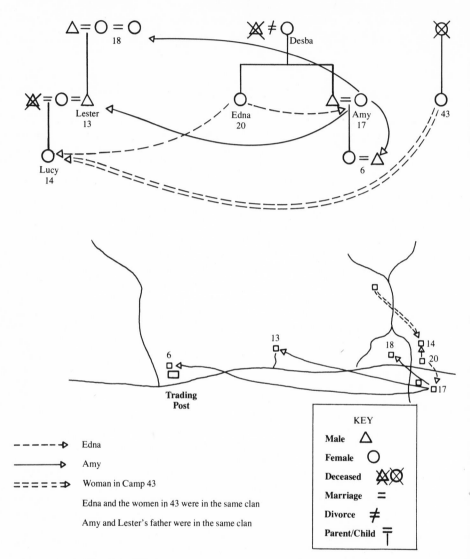

Fig. 7.1   *Transportation requests made by Edna and Amy*

group. Sometimes the car owner will transport his or her genealogical relatives or those of the spouse. Those in households without cars will usually get transportation from a household in the residence group with a car, but often they will call on someone outside the residence group if the usual transporters are not available.

If an entire extended family residence group of several households is without transportation, they will all have to depend on genealogical sets of primary or secondary kin or on more distant relatives and neighbors. Each adult will make his or her own arrangements as the situation arises. Since several households are involved and each adult has a different set of kin, members drawn from several sets may provide transportation for the residence group over a period of time. The following four cases have been selected to illustrate how transportation is handled in each of these four situations.

CASE I.   KEVIN AND LUCY'S TAXI SERVICE

Camp 14 was a nuclear family with its own transportation. Kevin and Lucy had a pickup and car; since both could drive, they were often called upon to take relatives and neighbors. Kevin had no genealogical relatives in Copper Canyon but was related by clan to members of Camp 58, and to two sisters who were married to Lucy's brothers in Camp 13. Lucy's mother, Nancy, and four married siblings lived in Camp 13. Three pickups and three cars were owned by members of this residence group, so Lucy rarely provided rides for them. The location of these residence groups is shown in Figure 7.2.

Some transportation services provided by Kevin and Lucy were the following:

(a) Lucy borrowed her stepfather Johnny's pickup to haul a refrigerator from Gallup; on another occasion she took her mother, Nancy, and her sister-in-law to Window Rock in her brother's car (Camp 13).

(b) The mother, Nelly Begay, and married daughter in Camp 19 were often transported by Lucy. Nelly was married to Lucy's *bidá'í* (mother's brother), now deceased. Their camp was near Lucy's.

(c) At times, Lucy provided rides for members of Camp 18. The two wives and children were the same clan as Lucy's father, and one of the older children was married to Lucy's mother and was the stepfather mentioned previously. They were also Lucy's neighbors; they owned one pickup, but on some occasions extra transportation was needed. In one instance, Lucy took the younger wife to Shiprock to notify her half-sister of the illness of her father.

(d) Lucy gave rides to the mother, son, and daughter-in-law in Camp 23. These people were not related, but lived nearby. The entire camp was without transportation, as were their close genealogical kin in nearby camps. Lucy also had provided rides for a maternal niece of the wife in Camp 23 and Kevin had taken her new husband to Farmington.

(e) The widow in Camp 32, Betsy, often was transported by Lucy. This camp also was without transportation, and few of the woman's more distant relatives could have provided it. She was not related to Lucy, though her deceased husband was the same clan as Kevin. They lived several miles from Lucy, and arrangements usually were made at public meeting places.

(f) Kevin took a nonresident son in Camp 58 to Shiprock to his job. This camp usually was well provided with transportation, but in this instance, the son's pickup had broken down and he walked to Kevin's house to make the request. He was related to Kevin as *bitsilí* (younger clan brother).

(g) The husband, Mr. Sage, and his son in Camp 22 requested that Kevin take them to Farmington to buy hay. They were related to members of Camp 23, but there was no transportation in either Camp 23 or 22, so they came to Kevin, who was a neighbor but not a relative.

(h) Lucy and Kevin sometimes provided transportation for Camp 20. The younger couple, Edna and Mike, were related to both; Mike was a clan sister of the *ahidiilchíín* relation to Kevin. This camp had two cars, but occasions arose when they were in need of transportation.

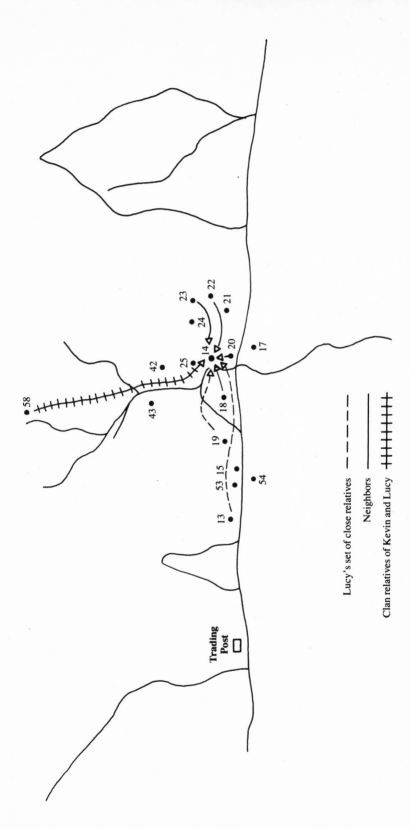

Fig. 7.2 *Spatial relations between Kevin and Lucy's camp and camps of persons they transport*

Lucy's set of close relatives — — —

Neighbors —————

Clan relatives of Kevin and Lucy ++++++++

In sum, Kevin and Lucy provided their own transportation and transportation for a wide range of Navajos, many of whom were not related but who lived in nearby residence groups. They gave rides to primary relatives (e.g., Lucy's mother and siblings) and to secondary relatives (e.g., the wife of Lucy's mother's brother) who lived nearby. In addition, they gave rides to clan relatives who were also neighbors and to some neighbors who were nonrelatives. They did not give rides to secondary relatives (e.g., Lucy's two maternal uncles) who lived in other neighborhoods nor to some of their neighbors who were not relatives (e.g., Camps 15, 43, 42, 21), though some of these were without transportation. They also did not give rides to clan relatives who were close neighbors but who usually had their own car (e.g., Camp 25).

In other words, given the need for transportation, kinship proximity and spatial proximity are both important and may reinforce each other. Requests by primary relatives are less affected by distance than are secondary or clan relatives. On the other hand, neighboring nonrelatives do request rides, though a request is more likely if the neighborhood tie is reinforced by clan relationship. Case J deals with contrasting circumstances. Unlike Kevin and Lucy's situation where requests were directed inward toward a couple, a couple without transportation in a nuclear family residence group, Fred and Janie, directed requests outward from their residence group and utilized ties with primary, secondary, and clan relatives.

CASE J. FRED AND JANIE'S REQUESTS FOR TRANSPORTATION

Fred and Janie, who did not own a car or pickup, often hitched a ride to Gallup with someone at the trading post. Fred also asked his sister in Camp 11 for rides, for example, to pick up his wife from the hospital in Gallup. This sister also took Fred and Janie to get their three children when boarding school was recessed for the summer. Other sources of transportation included Camp 49 (Fred's sister's daughter) and Camp 7. The latter was near Fred's house, and the wife was a parallel cousin (mother's sister's daughter) of Janie. Janie's brother in Camp 20 sometimes provided rides, but Janie's parents and married sister in Camp 12 had no transportation to share. Another sister, in Camp 17, drove a car, but rarely transported Fred and Janie. Fred traveled to California for seasonal agricultural work with a couple in Camp 36. The wife was a clan sister of Fred, and the husband was a clan brother of Janie. Fred returned by bus, as there was no room in the car.

This couple utilized almost all ties with those primary and secondary relatives who had transportation. Janie even requested rides from a tertiary relative (parallel cousin) who lived nearby, though there were other distant relatives and members of the same clan in the neighborhood of whom she did not request transportation. Fred and Janie did not ask nonrelated neighbors, but often hitchhiked instead. In other words, for this couple spatial proximity did not seem to be as important as genealogical proximity. When Fred asked clan relatives who lived several miles away to take him with them to California, this clanship link was reinforced by joint participation by both couples in the Pentecostal church.

The third example, an extended family residence group with transportation, concerns Edna and her relatives, many of whom were mentioned in Case H.

CASE K. EDNA AND MIKE'S TRANSPORTATION

Edna lived with her husband, Mike, and children in one household of Camp 20. An old lady of Edna's father's clan, Zonnie, shared the two-room house with them.

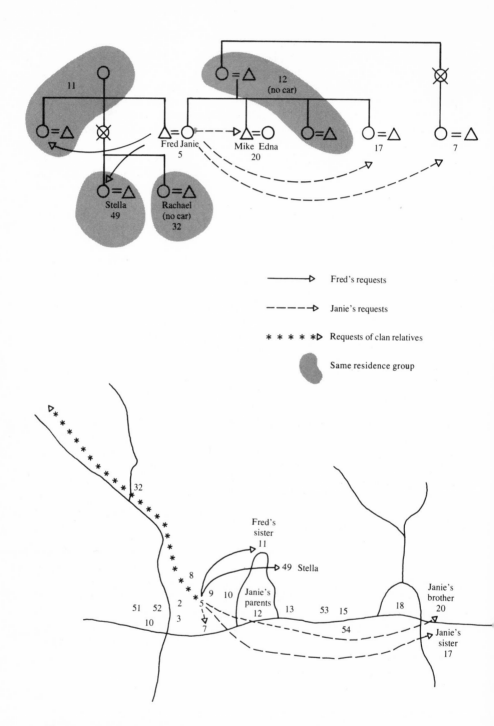

Fig. 7.3 *Spatial and genealogical relationships between Fred and Janie's camp and camps that provide transportation*

Edna's widowed mother, her divorced brother, and his daughter lived in a second household. Edna and Mike owned two cars, but only Mike and Susie, Edna's daughter, could drive. Mike was often away on railroad work and Susie was at boarding school, which meant that Edna had to get rides from other sources. Edna's sister, Evelyn, and her sister-in-law, Amy, lived in Camp 17 just across the highway. Evelyn's husband had a car as did one married, coresident son. Amy had a married son and a married daughter living in the camp, and both the son and son-in-law had cars. Much transportation-sharing took place between the two camps. Edna's mother received rides from members of Camp 17, and they picked up children at the boarding school. In turn, Mike and Edna gave rides to Amy, Evelyn, and their children. Requests were made by older members of the two camps through their siblings or children to the in-married males who owned and drove the cars. One exception was that Edna and Susie often made direct requests of Amy's son-in-law, who worked at the trading post. Amy had another son-in-law, in Camp 6, who had a pickup.

Mike also gave rides to his parents in Camp 12 and to a daughter from a previous marriage who was living temporarily with her grandparents in Camp 12. Transportation was often provided for Edna's brother and his wife in Camp 64, a clan sister (MMZDD) in Camp 43, and a clan relative (MMZD) and her husband in Camp 42. When Edna needed a ride, she depended on members of Camp 17 or on Lucy (a clan relative of her husband), who was also a neighbor (Camp 14). Edna and Mike also gave rides to the trading post to Edna's mother and to the old lady who lived in their household. The latter sometimes hitchhiked to Gallup to visit a granddaughter.

It is important to note that the pattern of giving and receiving rides was slightly different for each adult in this residence group, emphasizing the ego-centered nature of request making and the way in which the set of relevant kin shifts from individual to individual. For instance, Mike gave rides to his primary and secondary kin who were without transportation; Edna, his wife, was not asked to transport them, but gave to and received transportation from her set of kin. Even when Mike was driving the car, the request came from Edna's mother, sister, or sister-in-law to Edna, who made the specific arrangements with Mike. Edna's mother, who was frequently in the position of requesting transportation, sometimes asked her coresident daughter and at other times utilized ties with the daughter or daughter-in-law across the road in order to get a ride with a grandson or granddaughter's husband. Finally, Edna's sister-in-law, Amy, had a slightly different set of kin on which to draw. As mentioned earlier in this chapter, Amy had clan ties with Camp 18, which were reinforced by proximity, and she utilized them, while Edna was more likely to ask Lucy, her neighbor, or clan relatives.

While Edna and Mike both gave transportation to members of the other household in their camp and to members of their respective sets of kin *and* received rides from those kin who had cars, in the fourth example, an extended residence group without transportation, members of all households are necessarily in the position of always asking for rides from Navajos outside their residence group.

CASE L.   TRANSPORTATION DIFFICULTIES IN CAMP 32

As mentioned in Case E (Chapter 6), Camp 32 consisted of a widow, Betsy, and her adult granddaughter in one household and Betsy's son, Andrew, and his wife, Rebecca, in the second household. Betsy and her granddaughter often hitchhiked to their destination; other sources of transportation included the granddaughter's sister

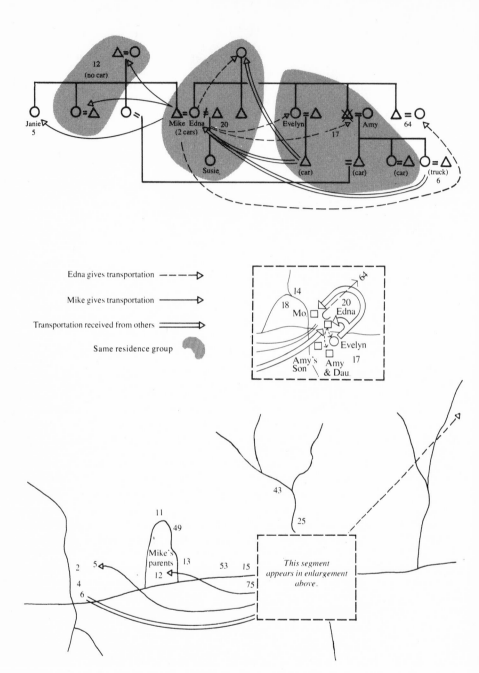

Fig. 7.4 *Spatial and genealogical relationship between Edna's camp and camps of those who share transportation*

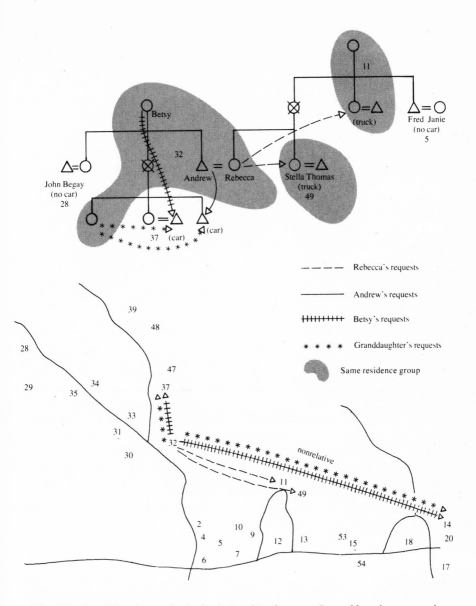

Fig. 7.5 *Spatial and genealogical relationships between Camp 32 and persons who provide transportation*

and husband in Camp 37 and Lucy in Camp 14. Rebecca and Andrew sometimes got rides from Rebecca's sister in Camp 49 or the couple in Camp 37. Another source was Rebecca's mother's sister in Camp 11, who took them to Toadlena to pick up the school children at the beginning of summer vacation. Rebecca and Andrew's nonresident daughter and son-in-law sometimes visited and provided transportation. A brother of the granddaughter took members of the camp on various errands when he returned for a two week vacation. Nonrelatives were sometimes relied on; for example, a couple in Camp 39 provided a ride home from the Pentecostal church.

Like the nuclear family without transportation, this extended camp used a variety of sources and often hitchhiked or walked if a ride could not be found. These adults tended to make requests of genealogical kin rather than neighbors, especially since, in this case, few neighbors were related by clan, so that spatial proximity was not reinforced by kinship and, hence, was rarely utilized as a principle of recruitment. Again, the composition of sets from which rides are requested shifts from individual to individual. Betsy and her granddaughter and married son relied on one set of kin, while Rachael obtained rides for her and her husband from another set.

In this analysis I have isolated request-making strategies that Navajos use in getting rides. The ideology of generalized reciprocity described in Chapter 3 provides the cultural context for the particular phrasing of the transportation request. The case material on Amy's and Edna's search for someone to pick up their children from boarding school illustrates that Navajos first consider ties within the residence group and, then, within their sets of primary and secondary kin outside the residence group. When these options have been eliminated, a clan relative in the same neighborhood is asked. Four cases amplify the way in which this strategy is influenced by (1) the composition of a residence group (whether a nuclear or extended family camp), (2) the presence or absence of transportation in the camp, and (3) the particular shape of an individual's set of kin. Genealogical and spatial proximity are both important. A Navajo without transportation is likely to ask coresident primary and secondary kin for transportation. If an inmarried affine owns the car or pickup, the request is made through the linking relative. Primary and secondary kin who are in other residence groups are then asked. Again, if the spouse of a relative owns the car, he or she is approached indirectly through the connecting relative. Neighbors are rarely asked for rides purely on the basis of spatial proximity: they are asked primarily when there is some clan relationship between the car owner or spouse and the Navajo in need of a ride.

Hauling Water and Wood

Obtaining a ride to or from a destination is a highly ego-centered and individualistic task. This means that a model of an ego-centered set is especially useful for analyzing the variety of requests made by a Navajo over a period of time. Requests for hauling wood and water also can be interpreted in terms of ego-centered sets, but an entire household benefits when these tasks are completed. Firewood and water are two commodities often not available at a Navajo camp site but essential for the performance of household-focused activities, such as cooking, eating, and sleeping.

The distribution of wood and water resources is related to ecological differences in summer residence areas (the Mountain and the Top) and winter areas (the Flats and the Gray Area). In the summer, every household is within one-half mile of an improved spring.[3] Those persons who have cars and wagons use them to haul large quantities of water, but many carry small amounts in buckets from a nearby water source. Wood is obtained from dead pine, piñon, and juniper trees near residence sites. A man often will cut and haul by hand several logs for the household wood pile; or he may use a wagon or truck to bring greater amounts. This distance is only one hundred yards to one-half mile in most cases.

In the winter areas water resources are much fewer and most households must haul their water from sources two to six miles away. Only a few households (24 out of 145) are near enough to a spring or well to haul water by hand in buckets. Wood must be hauled from the Mountain, usually ten to twelve miles from a residence group site. Two or three pickup loads of wood are needed by a household during the winter months. These are usually hauled in the fall before the first snowfall, while the roads on the Mountain are still passable. In the fall of 1965 several men were employed on a Tribal Works Project to cut and haul wood for chapter members. Members paid five dollars for a pickup load of wood if they got the wood at the chapter house, and two dollars if they went to the site where the wood was being cut. Differences in the ecology of summer and winter areas mean that households that can get along without transportation for hauling in the summer are forced to pay others for these services in the winter.

Before the advent of cars and pickups, every household or residence group had a wagon and team of horses with which to haul wood and water. Under conditions in the winter residence area, it would have taken one-half to a full day to haul water and a full day to haul a wagonload of wood. Each household had a good deal of autonomy since each owned, or could borrow from a relative in the same camp, the transportation needed for hauling.

The wagon has been replaced by a much quicker and more efficient method of hauling. Fewer people own the means of transportation, however, and hauling for many entails the time and labor of people in other households in the same or different residence groups. Those who own a pickup have a certain amount of freedom to get wood and water when needed, quickly, and without having to ask the aid of others. On the other hand, ownership of a car or pickup means acquiring financial burdens and accepting requests to haul wood and water for others. Some of these inconveniences are lessened by the fact that drivers receive ten to twenty dollars for a load of wood and two to five dollars for hauling water.

As with transportation in general, the pattern of hauling wood and water is related to two factors: (1) the presence or absence of transportation in the household, and (2) the isolation of the household as a nuclear residence group or its inclusion in an extended residence group. These two factors combine to form four possibilities, or categories as shown in Table 7.1

In category A are nineteen households which had transportation and which were nuclear residence groups; of these, four hauled wood and water by wagon, one used both a wagon and a car, and the remainder used pickups. All households were

TABLE 7.1
Distribution of Transportation for Hauling Wood and Water

Category	Camps		Households	
	Type	No.	With Transportation	Without Transportation
A	Nuclear	19	19	—
B	Nuclear	20	—	20
C	Extended	29	83	—
D	Extended	9	—	23

composed of couples and their children; the husband and wife consulted jointly on the need to haul wood or fill the barrels with water from the nearest well. The husband did the heavy work of cutting the logs and piling them in a pickup or wagon (perhaps with the help of a son or other close male relative). The wife often hauled water by hand, and the few women who drove could replenish the household water supply by themselves when needed, even though they might need help in removing full barrels of water from the truck. Arrangements for hauling wood and water were more stable for nuclear family households, since transportation was available within the household itself.

For households in the other three categories, hauling wood and water can be viewed as involving individual sets of genealogical kin, some of whom lived in the same residence group and some of whom lived in other residence groups. In a household with two adults, either the husband's set or the wife's set (or both) provided a pool of relatives on whom to call, while in the household of a bachelor or widowed or divorced Navajo, only one set was available.

In category B, the twenty nuclear camps without transportation, adults were necessarily forced to go outside the residence group to request aid from a member of the man's or the woman's set of kin or from nonrelatives. Eight of these twenty households could haul their water by hand from a nearby spring or well, even in winter. However, these households had to rely on others for hauling wood. Various primary and secondary relatives or their spouses were asked to help by one of the adults of the household. In Camp 76, the widow made requests of her sister's daughter; the divorcee in Camp 23 called on her brother; the wife in Camp 56 asked her sister; and the bachelor in Camp 9 relied on his brother-in-law to haul wood. Some adults requested help from more distant relatives: for example, in Camp 29 the hauling was done by the husband's clan brother.

Adults in the eleven remaining households in this category (nuclear camps without transportation) depended on relatives outside the residence group for *both* wood and water. Again, several different types of contacts were used. In one household (Camp 30) a widower called on his brother; in another (Camp 78) a widow asked her nonresident son-in-law to do the hauling. In some households, nonrelatives were used; for example, the widow in Camp 4 had the husband and wife in Camp 49 (both nonrelatives) haul water for her. Patterns in this category, of course, are much less stable than for the nuclear camp with transportation. One person will be asked on one occasion and someone else will be asked the next time. The variation in types of kin ties used is partly due to differences in the shape of kin sets of adults in the household. As with the problem of getting rides, Navajos tend to make requests of close kin, both genealogically and spatially, and if these possibilities are not workable, more distant kin, or even nonrelated neighbors will be asked. As with other requests, if an in-law is the owner of the car and hence *t'áá bee bóholnííh*, the request is made using the linking kinsman as an intermediary. The above data illustrate the kinds of kin and nonkin ties that are the outcome of this proximity strategy.

Category C, the third and most frequent situation (eighty-three households in twenty-nine residence groups), is that of an extended family residence group where there was some transportation.[4] In many cases the residence group was composed of an older couple and a married son or daughter. The son or son-in-law who owned the pickup hauled water and wood for his own household and for the parents. As usual, the request was made by the parents directly to the coresident son and indirectly to the son-in-law through the wife. In larger residence groups, this younger male might also have hauled for a third household, that of his sibling or sibling-in-law. In four cases, there were two or more pickups in the camp; thus, households without transportation in these residence groups had two options in making a request for hauling. Even so, some households without transportation went outside the residence group to have hauling done. In this category (extended camps with transportation), the pattern is most stable for households with pickups, as they hauled wood and water for themselves. Adults in households without a pickup had the option of asking a member of another household who had access to a pickup or to ask a relative outside the camp. Navajos will generally choose the former if this person is willing to accept the request, made directly if he is a kinsman or indirectly if an affine.

Category D is that of extended family camps with no transportation (twenty-three households in nine camps). Unlike extended camps with transportation, these Navajos looked for aid outside the residence group, from either genealogical relatives, clan relatives, or nonrelatives. The adults in each household made negotiations using their own kin ties so that members of a variety of sets were utilized within a camp over a period of time.

Strategies of using kin ties can be clarified by contrasting two extended camps without transportation. The kin sets of members of Camps 12 and 19 are shown in Figure 7.6. Camp 12 consisted of an older couple in one household and a daughter and son-in-law in a second household. The following have hauled wood or water for the two households: (1) Mike, a nonresident son of the older couple (Camp 20); (2)

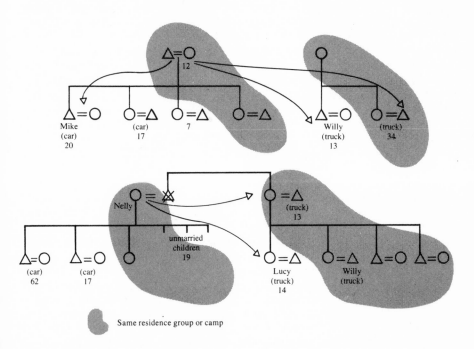

Fig. 7.6 *Genealogical relatives of members of Camps 12 and 19*

Willie, a brother of the son-in-law in the junior household (Camp 13); and (3) the husband of the same son-in-law's sister (Camp 34). The second two-household camp, Camp 19, utilized connections with relatives of the deceased husband of the widow, Nelly Begay. These included (1) his sister's present husband, Lester, in Camp 13, and his sister's daughter, Lucy, in Camp 14. The differences in the pattern of requests are related to differences in the shape of kin sets of adults in the two residence groups, and to the spatial proximity of these relatives. Nelly Begay had two nonresident sons and could make some of the same choices used by Camp 12. One son, however, lived ten miles away in *kindałizhini* (Camp 62), and the other was often at work on the railroad. Both had cars, which are not as efficient as a pickup for hauling water and are unsuitable for hauling wood.

Instead, the deceased husband's relatives were the most important to Camp 19, since Nelly was living near them and since there was a long history of disputes with her brother in Camp 28. Two married sisters, with whom there were also difficult relations, lived outside the Copper Canyon area. In turn, relatives of the husband were precisely the ones who were unavailable to Camp 12; here the husband of the older couple was born in another community and had few relatives in Copper Canyon. Relatives used by members of one camp may be exactly the ones which are unavailable—because they are nonexistent or too far away—to another camp.

Moving

Another activity that requires transportation and has an impact on the entire household is the moving of household goods between winter and summer residences. Again, the adults of the household (a couple, a widowed or divorced Navajo, or a bachelor) make the arrangements using either a pickup owned by a household member or asking for transportation from members of the same residence group or members of a kin set outside the residence group.

A Copper Canyon household moves its belongings twice a year, in May or early June, to a summer residence site on the Mountain or the Top, and in September or October back down to the winter residence site on the Flats or the Gray Area. Forty-five of 145 households did not move. Almost all of these contained adults who did not own livestock, which would need the grass available in the higher and wetter altitudes. A few had summer houses but had not moved in recent years because they did not own sheep. Other households were located in Black Mesa, a dry farming area where they remained during the summer to take care of their fields. The rest were younger couples who did not have summer houses on the Mountain, and who may also have had wage jobs at the trading post or in Gallup.

A pickup is the most efficient vehicle for moving, though a wagon also can be used. A car is adequate for transporting smaller items but cannot be used for hauling large pieces of furniture. Most families move beds, a table, a wood stove, cupboard, suitcases filled with clothes, dishes, bedding, and weaving materials.[5] The sheep are herded up to the summer area or back down to the winter area on the day that household goods are moved.

The married couple, widow, or bachelor in a household is responsible for moving the household's belongings, but it is often with aid from members of other households in a residence group or relatives outside the residence group. The indepen-

TABLE 7.2
Distribution of Transportation for Households
That Move Between Summer and Winter Homes

Category	Camps		Households	
	Type	No.	With Transportation	Without Transportation
A	Nuclear	10	10	—
B	Nuclear	16	—	16
C	Extended	23	59	—
D	Extended	6	—	15

dence of the household in moving is shown by the fact that in some residence groups one or two of the households will move and another will decide to remain at the winter residence site. Five extended family residence groups were separated in this manner during the summer months.

The same four situations are apparent as with transportation and hauling wood and water: (1) the nuclear camp with transportation; (2) the nuclear camp without transportation; (3) the extended residence group with transportation; and (4) the extended residence group without transportation. The distribution of these situations among one hundred households in fifty-five residence groups that move is shown in Table 7.2.

Again, each situation brought a characteristic solution. First, category A, couples in the ten nuclear camps with transportation moved their own household goods; seven used a pickup or car and three used a wagon. Those with pickups also helped Navajos in other residence groups to move.

Second, category B, the sixteen nuclear camps without transportation depended on those in other residence groups. In six cases this was a genealogical relative (or spouse of a genealogical relative) of the husband, wife, or isolated adult of the camp.[6] In four cases a clan relative or distant relative provided the transportation. (For six cases, the transportation is unknown.)

The third category, C, was the most commonplace: the extended camp with some transportation (fifty-nine households in twenty-three camps). The couple in a household where there is a pickup helped others in the residence group. In a few instances this within-camp transportation was supplemented by a close relative of the husband or wife who moved one of the households. The pattern may vary depending on the number of households in the residence group and the number of pickups available. As in hauling wood or water, if there is only an older parent or couple plus the household of a married son or daughter, the younger couple (who owns the pickup) will move themselves and the parent(s), making two trips in the same day. For larger camps the situation is more complex; an additional pickup from outside the camp may be used and moving takes place over several days.

In category D, there were six extended family residence groups (fifteen households in six camps) with no transportation. Three depended on genealogical relatives for transportation in moving. These were the sister of the younger wife in Camp 32; the parental wife's brother in Camp 47; and the sister's daughter of two brothers living in Camp 15. One residence group, Camp 12, depended on a clan relative and the other two on various nonrelatives. It should be emphasized that the situation is least stable for nuclear and extended camps without transportation, since the person who provides the transportation one time may not be available on the next occasion. There is always an element of chance in the arrangements that are finally made. One couple in Camp 32 had been prepared to pack their things in small bundles and hitchhike to their summer residence until the wife's sister stopped in her pickup. The wife quickly took advantage of the situation and asked her sister to move their belongings. The particular arrangements that are part of a move are illustrated by the following case.

CASE M.   AN EXTENDED FAMILY MOVES TO WINTER RESIDENCES

A snow in early October 1966 precipitated the move of residence group 28 to their winter home in the Gray Area. During a cold heavy rain on Saturday, one daughter, Joan, and her husband moved their belongings in their own pickup. They returned the next day and remained that night, since it was beginning to snow and the roads had become too muddy to return to lower elevations. On Monday morning, after the snowfall, Joan and her husband helped the mother, father, unmarried sister, and brother load their furniture and belongings into the back of the pickup. The males lifted most of the heavy things while the mother and younger daughter packed clothes and dishes into boxes and suitcases. The unmarried son drove the sheep down the road to the winter residence.

I was staying with another daughter, Sarah, and her children. The two of us were able to pack most of the clothes and dishes in boxes and put them in my car. Just after the parents, Joan, and her husband had left, a nonresident married brother from Camp 34 arrived in his pickup. He was hauling wood for another Navajo but had come to see if his mother needed help in moving. He had been to the camp the previous day, but had found his mother and sisters gone, so had not been able to help them move. Instead, he had moved his wife and mother-in-law to their winter home also in the Gray Area. He later agreed (at his mother's request) to take Sarah's furniture to her winter cabin as it could not be transported in my car.

A third married daughter and her husband, who also lived in the camp, had yet to pack their things and move. They owned a car but needed help with the bulky furniture. Joan and her husband returned later that day to move these possessions. The brother was unable to get Sarah's furniture until two days later. At that time he took Sarah and the mother back up to the summer camp and all three helped load the beds, stove, and table into the pickup. They also swept out the mother's and Sarah's house, burned some of the trash, and finished cleaning up the area. The moving of this camp, which included four households, took place over five days. One daughter and husband moved the mother and father and helped move another daughter and her husband, all utilizing the same pickup and making three separate trips. The remaining daughter was moved with my help and that of a nonresident brother who owned a pickup.

This case shows how the communication and authority patterns within an extended family camp and the use of an ego-centered set of kin came together in a concrete instance. Within this uxorilocal extended camp, with transportation, there was mutual aid between households, although members of each household were primarily responsible for packing their own things. As with activities like sheepherding or shearing, the parents, and especially the mother, served as a clearinghouse for coordinating the movements of households, using both Joan's pickup truck and that of the nonresident brother. The mother, in asking the brother to transport Sarah's furniture, from one point of view was using the closest tie within her set of genealogical kin. From another point of view, in her position as center of communication and as someone who was *t'áá bee bóholníih* for activities concerning the whole camp, it was appropriate for her, rather than Sarah, to make the request; that is, she was the proper person to activate a kin tie in this situation. Such mother-centered coordination of moving is, of course, not the only pattern at Copper Canyon. Members of different residence groups with different compositions and with different transportation resources, although following the same principles of authority and communication and also recruiting from ego-centered sets will, nevertheless, solve the problem of moving household goods in different ways.

That Copper Canyon Navajos use a "proximity strategy" in obtaining transportation is a constant finding in my analysis of requests for rides, for help in hauling wood and water, and for assistance in moving. Both kinship distance and spatial distance are important in understanding how this strategy is used. A Navajo without a car or pickup begins his search by investigating the possibilities for transportation among his nearest kin, that is, primary and secondary relatives living in his residence group. When these are eliminated, he is likely to ask a primary or secondary relative outside his residence group. The further away these relatives live, the more likely the requester is to ask a clan relative, or even a remote genealogical kinsman who lives in the same neighborhood. In other words, the ego-centered nature of transportation requests illustrates both the importance of ties within the residence group and the usefulness of the concept of set for analyzing the way ties to kinsmen outside the residence group are used. Ties to clansmen (and usually only to clansmen who are also neighbors) form, in my view, a reserve pool of individuals who can be called upon for aid when "nearer" possibilities are not available.

The increased use of motorized transport is one of the significant changes in Navajo life since 1940. Cars and pickup trucks are in constant use on eastern parts of the reservation and are also increasingly common in the more isolated areas. It is impossible to state whether or not patterns described in this chapter are typical in other communities, since I am not aware of any study that deals with requests for transportation. I would hypothesize that Navajos in other communities, as well as in Copper Canyon, get rides, haul wood and water, and move belongings using the same sort of "proximity strategy" I have outlined. A model incorporating the notion of ego-centered sets of kin has been useful in isolating this strategy of recruiting help in a new set of circumstances. In the next chapter I will show how the same model can be used to analyze cooperative patterns in more traditional contexts involving Navajo curing ceremonies and puberty rites. Other ceremonial settings—the peyote meeting, a mid-twentieth century innovation, and the funeral, which has changed much since World War II—will be analyzed in a similar manner.

Chapter 8

Ceremonials and Funerals

≈≈

As I have shown, agricultural and pastoral activities at Copper Canyon are handled by the residence group. Cooperation is organized along the lines of communication and authority that exist in each camp. In the nuclear family camp, there is joint consultation between a husband and wife regarding the handling of a herd or field. In an extended family camp, the older couple, or widow, makes requests directly to a coresident son or daughter and indirectly to an in-married affine through the connecting child. Transportation-related activities, as demonstrated in the previous chapter, are handled within the residence group, but since some camps are without pickup trucks or cars, arrangements are best viewed in terms of the recruitment of aid from an ego-centered set of primary and secondary kin who live outside the residence group. When these relatives are unavailable, a neighbor with whom ego has a clan tie is the most likely choice.

In this chapter, I will discuss cooperation concerning ceremonies and funerals. On these occasions, aid from a large number of Navajos is needed, usually over a period of several days, making participation of only residence group members insufficient. Consequently, the model of an ego-centered set of kin plays a more significant role in the analysis of recruitment for these activities than for those already discussed. Clan and neighborhood ties are also activated, especially for large ceremonies and funerals.

Requesting Aid for Ceremonies and Funerals

During my stay in Copper Canyon I collected data on twenty-nine ceremonial occasions. I observed who participated, and who did not, and in some cases was able to witness the entire process of making requests, mobilizing kin, and organizing (very indirectly) the progress of cooperation. Use of the English term "ceremonial" to describe these occasions is only an ad hoc category to describe situations in which Navajos, in addition to those living in a residence group, were called upon to provide goods and services. Specifically these situations included: (1) eight five-night sings, or *hatáál*; (2) six peyote meetings; (3) four girls' puberty ceremonies, or *kinaaldá*; (4) one Fire Dance (the nine-night version of Mountain Top Way); (5) two Squaw Dances (Enemyway); and (6) eight funerals.

All except the funerals involved a ritual and a ritual specialist (either a "singer," or *hataałii*, or a Peyote Road Chief). Even some funerals entailed rituals and ritual specialists. Other funerals, however, involved only the preparation of the deceased for burial and observance of the customary two- or four-day mourning period.

All of the occasions chosen for analysis have one important aspect in common: the preparation and eating of customary Navajo food (mutton stew, fried bread or flour tortillas, and coffee). These may be supplemented with delicacies such as braised ribs, liver, and intestines from freshly butchered sheep, and yeast bread baked in an earth oven. The major part of cooperation is focused on cooking and attendant activities such as hauling wood and water, butchering, and washing dishes. A major portion of the ingredients—flour, coffee, sugar, lard, potatoes, and sheep to be butchered—are donated by the cooperators. For traditional sings, cooperators also may aid in the ritual by collecting herbs for medicine to be administered to the patient, helping with the sandpaintings, and assisting in a ritual bath. Jewelry or clothing may be loaned for the patient to wear, and cloth or money may be given to help pay the singer.

Women prepare and cook the food while men usually haul the wood and water. Both share in the butchering, wood chopping, and ritual tasks. Men may also be called upon to build a ceremonial hoghan or a cooking shelter for a sing, or to dig the grave for a funeral.

Specific activities differentiate some ceremonial occasions from others. During a girl's puberty ceremony (*kinaaldá*), a large corn cake (*'ałkaan*) is baked in the ground, and the grinding, mixing, and pouring of the batter occupy most of the female helpers, especially on the last day of the ceremony. For a funeral, new clothes as well as a traditional blanket may be bought for the deceased; jewelry is often retrieved from pawnshops, and missionaries are often contacted to perform a burial service.

Each of the twenty-nine occasions studied focuses around one or two primary organizers. This individual or pair are *t'áá bee bóholnííh*; they make requests for aid from their kin, and they see that tasks are accomplished; they coordinate communications about what is to happen and who is providing which goods and services. As indicated in Chapter 2, this coordination and direction is extremely nondirective. Some direct requests are made, but more often the person who is *t'áá bee bóholnííh* makes his or her plans known and awaits general agreement and offers of aid from kinsmen who hear of the plans.

If the patient in the sing or peyote ceremony, or the deceased individual, is a child, it is the parents (both the mother and the father) who are *t'áá bee bóholnííh*. The same is true for the *kinaaldá*, in which a pubescent girl is the patient. There are two relevant sets of potential cooperators: kin and spouses of the mother and of the father.

If the patient is a married adult, he or she is the prime organizer, and his or her kin are potential cooperators. However, many decisions are made in cooperation with the spouse, and even the decision to have a ceremony is dependent on the consent and tacit support of this person. This gives direct access to a second set of potential cooperators: the relatives of the husband or wife.

When the patient is an older person with married children, or in the event of the death of an older man or woman, it is the children who are *t'áá bee bóholnííh*. Potentially, this may involve more than two individuals, but actually one or two of the children who live at the residence group where the ceremony is to be held make most of the arrangements. In the event of a death, the surviving widow may be *t'áá bee bóholnííh*. This means her kinsmen are potential cooperators, including the married children; the kin of the deceased (i.e., his siblings and their children) are a possible second set.

In sum, at almost all twenty-nine occasions there were two sets of potential cooperators, though the composition of these sets shifted with the age of the patient or deceased individual. At larger ceremonies (the Squaw Dances, notably), more sets of potential cooperators were made available by incorporating more patients into the ceremony. There are, of course, nonkin who often help, and at any ceremony one is likely to find neighbors, clan relatives, and relatives of the singer or Peyote Road Man who are attending and aiding in preparations.

Given two persons who are *t'áá bee bóholnííh* and the two sets of potential cooperators, goods and services are mobilized in much the same way that other requests are made (see Chapter 2). In the case of sings or a peyote meeting, the principal decision maker(s) decides to hold a sing or peyote meeting. (For a sing, this is often after consultation with a handtrembler or other diviner, to find out the supernatural cause of the illness and the appropriate sing which will cure it.) A *kinaaldá* follows the onset of the girl's first menses, and both the father and mother discuss and plan the ceremony, although much of the requesting and organizing is particularly the concern of women. Decision making concerning a funeral immediately follows the death of an individual and falls to the parents, spouse, or child of the deceased.

The prime organizers tell relatives and neighbors of plans for the sing, *kinaaldá*, or funeral. Patterns of communication follow lines of authority within the residence group. Parents, siblings, and children—primary kin—are notified directly; they, in turn, tell their spouses and children. The word is also spread at public places, such as at the trading post, laundromat, chapter house, and on the streets of Gallup when Navajos meet casually. As noted earlier, this "spreading the word" in a generalized way is a request for aid. Particularly for a large ceremony like a Squaw Dance, the news is circulated several weeks in advance that "X is planning to have a ceremony"; in letting everyone know of the plans, the patient or parents are asking for help. Kinsmen hear about the ceremony and may make a special trip to the hoghan of the patient to offer help. Also the patient and spouse, or the parents, will make special trips to relatives who do not live in the same residence group in order to tell them of ceremonial plans.

A consultation as to where to hold the sing or peyote meeting is a direct and crucial request. It usually entails a visit by the patient, spouse, or parents to the residence group where the sing might be held. Plans are outlined, and the request is made indirectly by stating that a hoghan is needed. Possibly the hoghan will be offered without mention by the prime decision maker of his or her need, but as a response to generalized talk about the plans. Lending a hoghan in a residence group to a nonresident daughter and son-in-law (as in three of the twenty-nine cases), or to a classificatory mother's sister (as in one case), commits the whole residence group to participation. It might be possible in an extended camp for one or two of the younger couples to ignore the ceremony and not commit their time and labor to preparations, but their aloofness would undoubtedly be commented upon as a show of uncooperativeness. A possible exception would be a young son or son-in-law who is away on wage work. Those who take over the sheepherding during the ceremony are considered to be helping in an indirect way, even though they are absent from much of the preparatory activity.

Agreeing to have a ceremony at the residence group also allows members access to attend it. In Copper Canyon, many of the peyote meetings are held at the residence group of the officiating Road Man. Sometimes a member of the Road Man's own residence group is the patient, but in the case of a patient from another residence group, holding the ceremony at his or her place encourages the attendance of coresident relatives (though they are not obligated to help in the preparation of the food for the morning meal). Relatives of an officiating singer (especially the wife and adult children) often attend part or all of the sing. They may even travel a great distance to attend; even though they may be strangers, they are treated as welcome guests, given food, and included in casual conversation.

The process of mobilizing aid and the indirectness of requests can best be illustrated by a concrete example.

CASE N. OFFERING AID FOR A CEREMONY

Desba, a Mountain-recess People woman about seventy years old, went to visit her clan brother (with whom she was brought up), and learned that Sam and his wife, Lois, were going to have a second puberty ceremony for their daughter. Sam was the son of a clan sister of Desba; this woman was not a genealogical relative but lived in the same neighborhood. The two women were quite close and helped each other on ceremonial occasions. Desba and her daughter, Edna, asked me to drive them to visit Sam, a Navajo policeman who lived in a modern house in a community ten miles north of Copper Canyon. The visit was made about a week after the original news was heard. By that time, Desba and Edna had learned that Sam's daughter had been stricken with a skin disease and a five-day sing was to be given instead of a *kinaaldá*. Desba and Edna consulted with Lois, and Sam joined in the conversation when he arrived home. Desba acted as spokeswoman and offered the use of her old hoghan, but Lois explained she wanted to have the sing at her mother's place because the girl's aunts and uncles (mother's sister and mother's brother) and grandmother (mother's mother) would be there. Desba agreed by stating, "It's ok with me" (*t'áá 'akót'é*), and offered to help out with some groceries and cloth for the singer. Sam and Lois said the sing would start in three days. That day, they planned to go to Gallup to get supplies; then, in two days, they planned to drive to Sam's mother's place and tell her and Sam's stepfather of the sing.

Arrangements had probably been made already with Lois' mother and siblings, both to use an empty hoghan at that camp and to get their cooperation in preparations. A singer had not yet been contacted. The beginning of a ceremony, of course, depends on when the singer can come, and he is contacted after most of the other arrangements are made. Often he arrives on the next day, but in this case he was unable to come until five days after Desba's and Edna's visit.

This example illustrates the diffuse nature of organizing ceremonial cooperation, due in part to the scattered settlement pattern that impairs rapid communication. The start of the ceremony may be postponed several days beyond the original date. A visit to tell of plans for a ceremony may be delayed because of transportation difficulties, or because the relatives are not at home when the requester arrives. This case shows the way in which word is passed indirectly and how relatives are contacted directly by visits. Both the husband's and wife's relatives were part of the requesting process and the couple worked as a team in much of the arranging (such as shopping, visiting, discussing plans). The wife's wishes about the location prevailed in this instance; she made the original request of her mother and siblings, though her husband may have accompanied her on the trip.

In view of this sketchy outline of how news of a coming ceremony is spread, and how both direct and indirect requests are made, which relatives actually attend and participate? A closer examination of the case material collected for each type of ceremony and for funerals will aid in elucidating some of the factors that influence the recruitment of kin from ego-centered sets and the participation of clan relatives and neighbors.

Five-Day Ceremonies

Of the thirty-eight Navajo song ceremonies (*hatáál*), many have two-, five-, and nine-night versions (Wyman and Kluckhohn 1938). The two-night versions can easily be handled by members of the residence group. Although visitors from outside the camp may come for the all-night singing the last night, the shortness of the sing means that a limited number of relatives will be involved.

Five-night versions, in contrast, require more preparation of food since they are longer. Attendance may be limited to members of the residence group or may include as many as fifty people who come during the course of the sing. Visitors are likely to arrive to take part in sub-ceremonies held each morning or evening. Copper Canyon people are enthusiastic gamblers and often pass the time between sub-ceremonies (e.g., in the late afternoon) playing cards. Shoe's Game (*késhjéé'*) is played in the evenings during the Ghostway ritual (*hóch'ǫǫjí*) and often involves a hoghan crowded with forty or fifty Navajos. Activity culminates on *hatáál bijį* ("the sing, its day," referring to the day before the last night of singing). On this last day, visitors and relatives may come for a sandpainting ceremony or an "unraveling"* and to bring food contributions. There is constant preparation of bread and mutton stew to feed those who visit and stay during the all-night singing.

Data were obtained from eight five-day sings, which were held during my stay in Copper Canyon (Table 8.1). In six cases I visited the residence group where the sing was held on *bijį*, obtaining information about the most important contributors. Since relatives come and go during a ceremony, those I have listed as not participating may have been present at other times when I was not observing.

Six cooperative activities are characteristic of five-day sings: (1) construction of a hoghan for the ceremony (this occurred only in Cases 2, 5, 7, 8); (2) hauling wood and water; (3) contributing mutton or groceries (usually flour, coffee, sugar, potatoes, and lard); (4) helping to butcher a sheep or goat; (5) preparing food; and (6) helping with the ritual (e.g., construction of a sandpainting or gathering materials to be used by the singer).

---

*"Unraveling" refers to pulling apart a bundle of ritually potent herbs or feathers wrapped with a reed, symbolically representing "pulling out" the disease-causing elements from the patient's body.

Those who take part in these activities include members of the patient's residence group as well as individuals drawn from one or two ego-centered sets. As pointed out in the previous section, composition of relevant sets shifts with the age of the patient. As Table 8.1 shows, if the patient is a child (Cases 1, 5, 7), the relatives of the father and the mother are the most important.[1] For the middle-aged male or female (Cases 2, 3, 8), the patient's own relatives and those of the spouse are most relevant. For the older man or woman (Cases 4, 6), the children and grandchildren are most important, with other members of their own and their spouse's set playing a secondary role.

As mentioned earlier, the decision to locate a sing in a residence group other than the patient's is important. In two instances (Cases 1 & 5), the same nuclear family, Sam and Lois, chose to give both sings at the camp of the wife's mother (the winter camp in Case 1 and the summer camp in Case 5). Because Sam was a Navajo policeman, the family lived in a modern house ten miles from Copper Canyon, in a neighboring community. Such a home is inappropriate for a traditional Navajo ceremony. The same applies to the couple in Case 2 who lived in a modern house in a community fifty miles north of Copper Canyon. They maintained a log cabin at Camp 18, and temporarily moved there for the duration of the ceremony. In these cases, granting permission to hold a sing implies that all residence group members will help and determines whose set of kin will be most directly involved. If the patient, or patient's parents, had selected a site in another residence group (e.g., with the father's or husband's relatives) different kinsmen would have performed the major cooperative chores.

The difference in cooperators due to changes in location of a sing is illustrated by Case 4 when compared with a two-night Little Enemyway (*ńda ýazhí*) held for the same patient, the oldest woman in the community. In Case 4, a Ghostway ritual (*hóch'ǫ́ǫ́jí*) was held at the winter home of the patient's daughter, Camp 35. As shown in Figure 8.1, important helpers were the daughters and married children in that camp and Camp 34. A son and wife from the patient's winter camp (Camp 15) aided, but a second son from Camp 15, a daughter's daughter from Camp 54, and a daughter's daughter from Camp 53 did not attend. Camps 54 and 53 were adjacent to Camp 15, the patient's residence group. In contrast, at the Little Enemyway held at Camp 15, the core work group consisted of the members of the camp (the two adult sons and the wife of one son) and of Camp 53 (a daughter's daughter and children). The daughter from Camp 35 also helped, but her married children were not present. In both cases the major helpers were drawn from the patient's set of primary and secondary kin (i.e., her children and grandchildren), but the composition of work groups in each ceremony shifted to include more of those in the residence group where the sing was held and less of those in more distant residence groups.

For those sings held at the residence group of the patient, the composition and location in relation to camps of other relatives is important. In the case of a female patient living virilocally (Case 8), those participating will be the husband's relatives who live in nearby camps. If she is living uxorilocally, her own relatives—for example, siblings, and sibling's children who live in the same neighborhood—will help.

When the patient is older (and has established a camp independent of his or her or the spouse's siblings), the neighborhood context is even more important. If a man has initially lived uxorilocally and then becomes an independent head of a residence

TABLE 8.1
Participation in Five-Day Sings

Case	Patient	Location of Sing	Residence Group Participants	Ego-Centered Sets		
				Participants	Not Present	Others
1	Navajo Wind Way for adolescent girl	Patient's mother's camp (uxorilocal extended)	Mother, father; MM & husband; MZ & daughter.	*Mother's Set* MZ & daughter; 2 Bs and wives. *Father's Set* Distant clan relatives (MMZD and MMZDD)	*Mother's Set* MZ & children; FB; MBD. *Father's Set* Mother & stepfather; MZ.	Singer & 2 adult sons; male relative of singer; husband of woman in father's set & his father.
2	Ghostway for adult male	Wife's camp (mixed extended)	Wife's mother; wife's sisters, brothers, & spouses.	*Wife's Set* All in residence group; brother & wife. *Husband's Set* None	—	6 neighbors not related by clan; 1 neighbor in clan related to wife's clan; 2 in clan of wife's father's clan; 1 whose father is in clan of wife's father; 2 non-kin, no neighbors.
3	Ghostway for adult male	Own camp (mixed extended)	Wife; married step-son; married daughter & husband.	*Patient's Set* Stepmother; MMZD & husband; clan brother MMMZDD(?). *Wife's Set* MZS	*Patient's Set* B; B; Z; ½Z. *Wife's Set* S of wife; MZD.	1 clan Z of wife; 2 non-relatives; widow of BS of wife & her 2 sons; 1 neighbor. (many clan relatives not present)
4	Ghostway for old woman	Daughter's camp (uxorilocal extended)	Daughter & husband; DD; DD & husband. (Unmarried son not present)	*Patient's Set* Son & wife; S (12 miles away); DS.	*Patient's Set* Son; DS; DD; DD; D (Gallup); D.	Mother-in-law of DS; 1 clan relative of D's husband; 1 clan Z of daughter; 1 nonrelative

5 Ghostway for adolescent girl (same patient as in Case 1)	Patient's MM's camp (summer) (uxorilocal extended)	Mother & father; MM & husband; MZ & child.	*Mother's Set* MZ; MZ; B. *Father's Set* Mother; clan relatives: MMZD, MMZDD, husband & children.	*Mother's Set* B (10 miles away); MB. *Father's Set* Stepfather; MZ.	*Brief visit* 3 "born for" clan of wife; MBD of wife; wife of clan relative of patient's mother; 4 nonrelatives. neighbor (Shoe's Game: several non-relatives & distant clan relatives)
6 Ghostway for older man	Own camp (summer) (uxorilocal extended)	Patient's wife; widowed daughter & son.	*Patient's Set* Sister; MBD. *Wife's Set* D	*Patient's Set* Sister & ZDS; ZD; brother. *Wife's Set* DD, DD, DS (living on other parts of reservation)	2 relatives in clan related to patient's clan; nonrelative; singer & wife.
7 Five-day sing for young boy	Mother's camp (sororilocal extended)	Mother & father; MZ & children (husband away); 3 unmarried adult siblings; married Z.	(Kept sing entirely within residence group; may have gotten some help from patient's mother's sister, who lives in another community.)	(Distant genealogical and clan relatives did not participate.)	—
8 Five-day sing for middle-aged woman	Own camp (mixed extended)	Husband & children; husband's sister and her husband; husband's mother & sister & her husband.	*Wife's Set* (?)	*Wife's Set* Sister; brother; brother; 3 siblings off-reservation	Some clan relatives present

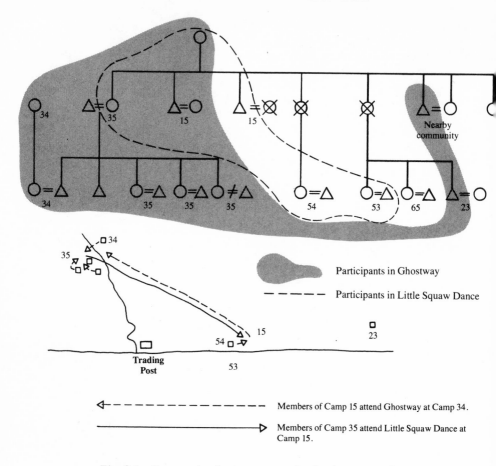

Fig. 8.1   Cooperation for two ceremonies for the same patient

group, it is likely that the wife's relatives (e.g., married siblings) are still in the same area and have nearby camps. His kin, on the other hand, may be located in another section of the community or even in another part of the reservation. Though the main helpers at the sing are his wife and married children (especially those who have remained in his residence group), secondary helpers and visitors include the wife's siblings who live nearby.

Case 3 is a good example. The patient had parents, several siblings, and many clan relatives in the Copper Canyon area. He was the head of an extended family residence group composed of his wife, a married daughter, and a married stepson. He lived nearer to his wife's relatives than to his own. Though his mother and some clan relatives came to the sing, just as many of the visitors were related through the wife or were from neighboring camps.

There is always a chance that Navajos from a neighboring camp will provide help, even if they are not related. The neighborhood effect seems strongest in Case 2 where the patient's wife's set of kin was small and consisted mainly of her own residence group and Camp 18, where her parents lived. Her mother came from another community, and her father only had clan relatives in Copper Canyon. The parent's residence group was in an area, however, where several camps (in turn related to each other) also cooperated with the patient's parents. Members of these residence groups were visitors and participants in the sing.

Case 7 also exemplifies a small set of kin, largely consisting of those in Camp 43 where the sing was held. This residence group chose not to publicize the sing and limited participation to the residence group. When I was told about the sing, the *bádí* (mother's sister's daughter) of the boy who was the patient cautioned me not to tell anyone, as they did not want visitors. This was an atypical attitude and can be traced to fear of witchcraft.[2]

In sum, the age of the patient is related to the composition of the residence group that will supply most of the help during the five-day sing. The decision to hold the sing in a particular residence group will bring participation of those relatives rather than others. The location of the patient's own residence group within a neighborhood of either own or spouse's kin may determine visitors and contributors. The actual size and shape of relevant sets of kin (i.e., those of the patient, spouse, or patient's parents) will often determine not only who comes but whether neighbors are important.

Even so, contributors to two sings given at different times for the same patient may be different. Cases 1 and 5 are good examples. In Case 1, the sing was held for the daughter in Camp 50 at the winter home of her mother's mother (Camp 75). In Case 5, the sing was held for the same daughter at the summer camp of her mother's mother (Camp 75). At the winter ceremony, the main helpers were members of Camp 54 and nonresident mother's brothers and spouses. In the summer, the patient's father's relatives in Camp 20 provided more help and had primary roles; the patient's mother's brother and spouse were not present, but another brother, who had left his wife at home, had a more peripheral role.

In sum, the couple most concerned with giving the ceremony have a wide range of relatives to call upon in addition to those living in their own residence group or the residence group where the sing is to be held. On one occasion they may obtain more aid from some relatives than from others. The latter may be important on another occasion. Despite this variability there are general principles of recruitment, which will be considered in the final section of this chapter when data from all twenty-nine ceremonies are analyzed.

Peyote Meetings

Peyote meetings, like five-day sings, are held in residence groups; however, they last only one night (beginning about 9 P.M. and concluding at dawn the next morning). The actual ceremony is followed by a customary Navajo meal of fried bread, stew, and coffee, often embellished with pop, candy, fruit, and jello.

Since the Native American Church is a membership organization, attendance at meetings consists of those who consider themselves members of the movement. Membership is based on attendance at meetings and acceptance of beliefs rather than any initiation or formal enrollment, and is, thus, very flexible. Relatives of peyotists may accompany them to a few meetings, though they may come only a few times before losing interest. On one hand, a limited number of Copper Canyon residents were regular peyotists and potential participants in the meetings; on the other hand, peyotists from other parts of the reservation were welcome. The first factor limited those likely to come from Copper Canyon; the second added diversity in attendance, which is not characteristic of five-day sings.

During the winter there were three concentrations of peyote cult participants. One was in the Gray Area (Camps 28, 36, and 38); one was near Blue Mesa and included Camps 13, 14, 17, 18, 19, 20, 42, 57, and 76. A third group was at Black House Mesa (Camps 64, 61, and 66). Each of these groups contained an interrelated set of kinsmen. Three Road Men, or Road Chiefs, who lived in the Copper Canyon area, conducted peyote ceremonies.[3] They led many of the meetings held in the community but also rendered service to those in other communities. Likewise, Copper Canyon peyotists sometimes obtained a Road Man from outside the community, often from the neighboring community to the south, though also from locations as distant as fifty miles. In general, the three Road Men did not attend meetings conducted by each other or other Road Men. The same was true for their wives and sometimes for other members of their residence group. Copper Canyon

TABLE 8.2
Peyote Meetings

Case	Patient	Location of Meeting	Food Preparation	Attendance
9	Middle-aged male	Residence group of Road Man (brother-in-law)	Residence group where held (i.e., patient's wife's mother & sister)	Primary & secondary kin of wife (wife's kin set); clan relatives; two nonrelatives
10	Adolescent child	Residence group of Road Man	Patient's M, F, and MM (i.e., patient's residence group)	Residence group; mother's primary relatives (her kin set); Road Man's residence group; peyotists from other communities
11	Two adolescents	Residence group of Road Man	Patient's M & Z (i.e., patient's residence group)	Residence group; kin set of the two patients' mothers; Road Man's residence group; other clan relatives
12	Older male	Residence group of wife's ZD	Residence group where held (wife's ZD & ZDD)	Residence group where held; genealogical relatives of wife's ZD & ZDD; Road Man & wife
13	Baby of young married woman	Residence group of patient's mother	Patient's residence group	Residence group; Road Man & wife, & other members of Road Man's residence group. (No detailed data on attendance)
14	Unmarried son	Residence group of Road Man's mother	Patient's residence group	Residence group of patient; Road Man & wife, & mother & siblings of Road Man. (No detailed data on attendance)

residents who did not have a Road Man living in their residence group attended meetings over a period of time conducted by a variety of Road Men; they would call on one of several men when holding a meeting at their own residence group.

Preparing the food for the morning meal is the most important cooperative activity outside of participation in the peyote ritual itself. This is always handled by members of the patient's residence group or members of the residence group where the ceremony is held. The latter was true for Cases 9 and 12, where the patient was residing in a nuclear family residence group. In both cases it was decided to hold the meeting at the residence group of a relative. In Case 9, it was the camp of the patient's wife's mother and married siblings; the camp also included a brother-in-law who acted as Road Man for the ceremony. In Case 12, it was the residence group of a daughter of the patient's wife's parallel cousin. This freed the wives of the two patients from doing the food preparation themselves and assured them of someone to take care of last-minute activities in the early morning, while they were still participating in the ceremony.

As Table 8.2 shows, most of the Copper Canyon residents who attended peyote meetings were relatives of the patient, kin of someone in the same residence group, or related to the Road Man or his spouse. It happens that in all cases for which I have data, help was recruited from only one kin set (rather than two)—that of the patient's mother or spouse. Most members of this set attend if they are peyotists and if they live nearby. For example, in Case 10, primary and secondary relatives of the patient's mother, Edna, attended and contributed some of the food. The father of the patient, Mike, attended and helped with the cooking; but most of his relatives were non-peyotists and would not be expected to participate. Likewise, in Case 9, only the relatives of the wife attended, since the relatives of the husband (who was the patient) were not peyotists.

If the peyote meeting is held at the residence group of the Road Man, more members of his residence group will probably attend than might accompany him to a distant meeting. In addition to members of the Road Man's residence group, possible participants are most likely to be peyotist families in the neighborhood of the meeting. They probably will be distantly related by clan to the patient, spouse, or parents of the patient, as well as residentially close.

Girls' Puberty Ceremonies

As described in Chapter 2, a *kinaaldá* is held at a girl's first menses. I observed portions of four puberty ceremonies during my stay in Copper Canyon. Three of these were held at the residence group of the girl's parents; two (Cases 15 and 17) were nuclear family camps. A third (Case 16) was an extended camp of two households: (1) a widow (Nelly Begay) and her unmarried children (including the *kinaaldá* girl), and (2) a married daughter with two children who was temporarily separated from her husband. The fourth ceremony (Case 18) was held at the residence group of the girl's father's parents (Mr. and Mrs. Sage). The family of the girl lived in Wyoming and was on vacation visiting the reservation when the ceremony was held.

The ceremony takes place over a four-day period, but the activity culminates on the final day and night when the corn cake (*'ałkaan*) is prepared and baked in the ground. Puberty ceremonies tend to be much larger than five-day sings, partly because of the work involved in making the corn cake batter. It is attended by many of the old women in the community. Since it expresses the values of womanhood and assures a good life for the adolescent girl, helping in the preparation is especially important to these older traditional females. This ceremony, more than any other Navajo ritual, is organized around women.

Important cooperative activities are:

1. Grinding the corn for the corn cake.*
2. Borrowing jewelry (turquoise beads, bracelets, pins) and clothing (a traditional velveteen blouse and three-tiered skirt) for the young girl to wear (usually done by the *kinaaldá*'s mother).
3. Digging the hole in which the cake is to be baked (a task done by males).
4. Hauling wood and water (usually done by males).
5. Mixing the corn cake batter and stirring it until smooth (done by females).
6. Pouring the batter into the hole and lining it with corn husks (Females participate, while males in the residence group carry the vats of batter to the hole, and help with the pouring).
7. Preparing food for visitors (done by females).
8. Cutting and distributing the cake in the morning.†

Since the residence groups are small—one or two households—many participants come from outside the residence group. The smallest number of participants were in Case 16, where work was handled by the residence group and siblings of the girl's father. The number of nonrelatives who were older women is especially prominent in Case 16. Though many older women were present in Case 18, they were distantly related to the *kinaaldá*'s father's father or father's mother. The former came from one of the largest clans in the community, and many older women who would have come to any puberty ceremony happened to be related to a member of the host residence group in this particular case.

Since the mother of the *kinaaldá* usually makes the requests for aid during the ceremony and sees that important tasks are accomplished, she is likely to call on her own and her husband's relatives who are the most available. The actual requests may be made by the woman or by an intermediary. For example, the husband or husband's parents make requests to their consanguineal kin. At Copper Canyon the cases exemplify four different patterns, depending on the situation of the wife and mother. (See Table 8.3.)

Since the central figure, or patient, for the *kinaaldá* is always an adolescent girl, the girl's parents are usually in the second phase of the residence group cycle and living independently of their natal camps. Rather than the composition of the residence group itself, the location of the camp in the same neighborhood as the husband's or wife's relatives influences which set of kin is most likely to be activated. This is shown in Table 8.3. If the couple is living near the husband's relatives, they will provide the most aid, as in Case 16. If they are living near some of the wife's primary and secondary kin, they will be the primary helpers, as in Case 17. In another case, the circumstances of a visit determined which set of kin were closest. The mother in Case 18 would have preferred to have returned to her own community in another part of the reservation for the ceremony. Then, she explained, her sisters and mother would have been able to help. Instead, her husband's parents wanted to have the ceremony; she consented, as it would have been

---

*At Copper Canyon the corn is taken to a commercial grinder in Farmington.
†It is cut by a male relative and distributed by the *kinaaldá* girl at the direction of her mother.

TABLE 8.3
Relation of Residence to Cooperation in Girls' Puberty Ceremonies

Case Number	Residential Situation of Wife (i.e., mother of *kinaaldá* girl)	Important Helpers
15	Nuclear family living near and in area of husband	Female siblings of husband; spouses of husband's male siblings (i.e., the husband's kin set)
16	Extended family living near a few relatives of her husband's and at a distance from her own relatives	Two married sons and spouses; mother-in-law of one married son; a few primary and secondary kin of the husband; many neighbors and nonrelatives.
17	Nuclear family living near kin of wife's deceased father. (Her husband's mother also lived in Copper Canyon.)	Siblings of the wife's father and other clan relatives (wife's kin set); husband's mother
18	Nuclear family visiting the husband's parents	Primary and secondary kin of the husband's parents: Paternal grandfather's sisters and sister's daughter (FF's set); paternal grandmother's mother and mother's sister (FM's set)

difficult to refuse without appearing uncooperative and mean. Her husband's mother made most of the arrangements, and the wife worked with strange and unrelated women, an awkward but not impossible situation. If they had returned to her community, the personnel and their kin relationship to the *kinaaldá* girl would have been quite different, though the tasks to be accomplished would remain the same.

The interest and participation of older women in the community who are nonrelatives illustrates—more than in any other ceremony—the influence of an ideology of generalized reciprocity. Their aid is not based on particular kin ties but on a generalized notion that cooperation is to be valued.

Fire Dance and Squaw Dance

Three large ceremonies were held at Copper Canyon, for which I have cooperative data. A Fire Dance (Mountain Top Way) (Case 19) was held September 17–26, 1965, for the fourteen-year-old daughter in Camp 41. A Squaw Dance (Case 20) was held June 16–18, 1966 for the husband in Camp 16. Another Squaw Dance (Case 21) was held August 19–21, 1966, for the same daughter in Camp 41.

The nine-night version of the Mountain Top Way is similar to a five-night version of the same sing, except that there are public performances of dancing on the last night after a bonfire is lighted in a large brush corral (*ił náásh jiin*) near the ceremonial hoghan (Haile 1946). The Copper Canyon Fire Dance was held at a ceremonial hoghan and cooking shelter constructed during a Tribal Works Project in August 1965 in the summer residence area near the chapter house. Data on cooperation are meager, since my knowledge of the community and its members was slight at the time.

The main cooperators came from households within the patient's residence group (her parents, sisters, brother, and spouse) and residence groups of the patient's mother's sisters (i.e., the mother's set of primary and secondary relatives). Other assistance came from clan relatives of the patient's mother and father. In general, the bulk of the work was done by the residence group and genealogical kin of the parents. More distant relatives contributed smaller amounts of food and aid. Some contributed just for the sake of helping and not because they had been asked or had a close kin tie. The last night when dancing was held, the area near the ceremonial hoghan was crowded with pickup trucks. These were filled with spectators from Copper Canyon and neighboring communities who had come to sit inside the brush corral and watch the dancing. Some of the men participated in the all-night singing. Several hundred Navajos often gather at such large ceremonies; most of them are not relatives and have not contributed to the ceremony; rather they are spectators who have come for the more public aspects of the occasion.

Patterns of cooperation are more clearly seen by examining the two Squaw Dances. The Enemyway is a three-day ceremony that usually takes place in the summer for the purpose of curing illness caused by a ghost, an alien, or an enemy. The ceremony requires the participation of two groups: the patient and his relatives and the Stick Receiver and his relatives. (See Jacobson 1964 for details of the ceremony and exchanges made between both sides.) My data describe cooperation among relatives of the patient. The Squaw Dance (Case 20) for the husband in Camp 16 (Dan Grant) was held at his mother's and sister's summer camp. It was near his own camp but provided more room for the building of ceremonial and cooking shelters. The Squaw Dance (Case 21) for the daughter in Camp 41 was held at the site of the Fire Dance.

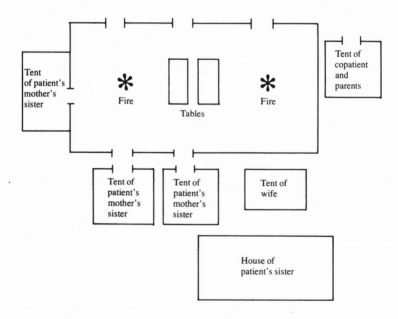

Fig. 8.2 *Arrangement of facilities at Squaw Dance (Case 20) for middle-aged man patient and adolescent girl copatient*

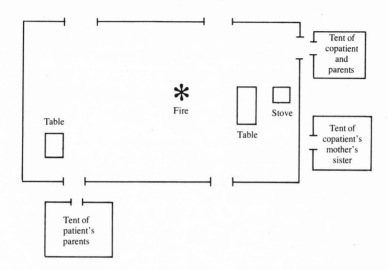

Fig. 8.3   *Arrangement of facilities at Squaw Dance (Case 21) for adolescent girl patient and adolescent girl copatient*

The organization of fires in the cooking shelter and the location of tents show which relatives are most important. In the Squaw Dance for Dan Grant (see Figure 8.2), the cooking shelter was divided between his relatives and his wife's relatives. (If a male is the patient, his wife must act as copatient; two separate cooking fires must be maintained.) Dan's mother, and two sisters of his mother, occupied tents near his cooking fire on the north end of the shelter. The wife's relatives had a tent adjacent to the south end of the shelter, as did the relatives of another co-patient (a girl from a neighboring community to the north).

One way of assuring a large amount of cooperation and a big ceremony is to include additional patients. In the Squaw Dance for Dan Grant there were two co-patients in addition to Dan and his wife.

In the Squaw Dance for the daughter in Camp 41, the copatient was Edna and Mike's daughter, Susie, in Camp 20. Kinsmen of the two patients shared the cooking shelter at the Fire Dance site. One tent on the north end was maintained by the patient's parents and older siblings. On the south end were tents of the co-patient's mother and mother's sister (see Figure 8.3). Most of the work was done by the patient's residence group and her mother's other genealogical relatives (as in the Fire Dance) and by the copatient's residence group and her mother's kin. The copatient's father's relatives also helped, but not as much. Contributions came from most of the residents in the area who were connected by clan to one parent of the patient or copatient. Clan affiliations of the four parents included the most important clans in the community; large amounts of money and food were donated. It is these contributions from more remote kinsmen that distinguish the large ceremony from the five-day sing. Still, the patient's residence group and the kin sets of the patient, the spouse, or parents of the patient, are the most important; other kin ties supplement and expand the goods and labor contributed by closer kin.

Navajo Funerals

Traditional burial rites for Navajos have been described by the Franciscan Fathers (1910) and Reichard (1928: 141–43). In the old pattern, a Navajo died in the hoghan or was removed to a shelter nearby just before death. Sometimes the individual was interred in the hoghan itself and the building allowed to collapse. In other cases, the body was carried to a grave in a rocky crevice or some other safe place nearby. The body was washed and dressed in new garments by two to four mourners. (They stripped off their clothes to the breech cloth and observed many taboos to protect them from the danger of dealing with the dead.) Jewelry or other valuables were buried with the person, and the deceased's horse or other favorite animal was killed. The mourners traveled to the north to bury the body and returned so as to make a circular route. The family observed mourning for four days and then ritually washed. Their activity was curtailed, as they did not work, talk unnecessarily, or say "bad things" to each other.

Many changes have taken place in Navajo burial practices. In the 1960s, most Navajos died in the hospital; the body was taken to a funeral home where it was embalmed and placed in a casket. Most families arranged for missionaries to bury the deceased.

Navajos still bury the individual in new clothes; jewelry is taken out of pawn and a new Pendleton blanket is purchased to be placed in the casket. Jewelry or clothing may be defaced so that it will not be stolen from the grave by werewolves (*yeenaaldloozhii*). John Begay (Case 29) was buried with a television set that had recently been given to him. It, too, was defaced and the glass broken in front of the picture tube. A horse or sheep is often killed, according to custom. The residence group of the deceased observes mourning for two to four days and washes at the end of the mourning period. Usually a sheep is butchered and food is provided for those who come to comfort the family; there is a feeling that relatives should come to the funeral or to visit the family. They should also bring food and help with the cooking.

Eight Navajos died in Copper Canyon during my stay. Funeral arrangements varied as shown in Table 8.4. The most traditional funeral was held for the oldest woman in the community, Cross Hills Lady (Case 27). She was buried near her hoghan after two of her daughters washed and dressed the body. The clothes were ripped and the jewelry defaced; other belongings were burned after the burial. The only modern touches were a casket, purchased by the Anglo husband of one of the daughters, and a short talk and prayer given by a missionary who arrived with a distant relative just as the grave was being filled.

The Mormon elders at Copper Canyon arranged four funerals (Cases 24, 26, 28, 29). Relatives had first contacted the trader, who was a Mormon, regarding a funeral, and he turned the arrangements over to the elders. These funerals ranged from a short graveside ceremony (Case 29) to a service in the Gallup Latter-day Saints church, complete with a speech by the trader, prayers by the elders, and singing by several other young missionaries (Case 26).

A Catholic ceremony was held for one woman (Case 22), and the residence group of the deceased handled the burial at public cemeteries in two cases (23 and 25).

Cooperative activities include the following: (1) arranging with a hospital or funeral home to get the body and/or purchase a casket; (2) arranging for new clothes, blanket, and obtaining jewelry from pawn; (3) digging the grave; (4) arranging for the ceremony with the trader and/or missionaries; (5) acquisition and preparation of food for the mourning period; and (6) attending the ceremony.

The first five activities are managed by members of the residence group of the deceased, although genealogical kin sometimes assist. The kin relationship and number of people involved varies from case to case. For instance, in Case 25—the funeral of a young thirty-two-year-old man—his wife made most of the arrangements. She hitchhiked to the hospital where her husband had died to see about his funeral and burial at the Gallup cemetery. Members of the residence group (including his mother, two half-sisters, one sister-in-law, and all their children) observed the mourning period, but there was minimum participation in any sort of funeral.

In contrast, for old Jim's funeral (Case 29), several Navajos outside the residence group helped with arrangements. A nonresident son, Lester, of Camp 13, asked several clan-related kinsmen for help. A clan sister, Amy, of Camp 17, and her married son and daughter, traveled to Gallup to get flowers for the funeral. One son in Camp 18 brought a suit of clothes from California in which to dress the deceased. Lester of Camp 13 and the wife of the deceased made a trip to Gallup to buy clothes and two blankets and to retrieve jewelry that had been pawned. Three nonrelations donated mutton (Camps 58, 23, and 13); it was cooked for a meal after the funeral by three nonrelated women, Edna and Desba, from Camp 20, and a woman from Camp 76.

Attendance at the funeral usually includes more than those who make the arrangements. In addition to the residence group, other genealogical relatives of the deceased, clan relatives, and nonrelatives may come.

The kin relationships of participants are different in each case, but they follow expectable shifts in the shape of the kin set of the deceased determined by his or her age at death. The main participants for the three younger Navajos (two males and one female) were primary relatives (i.e., parents and siblings) and the spouses. When primary relatives were not present it was because the relevant individual was deceased or lived off the reservation. In some cases, secondary kin of the deceased (e.g., parents' siblings) participated, but not all members of these categories. In general, the funerals for young Navajos were handled by the residence group, with some participation from nonresident siblings and parent's siblings.

The set of relevant primary and secondary kin of an older Navajo has a much different composition. Rather than from siblings, parents, and parents' siblings, the major help comes from the spouse, children, siblings, and siblings' children. Funerals for young Navajos are small affairs, while those for older Navajos bring together a large number of kin. This is especially true for respected members of the community, those who are cooperative, sociable Navajos with "no faults" (*bá'ate' 'adin*). (Examples are Cases 26 and 27). If funerals for older Navajos are small, it may indicate quarreling among the kin, as in Cases 28 and 29 (presented as Cases A and B in Chapter 2). In addition to disputes over cooperation in Case 29, and over inheritance in Case 28, both men were suspected of witchcraft. A funeral is a showing of social solidarity and an effort on the part of more distant relatives to help those of the deceased's household and residence group. Willingness to participate and help shows respect for the deceased. Quarrels and lack of cooperation, on the other hand, are the antithesis of Navajo ideals. They indicate that the ideology of generalized reciprocity is not always followed and that Navajo behavior exhibits aspects of conflict as well as solidarity.

TABLE 8.4
Participation in Funerals

Case	Deceased	Residence Group	Ego-Centered Kin Sets		Others Present
			Present	**Not Present**	
22	Widow; died Oct. 26, 1965; buried Oct. 27, in neighborhood community (anthropologist did not attend)	*All participated* Son and wife; DD and husband	*Deceased's Set:* Secondary Kin: BS and other relatives from neighboring community; DD from Albuquerque. *Husband's Set:* Primary Kin: His B, wife and daughter, also B's stepdaughters; possibly husband's two sisters.	No significant relatives missing	Others from community bordering on Copper Canyon
23	Young married male; died Nov. (?), 1965; buried Nov. 29, 1965	*All participated* Mother & father; Z and children; Z, husband & child; widow of ½B and child; wife and children	*Mother's Set:* Only those in residence group. *Father's Set:* Secondary Kin: Father's Z.	*Mother's Set:* Primary & Secondary Kin: ½Z of deceased; MZ of deceased. *Father's Set:* Secondary & other: FZ of deceased; FMZS of deceased. (None of wife's relatives helped; many of clan relatives did not help.)	2 clan relatives (1 own clan; 1 *ahíídilchíín* relationship, i.e., "born for" ego's father's clan)
24	Young mother; died Jan. 18, 1966; buried Jan. 20, 1966, in neighboring community	*All participated* Father and stepmother, 3 stepchildren; 2 small children of deceased	*Deceased's Set:* Primary & Secondary Kin: B and wife (from Los Angeles); FZ and husband (25 miles away)	*Deceased's Set:* Primary & Secondary Kin: Z and husband (Los Angeles); FZ (in neighboring community); FZ (in Copper Canyon); MB (in Shiprock)	No other relatives or neighbors
25	Young unmarried male; died in Oregon; body	*All participated* Father and unmarried	*Deceased's Set:* Primary & Secondary Kin: B and	No significant relatives missing	Clan MZ and Z came to visit

		Deceased's Set		Clan Relatives
	children, including son working in Oregon		wife; Z; MB, married daughter & husband, from neighboring community	
shipped to Gallup; buried Mar. 21, 1966				
26 Older man; died May 6, 1966; buried May 10, 1966	*All participated* Wife; younger wife (daughter of above by previous marriage); married daughter, husband, and children; 2 married sons, wives and children.	*Deceased's Set:* Primary Kin: Son and wife; son (by a 3rd wife). (Wives had no local relatives)	(No significant relatives absent) *Cooking and Food Contributions:* 2 neighbor women (1 clan relative); 1 affine (son's wife); 1 same clan as deceased; 1 related clan	*Clan Relatives* Clan Z, her daughters, 1 son from Ft. Defiance, 1 daughter & husband from Denver; Clan SD; Clan B, 2 clan Zs; Clan BD & ZD; 1 related clan.
27 Old widow; died May 21, 1966; buried on Mountain	*All participated* 2 sons & one son's wife	*Deceased's Set:* Primary Kin: Daughter, husband, 2 married daughters; daughter, husband (Gallup); son, wife (Ft. Defiance). Secondary Kin: DD; 2 DS; 1 DD (12 miles away); SD (25 miles away); SD.	(No primary or secondary relatives absent)	*Clan Relatives* 2 from same clan; 5 from related clans; 1 nonrelative; 1 spouse of secondary kin.
28 Old man; committed suicide on July 19, 1966; buried in neighboring community, July 22	*All participated* Wife; Stepchildren; Children of deceased daughter.	*Deceased's Set:* Primary Kin: S and wife (Los Angeles); D and husband (Los Angeles); D; Sister. *Wife's Set:* Mother; B and wife.	*Deceased's Set:* Primary and Secondary Kin: Daughter; sister; sister's son.	
29 Old man; died July; buried north of Copper Canyon, July 22, 1962	*Not all participated* Stepdaughter; married stepdaughter; widow of stepson and child; Widow of son and children (Wife hardly helped.)	*Deceased's Set:* Sister, ZS; ZDD; ZD (Shiprock); BD. *Wife's Set:* B and wife; her daughter by another man.	*Deceased's Set:* Primary and Secondary Kin: Sister; ZD and MZD.	1 Clan relative

Principles of Recruitment From Kin Sets

The previous analysis of five-day sings, peyote meetings, puberty ceremonies, a Fire Dance and two Squaw Dances, and funerals has stressed the usefulness of a model based on ego-centered sets of primary and secondary kin, in addition to the residence group. Considering all twenty-nine occasions together, it is possible to isolate principles of recruitment that account for participation of some members of sets and not of others. Since ceremonial cooperation shows a great deal of flexibility, I will attempt to isolate only a few simple and very general principles, concentrating on two variables: kinship proximity and spatial proximity.

As stressed previously, the model calls attention to a potential set of cooperators available to an ego, who is a prime decision maker or *t'áá bee bóholníih*. For each occasion there are usually two of these decision makers. Their kin can be divided into those which are primary kin (parents, siblings, and married children) and those which are secondary (grandparents, parents' siblings, siblings' children). Some of these live within the same residence group as the prime decision makers and are classified as coresident kin. Others live in the same neighborhood or community and are considered local kin. Those living outside the community are nonlocal kin.

Using these categories, I have tabulated the number of kin who were potential cooperators in comparison to those who actually participated for all the twenty-nine occasions studied. Only adults have been counted; there are always a number of children and teen-agers present at ceremonies, who herd sheep, aid in the cooking and dishwashing, or run errands. They come, however, with their parents and would not be there without them; the recruitment of the parents, who are the adult kin linked to one of the central egos, is thus more crucial than the absolute number of individuals present. Likewise, a spouse will not participate unless he or she comes with the linking kinsman, a relative of one of the individuals who is *t'áá bee bóholníih*. For this reason the possible number of spouses has not been tabulated, but spouses have been counted when they did appear to aid in cooperative activities.

Table 8.5 focuses only on the primary and secondary kin who participated in twenty-nine ceremonies. It shows the proportion (given in percentages) of the actual cooperators to the total number of potential cooperators of primary and secondary kin (coresident local and nonlocal).[4] The data in Table 8.5 can be summarized according to the following principles. First, as might be expected, a larger proportion of primary kin (parents, siblings, and adult children) than secondary kin (parents' siblings, siblings' children, and grandchildren) are recruited. In other words, the more distant the kinsman in terms of genealogical linkage, the less likely that he or she will be recruited. Second, spouses of primary or secondary kin often attend and cooperate. Third, nonlocal kin (those not residing in the community) are rarely recruited. If they are, they are likely to be primary kinsmen of one of the individuals who is *t'áá bee bóholníih*. Nonlocal attendance is especially marked for funerals where, as in several cases presented, a special effort was made to bring the primary kinsmen of the deceased from distant points for the burial and part of the mourning period.

Table 8.6 shows the distribution of all adults, both kin and nonkin, observed in cooperative tasks in the same twenty-nine occasions. The chart indicates that almost one-half of those participating were not primary or secondary kin but were either clan relatives[5] or nonrelatives, including neighbors. There are several notable points concerning these cooperators.

First, the clan relatives who come are not necessarily from ego's own clan, nor do they represent a substantial proportion of the members of ego's clan in the commu-

TABLE 8.5
Actual and Potential Kin Cooperators for Twenty-nine Ceremonies

Type of Ceremony	Cases (No.)		Primary and Secondary Kinsmen				Total Adult Kin Participating	
			Active	Potential	%	Spouses	(No.)	(%)
Five-day sings	8	*Local*					62	53
		Primary	45	63	71.4	5		
		Secondary	7	21	33.0	1		
		Nonlocal						
		Primary	4	18	22.2	0		
		Secondary	0	0	0	0		
Peyote meetings	6	*Local*					39	48
		Primary	29	50	58.0	8		
		Secondary	1	10	10.0	1		
		Nonlocal						
		Primary	0	9	0			
		Secondary	0	5	0			
Girl's puberty ceremonies	4	*Local*					37	48
		Primary	20	32	62.5	6		
		Secondary	9	24	37.9	1		
		Nonlocal						
		Primary	1	6	16.6	0		
		Secondary	0	5	0	0		
Squaw Dances and Fire Dances	3	*Local*					58	51
		Primary	28	33	84.8	13		
		Secondary	11	25	44.4	1		
		Nonlocal						
		Primary	0	3	0	0		
		Secondary	5	15	33.3	0		
Funerals	8	*Local*					92	66
		Primary	30	41	73.2	12		
		Secondary	14	30	46.7	4		
		Nonlocal						
		Primary	11	17	64.7	5		
		Secondary	10	22	45.5	6		
TOTALS	29	*Local*					288	55
		Primary	152	219	69.4	44		
		Secondary	42	110	38.2	8		
		Nonlocal						
		Primary	12	53	22.6	5		
		Secondary	15	47	31.9	6		

nity. It is equally likely that a clan cousin (*bizeedí*: either someone "born for" ego's clan or someone belonging to the clan ego is "born for") will attend as will a member of ego's own clan. Recruitment is on the basis of particular ties rather than universalistic principles (such as a norm that all members of ego's clan should attend).

Second, distant relatives or nonkin often appear for a sing, especially a large one, or a peyote meeting, since it is consistent with the ethic of generalized reciprocity

TABLE 8.6
Cooperators in Twenty-nine Ceremonies

Type of Ceremony	Primary and Secondary Kin					Clan Relatives and Others					TOTAL
	Primary	Secondary	Spouse	Subtotal	% of all	Relatives	Spouse	Non-Relative	Subtotal	% of all	
Five-Night Sings	49	7	6	62	53	21	3	30	54	47	116
Peyote Meetings	29	1	9	39	48	17	0	25	42	52	81
Girl's Puberty Rite	21	9	7	37	48	12	0	28	40	52	77
Squaw Dance and Fire Dance	28	16	14	58	51	17	9	29	55	49	113
Funerals	41	24	27	92	66	32	7	8	47	34	139
TOTALS	168	57	63	288	55	99	19	120	238	45	526

described in Chapter 2, and since there are benefits to the individual's health and security that accompany participation in the ritual aspects of the occasion. They often bring food or pitch in without being asked, because this sort of behavior is considered a good thing.

Third, participation of nonrelatives is a regular feature of some kinds of ceremonies. One half of the nonkin attending peyote meetings include the Road Chief, his spouse, and other relatives. The other half consists of Copper Canyon peyotists who are welcome as members of the cult. Older women are particularly interested in the *kinaaldá* ceremony, which stresses the values and attitudes of womanhood to the young girl who is the patient. These *sáanii* (or older women) and their children from all over the Copper Canyon area account for many of the nonrelatives or clan relatives who come to prepare the corn cake for this ceremony.

Table 8.7 reveals an additional factor in the recruitment of clan and nonkin: where primary and secondary kin of one or both egos are lacking, clan kin, neighbors, or nonkin will constitute a major portion of the participants. This table presents three cases, each representing a different type of ceremony: a five-day sing, a peyote meeting, a girl's puberty ceremony; in each, nonkin make up more than 60 percent of those involved. In addition to the importance of these nonkin, it is also clear that when the primary and secondary kin of one ego are lacking, those of the other ego will be utilized. In other instances, where each ego has potential local kin on whom to call, participants are more evenly distributed among relatives of both egos. Table 8.7 also shows that locality *within* the community plays an important role, as expected from cases examined earlier in this chapter. If there is a decision to locate the ceremony in the residence group of one ego's relatives rather than in a residence group where relatives of the second ego live (e.g., in the camp of the husband's kin rather than in that of the wife's kin), it is this first set of kin which is more heavily involved in cooperation.

TABLE 8.7

Comparison of Cooperation in Three Ceremonies

Case Number	Central Egos	Location	Cooperators (no.)	Kin (%)	Other (%)		Description of Kin							Spouse	Description of Other
							Active	Poten-tial	%	Spouse	Active	Poten-tial	%		
#2 Five-day sing	Wife & patient	Camp of wife	22	27.3	73.7	*Local* Primary	5	5	100	2	1	1	100		6 distant clan relatives; 8 neighbors
						Secondary	0	0	0		0	?	0		
						Nonlocal Primary	0	0	0		0	?	0		
						Secondary	0	?	0		0	?	0		
#12 Peyote meetings	Wife & patient	Camp of wife's clan relatives	17	17.7	82.3	*Local* Primary	2	4	50		0	0	0		5 clan relatives, plus 3 spouses; 3 nonrelatives: Road Man, wife, & sister
						Secondary	0	0	0		0	0	0		
						Nonlocal Primary	0	0	0		0	0	0		
						Secondary	0	0	0		0	0	0		
#16 Puberty ceremonies	Mother & deceased father	Camp of mother; near relatives of deceased father (virilocal)	22	31.4	68.6	*Local* Primary	4	5	80	2	0	2	0		1 ego's own clan relative; 2 distant clan relatives; 9 nonrelatives (many of whom were neighbors); 1 affine
						Secondary	0	1	0		1	5	20	1	
						Nonlocal Primary	0	3	0		0	1	0		
						Secondary	0	2	0		0	2	0		

In sum, there is a hierarchy of priorities in the recruitment of actual cooperators: primary kin over secondary kin, coresident and local over nonlocal kin. Since there are usually two egos who are organizers, more members from one set of primary and secondary kin may be activated than from the other. This occurs under two conditions: (1) if one ego has few kin, or (2) if his or her kin are residentially distant from the camp where the ceremony is held.

In this chapter I have demonstrated the usefulness of a model based on ego-centered sets in analyzing the recruitment of aid for twenty-nine ceremonies. The patient and spouse, or the patient's parents, are the main decision makers, who communicate plans to and coordinate activities among members of their residence group and their primary and secondary kin. These close relatives and their spouses perform the major nonritual tasks necessary to carry out a ceremony or funeral, while clan relatives and neighbors are auxiliary participants.

I have also isolated several principles that predict which kin are most likely to be recruited from these ego-centered sets. The operation of these principles produces an organization fundamentally different from one based on large corporate kin groups. The community of Copper Canyon is best characterized in terms of an unbounded network of ties; this network is the sum of individual cooperating sets, which are activated, particularly in ceremonial situations, and which acquire a certain amount of regularity over a period of time. Each residence group is connected with others in the community, since residents have primary and secondary kin in other locations in the Copper Canyon area.

A model using ego-centered sets combined into an unbounded network overcomes the weaknesses of concepts like outfit, matrilineage, and Local Clan Element, since it (1) more closely parallels the ego-centered nature of Navajo request making, and (2) more closely fits the data on who cooperates with whom. Those who, according to published definitions of outfit, matrilineage, or LCE, might be likely to participate in a ceremony, are actually differentially recruited depending on the genealogical and spatial proximity to the patient, his or her spouse, or parents. If lineage or clanship provided the principles for recruitment, I would expect a larger proportion of an individual's own clan to participate than actually do. Since any ego has four types of clan relatives (those in one's own clan, one's father's clan, those "born for" one's clan, and those "born for" one's father's clan), I would expect significant proportions of these clans to help at ceremonies, especially large sings like a Fire Dance or Squaw Dance. However, this is not the case; clan relatives who attend tend to be primary and secondary, or more distant, genealogical kin, or those clan relatives who live in the same neighborhood. The kin set of a spouse is much more likely to be activated than are ties to the patient's clan relatives, especially those who live in a distant part of the Copper Canyon community.[6]

Part V

CONCLUSION

Chapter 9

New Perspectives
on Navajo Studies

〰〰〰〰〰〰〰〰〰〰〰〰〰〰〰〰〰〰〰〰〰〰〰〰〰〰〰〰〰〰〰〰〰〰〰〰

The data on cooperative activities presented in this study and the cultural and social structural models used to analyze these data have important implications for assessing previous studies of Navajo culture and society. Publications that treat aspects of the Navajo cultural system include studies on three broad topics: (1) religion, including myth and ritual; (2) witchcraft; and (3) philosophy, morals, and values.

The extensive literature on Navajo religion has three major characteristics. First, many accounts are descriptive; either they provide minute details of particular chants (e.g., Matthews 1887, 1897, 1902; Stevenson 1886; Kluckhohn and Wyman 1940) or they are texts of the myths that account for the origin of various chants (e.g., Haile 1938, 1943b; Newcomb and Reichard 1937; Reichard 1939; Wyman 1957, 1970). Most chants and myths have been described, making available a nearly complete ethnographic record.

Second, the few general statements about Navajo religion as a cultural system consist largely of highly abstract characterizations using concepts derived from Anglo-American culture. For example, many studies have stated that the purpose of a Navajo chant is to bring the patient into "harmony" with the universe (e.g., Kluckhohn and Leighton 1962: 231–32). This alludes to the Navajo concept of *hózhǫ́*, which is often translated as "harmony," "goodness," "happiness," and "beauty," all of which imply Western philosophical and theological concepts and do not provide an accurate rendering of the Navajo meaning. In other words, Navajo religious beliefs could be more carefully treated as a self-consistent system and analyzed in their own terms, as I have suggested elsewhere (Lamphere 1969).

Third, explanatory statements made about the persistence of Navajo religion stress the psychological or sociological functions of myth, ritual, and belief systems (Kluckhohn and Leighton 1946; 1962 edition: 229–40).

Two of these three characteristics are found in Kluckhohn's study of Navajo witchcraft (1944; reprint 1967). On one hand, the book contains a large quantity of descriptive material including (1) native definitions of the types of witchcraft, (2) details of the practices in which witches and werewolves are supposed to engage, and (3) case material on witchcraft accusations. On the other hand, almost unconnected with the descriptive material, is an explanation of witchcraft in terms of its psychological and social functions.

Publications on Navajo morals, philosophy, and values are also either concrete and extremely descriptive or consist of highly abstract characterizations of Navajo values that are fit into a universalistic classification. The best descriptive data on Navajo morals and philosophy are contained in Ladd's study[1]; but three articles by Clyde Kluckhohn (1949 and 1956a and b), one article by Haile (1943a), and a monograph by Hobson (1954) contain data on these topics. Theoretical work has been mainly on values rather than on Navajo philosophy. Three schemes to characterize value systems have been proposed and applied to Navajo data by Ethel Albert (1956), Florence Kluckhohn (1950), and Clyde Kluckhohn (1958). The difficulties inherent in describing and comparing values have been excellently summarized by Vogt and Albert (1966: 2–20), including the lack of congruence between classification schemes derived from Western European thought and native modes of using value terms.

Three conclusions are apparent from the literature on the Navajo cultural system. First, many descriptive data have already been published and can be used in reinterpreting aspects of Navajo culture. In fact, several articles were useful in outlining the Navajo concepts of cooperation and authority presented in Chapter 2. Second, data have been used to construct abstract generalizations about aspects of the cultural system itself; for example, Navajos emphasize harmony with the universe (Kluckhohn and Leighton 1946; 1962 ed.: 232); Navajos are egoistic, utilitarian moralists (Ladd 1957: 212, 278–81); and Navajo value orientations emphasize collateral relationships, a present-time orientation, harmony with nature, and a "doing" rather than a "being" orientation to activity (Kluckhohn and Strodbeck 1961: 319). Third, when explanations have been offered, they have been in terms of the psychological and social functions of various aspects of culture (e.g., witchcraft beliefs, mythology, and relgious beliefs). The functional approach has, in recent years, been criticized by philosophers of science, anthropologists, and sociologists.

In avoiding the weaknesses of functionalism and the use of Western concepts, this book stresses aspects of Navajo culture that form a self-consistent system closely related to social behavior. Chapters 2 and 3 discuss concepts of cooperation and authority, social and antisocial behavior, particularly as these are communicated in gossip and witchcraft suspicion. The book also treats the etiquette of request making, which is congruent with the Navajo ideology of cooperation. Many aspects of my analysis have been recognized and described in previous publications, but these particular concepts have not been seen as interrelated or as having implications for social relationships.

Thus, the importance of my cultural analysis is twofold. First, in treating Navajo concepts as part of an integrated cultural system I suggested a new view of Navajo witchcraft that expands on Kluckhohn's original interpretation. Like Kluckhohn, I have shown how witchcraft beliefs are related to the Navajo view of bad, antisocial behavior, but, in addition, I have related these beliefs to other definitions of antisocial behavior (such as meanness, laziness, stinginess, and craziness). This indicates a much closer connection between witchcraft beliefs and social organization than Kluckhohn suspected; it also leads us to see that the vagueness of witchcraft accusations is connected with the maintenance of an idea system of generalized reciprocity. Vague accusations imply that punishment of deviant behavior is not as important as the explanation of illness and the definition of cooperative and un-cooperative behavior.

The second implication deals with the relationships between ideas and behavior that are highlighted by the models of the cultural system and social structure I have proposed. In a system that stresses both an uncalculated notion of cooperation (that is, generalized reciprocity) and autonomy, it follows that any individual Navajo should act to retain as many potential cooperators as possible. All are obligated to help, but there is no way of making sure that any particular individual will, in fact, give aid. As many options are needed as possible, so that if one kinsman or neighbor refuses or gives an excuse there are others on whom to call. Hence, one would not suspect a sharp line between those who help and those who do not help in any given situation. Rather than a dichotomy between cooperators and non-cooperators or between members of groups who aid and members of other groups who do not, one would expect a shading from those who might be more likely to cooperate to those who are less likely. That this "shading off" does occur is clear from the analysis of social structure and cooperative activities I have presented.

My treatment of both structural and organizational properties of the social system, like my model of aspects of Navajo culture, varies considerably from the published literature. Previous studies of the Navajo social system have stressed the definition of social groups and a description of the activities handled by each. There has been a great deal of disagreement as to the criteria to be used in defining a particular group and what it should be called. Table 9.1 is a summary of the various terms used in Navajo community studies and articles on social organization. The majority of authors define groups that can be arranged according to size into four categories: the first two levels correspond roughly to what I have called Navajo domestic groups—the household and residence group. The third level I have treated using the concepts of set and network, while the fourth level I have dealt with by using the terms clan and Local Clan Element.

Variations in both the terms shown in Table 9.1 and their definitions depend on which of the following factors is stressed by the investigator: (1) kinship or genealogical affiliation; (2) spatial or residential affiliation; or (3) type of cooperation within the group. For example, terms and definitions given by Kluckhohn and Leighton (1962 ed.) emphasize genealogical relationships in defining the groups in Levels 1 and 2. The biological family consists of "husband, wife, and unmarried children" (1962: 100), while the extended family commonly consists of "an older woman with her husband and unmarried children, daughters and their husbands and unmarried children" (1962: 102). The authors also specify several variations that are found.

In another example, terms used by Adams, household and residence group, stress the spatial nature of the two smallest groups, rather than their kinship base. His definitions seem to combine both locality and cooperation, though kinship criteria are often mentioned. "A household is defined here as a group of people who regularly eat together and share food resources in common, thus constituting a minimum subsistence unit. . . . All Shonto households are comprised [sic] basically of nuclear families or remnants thereof" (1963: 64–65). "A residence group comprises one or more closely-related households living in close proximity (within 'shouting distance') and sharing certain basic resources in common" (1963: 57).

Despite these differences in terminology and emphasis on one or another of three criteria, there is a fair amount of agreement on groups in Levels 1 and 2: the household or nuclear family and the residence group or extended family. I chose to

TABLE 9.1
Terms for Navajo Social Groups

Author	Level			
	1	2	3	4
Reichard (1928)		Family		Clan (Clan group)
Kimball and Provinse (1942)	Family	Family group	Land-use community	
Collier (1966)	Household	Camp	Cooperating unit	
Kluckhohn and Leighton (1962 ed.)	Biological family	Extended family	Outfit	Clan
Bellah (1952)	Biological family	Extended family	Land-use community (local group)	Clan
Ross (1955)	Hoghans/ nuclear family	Households (extended family)	Outfits	Local Clan Segment
Adams (1963)	Household	Residence group	Resident lineage	Clan
Kluckhohn (1966)	Unit	Extended family group	Outfit	
Aberle (1961)	Single hoghan unit	Extended family (cooperating group and outfit)		Local Clan Element
Levy (1962)	Biological family	Extended family (camp, household)	Outfit	Community (Local Clan Element, or extended outfit)
Downs (1964)	Family	Homestead group (outfit)	(Denies function of outfit and land-use community)	
Shepardson and Hammond (1970)	Nuclear family	Camp		Clan
Edmonson (1966)	Household		Local group	
Witherspoon (1975)	Household	Subsistence Residential Unit	Outfit	Clan (Descent Category)

utilize the terms household and residence group only after I had carefully surveyed published studies and statements of Copper Canyon informants for information on the Navajo actors' view, or model of residential arrangements. Although there is no Navajo label for either domestic unit, I attempted to take into account Navajo ways of expressing spatial and kinship relationships and used these two criteria in settling on a definition. In order to classify data on the structure of these groups and to understand variations in their composition, it was necessary to use the anthropological concept of a developmental cycle of domestic groups. This model, I would argue, gives a much clearer picture of the dynamics that produce the particular configuration of various residential groupings in the Copper Canyon community. I also feel that its application to data already collected from other communities on the reservation would help clear up many aspects of the debate over flexibility or variation, as this controversy applies to the household and residence group levels of organization.

There is much greater disagreement, as Level 3 in Table 9.1 shows, concerning relationships between kinsmen beyond the domestic group level. In Chapter 4 I reviewed the terms used in many community studies and journal articles and strongly argued that an analysis in terms of groups is inappropriate. The concepts such as outfit, matrilineage, and cooperating group neither approximate Navajo discourse (since there are no terms which describe such groups) nor accurately reflect the way in which Navajos recruit aid and organize activities that require the cooperation of a large number of genealogical kinsmen, neighbors, and clan relatives. Instead of basing my analysis on groups, I utilized the concepts of set and network. These two concepts are also not isomorphic with Navajo terms per se, but are consistent with Navajo ideas about cooperation and ego-centered methods of recruiting aid.

I also discussed the treatment of clan relationships in the anthropological literature and analyzed the residential distribution of members of three Copper Canyon clans, or Local Clan Elements. The dispersion of members of a clan into different neighborhoods within the community can best be interpreted in terms of the expansion and fission of domestic groups using the model of a developmental cycle over several generations. That clans do not become highly localized units monopolizing a contiguous land base is congruent with the view that ego-centered sets of kin provide a fruitful way of analyzing the recruitment of aid. In turn, sets are overlapping and produce a network of ties that link together domestic groups throughout the community. My analysis substantially differs from the view that Navajo social structure is composed of a series of groups of increasing size—for example, household, residence group, outfit, or matrilineage, and clan.

I have supported my model of Navajo social structure with data on the organizational aspects of Navajo social life. I analyzed concrete cooperative patterns for a series of activities and have shown that some activities illuminate the structure and authority of the residence group, while others illustrate the importance of the set/network model. Thus, livestock and agricultural tasks in Copper Canyon are mainly handled within the residence group whether it is composed of one nuclear family household or several households of an extended family. Getting rides, hauling wood and water, and moving to summer and winter residence sites are activities sometimes organized within a residence group and sometimes using an individual's set of kin who live outside his or her residence group. The important factors that channel the direction of requests for help in these activities are the presence or absence of transportation in ego's residence group and the composition of the residence group itself. The primary strategy for obtaining rides is for an individual to work from close genealogical and spatial kin to more distant relatives and nonkin. In other words, a Navajo without transportation is likely to ask coresident primary and secondary kin for a ride or aid in hauling wood and water or moving. Neighbors are rarely asked purely on the basis of spatial proximity, but because there is some clan relationship between the requester and the car owner (or his or her spouse). A close examination of the way moving is organized in an extended family camp with transportation shows that it follows the lines of communication and authority within the residence group, as do such pastoral activities as sheepherding, shearing, and dipping.

The usefulness of the model based on ego-centered sets emerges even more clearly in the analysis of ceremonial cooperation and funerals presented in Chapter 8. In recruiting aid there are usually two primary decision makers who operate within the cultural system of cooperation and the etiquette of request making described in Chapters 2 and 3. These two decision makers request help from members of their respective sets of primary and secondary kin. Principles of recruitment are as follows: primary kin are recruited before secondary kin; coresidents and kin who live in Copper Canyon are asked before nonlocal kin. Since there are usually two egos who are organizers, more members of one set may be activated if (1) one ego has few kin, or (2) if his or her kin are residentially distant from the camp where the ceremony is held.

Thus the analysis of participation in ceremonies further delineates the same "proximity strategy" described in Chapter 7 on transportation. Residence group members are the "closest" and most easily recruited participants; next to be activated are ties to primary and secondary kin outside the residence group, with those who live in the same neighborhood being the most likely to participate; then, neighbors with whom the organizers have clan ties are recruited; finally, distant clan relatives (of one's own clan) are likely to participate only in funerals or large ceremonies.

This study casts the role of matrilineality in Navajo society in a much different perspective. I have emphasized that an individual not only has potential ties with members of his or her own clan, but also with those in three other clans to whom ego is "related." Rather than members of one clan forming a block of cooperators on a particular occasion, a Navajo draws upon clanship as a principle for recruiting a wide range of individuals, usually those who are in ego's own or a related clan and who also live in ego's own neighborhood or an adjacent one. Clan ties, along with neighborhood ties, serve as a reserve system for occasions when a great deal of help is needed or when genealogical kin are lacking. Recruitment is on the basis of dyadic relationships rather than as part of an allegiance to a group such as Local Clan Element.

I should again emphasize that I have proposed an observer's model of how the system works. Although I have gone beyond Navajo terminology for kinship, residence, and clanship, I have carefully considered these concrete representations of the Navajo model of their system as a basis for my own interpretation. Although the Navajo do not have sets and networks, a network analysis reveals important regularities in data on cooperative patterns with more success, I would argue, than previous analyses based on the notion of groups.

As I have interpreted my data, aspects of the Navajo cultural system are related to the social system. Concepts for interpreting and organizing behavior are used in conjunction with the structural situation in which an individual finds himself or herself (given his or her household, residence group, and set of primary and secondary kin). Both are important in understanding how help is recruited for a particular task. A cultural system of generalized reciprocity and universally applied concepts of cooperative and uncooperative behavior is, thus, congruent with a social system based on ego-centered recruitment of aid that in turn creates an unbounded network of residence groups In a social system where obligations to provide goods and services are not part of a well-defined set of kinship roles or large corporate groups, it is advantageous to have as many kinsmen as possible available to help and to have obligations that bind all equally, regardless of kinship role or type of task. A generalized notion that everybody helps combined with concepts of unhelpful behavior, which are also not role-specific, provide the very diffuse system of norms and sanctions necessary to back up an open-ended, flexible social system.

There are two sets of reasons why anthropologists who have studied Navajo kinship have been led to conflicting conclusions. First, anthropology in the United States developed with certain theoretical biases and approaches to data collection. Much of the early research on American Indian groups by travelers, missionaries, and, later, by anthropologists under the influence of Franz Boas, was "salvage anthropology" focused on recording the ethnographic details of dying Indian cultures. Early Navajo ethnography and some of Kluckhohn's first studies are of this kind. The concept of culture has long dominated American anthropological thinking, and, especially, Kluckhohn's interest in culture patterns and values is an outgrowth of this trend (Lamphere and Vogt 1972). The study of kinship was seen as only one aspect of culture, and concepts like social structure and social organization were used only by those influenced by Radcliffe-Brown during his years at the University of Chicago. British anthropologists, in contrast, working in African and South Asian colonial settings, developed a much more comprehensive framework for the study of kinship, family groupings, lineage systems, and political systems. In part, American anthropologists working with Navajo data in the 1930s, 1940s, and 1950s were not well trained in the analysis of kinship and social structure.

A second set of reasons for conflicting analyses is related to the nature of American Indian societies in general and the Navajo in particular. Most American Indian groups, at contact, were hunter-gatherer or tribal societies with a low level of social or political complexity. Even the more developed political systems—of the Iroquois in the Northeast and the Creek, Cherokee and other tribes of the Southeast—were only roughly comparable to the acephalous political structures in Africa. Certainly the wide variety of acephalous, centralized, and hierarchical societies found throughout South Asia and Africa provided data on the kinds of kinship systems where systematic and orderly patterns were easily apparent. In addition, by the time American anthropologists began to study American Indian groups, these had changed significantly through contact, defeat, and the advent of the reservation system. Kinship and family patterns in these small-scale, rapidly changing societies did and still continue to exhibit a variety of patterns. Thus, not only were American anthropologists relatively untrained in the analysis of social organization, but many of the groups they studied, including the Navajo, were particularly "unstructured."

Recent changes in theoretical perspectives both in British and American anthropology have provided new ways of examining kinship and social structure that make it possible to resolve the confusion present in Navajo studies. On one hand, the analysis of cultural patterns has moved from a consideration of either culture traits (the minutiae of learned behavior) or the study of values and world view in broad, abstract terms to analysis of the "middle range," such as those of Schneider (1968) and Geertz (1964). It is this view of culture as a system of ideas that I have used in building my model of Navajo cooperation. On the other hand, British structural-functionalism has been criticized both as an over-rigid view of rural tribal systems at a particular point in colonial history and as inadequate for the study of kinship in other parts of the world (e.g., New Guinea) or in changing urban situations. Structural-functional theory as typified in the work of Radcliffe-Brown, Evans-Pritchard, and Fortes would have provided models inapplicable to Navajo patterns.

Two developments in British anthropology have dealt with some of these limitations. The dynamic aspects of social structure at the domestic level have been conceptualized by the notion of a developmental cycle model, first proposed by Fortes and expanded by Goody and others. Also, the concepts of set and network have proved useful in analyzing social relationships in urban settings both in Western complex societies and in Third World nations. I have used both approaches in building a model of Navajo social structure based on data on cooperative activities in an eastern reservation community.

I have argued that this model is useful in comparing and reinterpreting data from other Navajo communities, both those collected in the 1930s and those more recently reported. There are differences between present-day communities in population density, economic base, and level of acculturation. There have also been changes throughout the reservation during the past thirty years as population has continued to grow on a stable land base, pastoral and agricultural activities have declined, education has led to off-reservation migration and the increased use of motor vehicles has given the Navajo access to their distant neighbors and relatives and to facilities on and off reservation. The model I have suggested can interpret both differences between communities and recent changes, while at the same time pointing to the overall similarities in Navajo culture and social structure.

REFERENCE MATERIAL

Appendixes

Comparison of Copper Canyon Households With Other Households

I. Shonto and Copper Canyon Household Types (Shonto data from Adams 1963:56; data collected in 1954)	Shonto Households		Copper Canyon Households	
	No.	%	No.	%
1 adult male, 2 adult females, and children	9	9	0	0.0
1 adult male, 1 adult female, and children	77 { 66 } 77		108	75.5
1 adult male, 1 adult female, without children	11			
1 adult male and children	1	1	4	2.9
1 adult female and children	11	11	17	11.8
2 adult females and children	1	1	3	2.1
1 adult male without children	1	1	3	2.1
1 adult female without children			8	5.6
Totals	100	100	143	100.0

II. Rimrock and Copper Canyon Household Types (Rimrock data from Kluckhohn 1966:368; data collected June 1950)	Rimrock Households		Copper Canyon Households	
	No.	%	No.	%
Nuclear families	39		108	75.5
Nuclear families with children not from 1 spouse	25			
Nuclear families with children not of either spouse (2 where children were grandchildren of spouses)	75 { 5 } 60.0			
Nuclear family and unmarried adult	6			
Polygamous families	11	8.8	0	0.0
Single parent and minor children	17	28.8	32	22.4
Relict units	19			
Isolated individuals	3	2.4	3	2.1
Totals	125	100.0	143	100.0

III. Navajo Mountain and Klagetoh Household Types (from Collier 1966, appendixes; data from 1938)	Navajo Mountain Households			Klagetoh Households		
	No.	%	People	No.	%	People
Nuclear family (husband, wife, and minor children)	15	68.2	73	19	50.0	104
Polygamous (husband, 2 wives, and minor children)	1	4.5	23	3	7.9	30
*Nuclear plus**						
a	1⎫	9.1	4	1⎫		6
b	1⎭		8	1⎪		3
c				1⎪	15.8	8
d				1⎪		5
e				1⎪		12
f				1⎭		11
Three generations†						
a	1⎫	9.1	8	2⎫		8
b	1⎭		3	1⎬	10.5	10
c				1⎭		4
Women and children (Mother, children, married son and wife)	2	9.1	12	4	10.5	16
Women alone				1	2.6	1
Men alone				1	2.6	1
Totals	22	100.0	131	38	99.9	219

*_Nuclear plus_ indicates a nuclear family plus nonimmediate relatives. The nuclear plus households in Navajo Mountain were (a) husband, wife, minor child, and niece; and (b) husband, wife, unmarried daughter, and her minor children.

In Klagetoh, the nuclear plus households included (a) husband, wife, minor children, wife's brother and sister; (b) husband, wife, and wife's father; (c) husband, wife, minor children and wife's sister; (d) husband, wife, minor child, and husband's child by previous marriage; (e) husband, wife, and daughter's children; and (f) husband, wife, niece's children, and daughter's children.

†In Navajo Mountain, the households of three generations were (a) mother, unmarried daughter, and daughter's children; and (b) mother, married son and wife.

The three generation households in Klagetoh were (a) mother, unmarried daughter, and daughter's children; (b) mother, married son and wife, and minor children; and (c) mother, minor children, and daughter's children.

The main differences seem to be, first, that polygamous households were more common in communities studied earlier. Between 5 and 10 percent of the households were polygamous at Navajo Mountain (1938), Klagetoh (1938), Shonto (1954), and Rimrock (1950), but such households no longer exist at Copper Canyon, the most recently studied community. This probably reflects the official tribal ban on polygamous marriages, in addition to the influence of welfare agents and missionaries who discourage such unions.

Second, in Klagetoh, there were more nuclear families with additional relatives (such as wife's sister's children, wife's siblings, wife's father, and wife's daughters' children). If such families (14.6 percent) were added to the percentage of nuclear families (53.7 percent), the total (68.3 percent) would be closer to the percentage of nuclear families in other communities. Possibly because of demographic characteristics, more non-nuclear family relatives have attached themselves to a nuclear family in Klagetoh than in other communities.

Third, in Rimrock, there was a greater percentage of households composed of single parents and minor children (28.8 percent) as compared to other communities (Shonto, 13 percent; Navajo Mountain, 18.2 percent; Klagetoh, 19.6 percent; and Copper Canyon, 22.4 percent). Most of these households were headed by women; their composition is probably related to the excess of older women over older males in the community population.

APPENDIX 2

Copper Canyon Camps and Membership

I-A. Nuclear Camps: Men, women, and children
(28 camps, 195 members; 6.96 persons per camp)

Camp No.	Members	Camp No.	Members	Camp No.	Members
5	9	38	14	62	3
6	4	42	2	63	5
14	12	45	2	65	10
16	10	49	6	68	2
21	9	50	10	70	12
22	3	53	10	71	2
26	6	54	9	72	4
29	6	56	15	74	6
31	11	59	3	77	2
		61	8		

		Camp No.	Members
I-B.	Nuclear Camps: Women and children	2	10
	(3 camps; 16 members;	4	4
	5.33 persons per camp)	67	2
I-C.	Nuclear Camps: Men and children	30	7
	(2 camps; 9 members; 4.5 persons per camp)	24	2

I-A, B, & C		
Total		220
(33 camps; 220 members; 6.66 persons per camp)		

II-A. Isolated Individuals (5 camps)					
Camp No.	Members	Camp No.	Members	Camp No.	Members
9	1	33	1	78	1
10	1	76	1		

III-A. Extended Camps: Uxorilocal
(22 camps; 241 members; 10.9 persons per camp)

Camp No	Younger Households (no.)	Camp Members (no.	Camp No.	Younger Households (no.)	Camp Members (no.)
3*	1	11	44	1	10
8	1	4	48*	1	16
11*	1	4	51	(s)†	10
19*	1	13	52*	1	9
25	1	10	55	1	11
27	3	21	58	1	5
28*	1	6	60*	1	3
34*	1	9	64	2	12
12	1	9	69	2	16
35	2	19	73	2	14
43	(s)†	18	75	1	12

		Camp No.	Younger Households (no.)	Camp Members (no.)
III-B.	Extended Camps:	7*	1	4
	Virilocal	46*	1	4
	(6 camps;	47	1	12
	54 members;	66	1	5
	9 persons per	15	(f)†	10
	camp)	39	2	19

III-C.	Extended Camps: Mixed:	1*	1V, 2U	20
	Virilocal and Uxorilocal	13	3V, 1U	30
	(12 camps;	17*	U, 3V‡	28
	234 persons;	18*	1U, 2V	18
	19.50 persons	20*	1U, 1V	11
	per camp)	23*	1V, 1U (ZD)	14
		32*	1V, U (DD)	13
		36*	1U, 1V	16
		37	1U, 1V	18
		40*	1V, 3U	29
		41	1V, 2U	19
		57*	2U, 1V	18

III-A, B, & C Total (78 camps; 754 members; 9.66 persons per camp)	754

NOTE: Maps 1.1 and 1.2 show the location of these camps in winter and summer.

*Widow was head of camp. No asterisk means a couple was head of camp.

† (s) indicates sororilocal; (f) indicates fratrilocal.

‡This camp was composed of a woman and her married sons (living virilocally),
 plus the woman's sister-in-law and her married son (living virilocally)
 and her married daughter (living uxorilocally).

Comparative Data on Residence Group Composition

I. Navajo Mountain (from Shephardson and Hammond 1964: 1035–41) compared with Copper Canyon

| | Navajo Mountain | | | | Copper Canyon | |
| | 1938 | | 1961 | | 1966 | |
	No.	%	No.	%	No.	%
Nuclear families	2	22	5	24	37	47.3
Matrilocal	1	11	9	43	23	29.4
Patrilocal	1	11	1	5	6	8.0
Mixed	5	56	6	28	12	15.3
	9	100	21	100	78	100.0

II. Shonto (from Adams 1963: 59) compared with Copper Canyon

| | Shonto | | Copper Canyon | |
	No.	%	No.	%
Nuclear derivation:				
1 generation: siblings	2	5.2	3	4.0
2 generations: parents and married children	17	45.0	38	48.4
3 generations: parents, married children, and married grandchildren	6	15.8	0	
3 generations: remnant grandparent and grandchildren (middle generation deceased)	1	2.6	1	1.3
Extended derivation:				
Parents, married children, and married niece	1	2.6	0	
Uncle and aunt, and married nephews and nieces	2	5.2	0	
Uncertain (apparently affinal relation)	1	2.6	0	
Isolated: 1 household	7	18.4	32	41
Not kin determined (Shonto School)	1	2.6		
Isolated individuals			4	5.3
	38	100.0	78	100.0

III. Rimrock (from Lamphere and Reynolds 1963) compared with Copper Canyon

	Rimrock No.	Rimrock %	Copper Canyon No.	Copper Canyon %
Nuclear camps	49*	47.6	37*	47.3
Extended camps				
Uxorilocal	32‡	31.1	23†	29.4
Virilocal	7	6.8	6	8.0
Mixed	10	9.7	12	15.3
Affinal	5	4.8		
	103	100.0	78	100.0

NOTE: *Isolated individuals: Rimrock (3) and Copper Canyon (4).
     †Includes three sibling groups, two sisters or two brothers.
     ‡Includes nine sibling groups, either two sisters or brother and sister, and children.

IV. Government Survey (Aberle 1961:187) compared with Copper Canyon. Survey includes 3,700 family units, which here are equated with camps or residence groups.

	Government Survey %	Copper Canyon No.	Copper Canyon %
Biological family (1,958 nuclear families or 81%; remaining are probably one parent and children)	53	37*	47.3
Matrilocal	32†	23†	29.4
Patrilocal	5	6	8.0
Mixed	10	12	15.3
	100	78	100.0

NOTE: *Includes four isolated individuals.
     †Includes grandmother-grandchild units.

The major differences can be summarized as follows:

1. In western Navajo communities (Navajo Mountain and Shonto), data on the size and structure of residence groups show more clustering than at Copper Canyon. There are more matrilocal extended camps and fewer nuclear camps at Navajo Mountain. At Shonto, there are more three-generation residence groups (parents, married children, and married grandchildren) and fewer isolated households. This, in combination with the sparse population of the western reservation, suggests that residence groups are larger but farther apart than at Copper Canyon.

2. Copper Canyon figures are similar to those for Rimrock, using data collected by Lamphere and Reynolds in 1963. This may reflect the fact that the same coding scheme was used in both cases.

3. The size and structure of residence groups for the reservation as a whole as reported in the Government Survey differs only slightly (from 3 to 5 percent in each category) from the figures from Copper Canyon. In the 1930s there seem to have been more nuclear and uxorilocal camps on the reservation and a smaller proportion of virilocal and mixed camps than in the 1960s at Copper Canyon.

As mentioned in the above summary, residence group classifications from Navajo Mountain and Shonto report a greater percentage of extended camps than at

Copper Canyon. This suggests that in working with the Copper Canyon data, I may have split ambiguous cases into two groups when they could have been counted as one residence group. Thus, I reclassified households, putting together the maximum number of households in an area, provided members were related and cooperated in herding, farming, transportation, or ceremonies. The following table shows the results:

Nuclear camps
1. Husband, wife, and children   21
2. Wife and children   1
3. Husband and children   1
    23   35%

Isolated individuals   3   4%

Extended camps
1. Uxorilocal   23
2. Virilocal   5
3. Mixed   13
    41   61%
    67   100%

The classification reduces the number of camps from 78 to 67 by merging 10 nuclear camps and 2 isolated individuals into existing extended camps. The number of uxorilocal extended camps is increased only by one, and one virilocal camp is changed to a mixed extended camp. The new classification only widens differences between Copper Canyon and data for the reservation as a whole (reported in the Government Survey), and differences between Copper Canyon and Navajo Mountain still remain. Thus, the initial classification was retained since it more closely approximates the norm for the general Navajo population.

V. Data on heads of camps (from the Government Survey, reported in Aberle 1961:190) compared with data from Copper Canyon

	Government Survey %	Copper Canyon No.	Copper Canyon %
A. Nuclear families (i.e., camps) total = 1,958			
1. Man, wife, and children (if they have any)	89	28	76
2. Woman and children (no husband)	6	3	8
3. Man and children (no wife)	4	2	5
4. Solitary individual	1	4	11
	100	37	100.0
B. Extended families (i.e., camps) total = 1,712			
1. Headed by husband and wife	62	20*	48.8
2. Headed by widow	31	20	48.8
3. Headed by widower	7	1	2.4
	100	41	100.0

NOTE: *Two camps were of households of two sisters and husbands. One camp had two brothers and included the wife of one; the other brother was a widower. Rather than one head of the camp in these cases, both couples probably had equal authority.

Settlement Patterns in Three Copper Canyon Clans

A. *Within-his-Cover People*
(Bit'ahnii) Genealogy

I. *'Asdzáán Bit'ahnii Tso* (founder deceased)

	Camp and Household Number	Residence
1. Sibling Group 1		
*1. Son	1–2†	Uxorilocal
2. Daughter (deceased)		
*2.1 Nancy	13–1	Independent
2.1.1 Daughter	Nonlocal	Neolocal
2.1.2 Lucy	14	Independent
2.1.3 Son	13–5	Virilocal
2.1.4 Daughter	13–3	Uxorilocal
2.1.5 Son	13–2	Virilocal
2.1.6 Son	13–4	Virilocal
2.1.7 Son	13–1	
2.2 Son (deceased)		
*Widow lives at	19–1	Virilocal
2.3 Son	Nonlocal	Uxorilocal
*2.4 Son	36–2	Uxorilocal
3. Daughter	8–1	Independent (uxorilocal)
3.1 Daughter	8–2	Uxorilocal
3.2 Daughter	Nonlocal	Virilocal
3.3 Son	48–1	Uxorilocal
3.4 Daughter	Nonlocal	Neolocal

II. *'Asdzáán Bit'ahnii* (founder and sister of *'Asdzáán Bit'ahnii Tso;* deceased)

	Camp and Household Number	Residence
2. Sibling Group 2		
1. 'Asdzáán Yazhi (deceased)		
1.1 Daughter	12–1	Independent (uxorilocal)
1.1.1 Son (Mike)	20–1	Uxorilocal
1.1.2 Son (deceased)		
1.1.3 Daughter	5–1	Independent
1.1.4 Daughter	12–2	Uxorilocal
1.1.5 Daughter	Nonlocal	Neolocal
1.1.6 Daughter	17–1	Virilocal
1.2 Daughter (deceased)		
1.2.1 Son	9	Independent (virilocal)
1.2.2 Iris	57–3	Virilocal
1.2.3 Son	38–1	Uxorilocal
1.2.4 Daughter	7–1	Uxori-virilocal
1.2.5 Son	10	Independent (uxorilocal)
1.2.6 Daughter	Nonlocal	Neolocal
1.2.7 Son	Nonlocal	Neolocal
1.2.8 Daughter	Nonlocal	Neolocal
1.2.9 Daughter	Nonlocal	Neolocal
2. Second daughter of *'Asdzáán Bit'ahnii*		
2.1 Daughter	25–1	Independent (virilocal?)
2.1.1 Daughter	25–2	Uxorilocal
2.1.2 Son		
2.2. Son (deceased)		
3. Third daughter of *'Asdzáán Bit'ahnii*		
*(Mrs. Silversmith)	40–1	Independent (virilocal)
3.1 Daughter	3–1	Independent
3.2 Daughter	40–2	Uxorilocal
3.3 Daughter	40–3	Uxorilocal
3.4 Son	40–5	Virilocal
3.5 Son (deceased)		

NOTE: *Indicates individuals who have moved away from original area.

†The first number designates the residence group and the second number designates the household within the camp; for example, 1–2 is the second household in camp number 1. Where there is only one household in a camp, only the camp number is given.

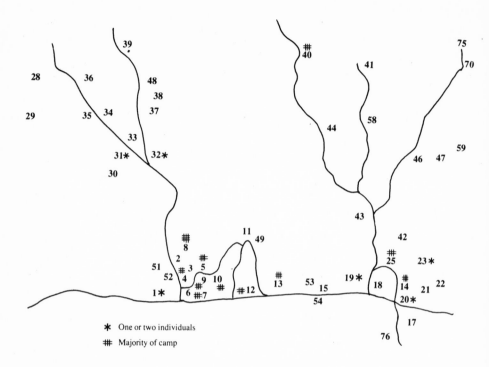

Map A 4.1   *Within-His-Cover people winter residences*

SETTLEMENT PATTERNS

Many of the winter residence groups that were headed by second and third generation Within-his-Cover people were located near the original settlement area adjacent to the trading post. These include Camps 8 and 12, which were headed by two second generation women and their husbands, and Camps 9, 10 and 7, which contained third generation Within-his-Cover people. See map A4.1.

Those who have moved away from this original area are as follows:

Camp of Present Residence	History of Movement
Camp 10	The son of 'Asdzáán Bit'ahnii Tso married into a family living adjacent to his own. He was technically living uxorilocally, but he was still near the original area.
Camp 13	The daughter's daughter of 'Asdzáán Bit'ahnii Tso, Nancy, first moved near Blue Mesa where her first husband's father was living and had a field. Later she moved to her present location, where she had no claims, but apparently gained the consent of her neighbors. One of her older daughters, Lucy, and her husband, Kevin, remained near the field (Camp 14).
Camp 19	Nancy's brother also lived near Blue Mesa (after residing uxorilocally with his father-in-law near the present Camp 29). This brother died, but his spouse, Nelly Begay, and children remained in the same area.
Camp 36	A second brother of Nancy's lived uxorilocally. (A third brother lived uxorilocally near his wife's relatives in another community.)
Camp 25	'Asdzáán Bit'ahnii's daughter's daughter moved near Blue Mesa. She may have claimed this residence site either through her husband's brother or her mother, since both had fields there. She and her husband originally lived near the trading post, and their move was precipitated by the burning of their hoghan and several other incidents of bad luck.
Camp 40	'Asdzáán Bit'ahnii's daughter, Mrs. Silversmith, lived in an isolated camp in the Gray Area with her married children. It is likely that she and Mr. Silversmith settled here through his claim to use rights in the area. His sister and husband lived and herded nearby in the spring and fall.

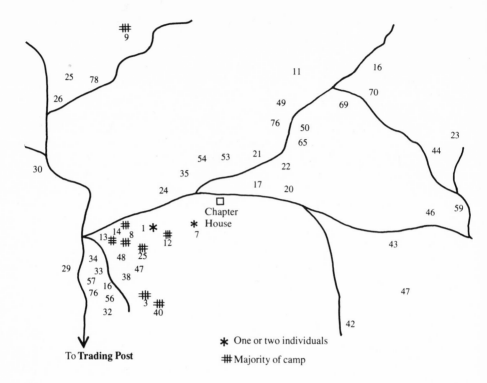

Map A 4.2   Within-His-Cover people summer residences

In summer, residence groups of Within-his-Cover people are still clustered at Cottonwood Pass. The only exception is Camp 9, a single male who herded his sheep on top of the mountain. He may have had claim to this grazing area since the founding sisters also herded there. Cottonwood Pass was the most densely populated summer neighborhood, and Within-his-Cover people residence groups shared it with residence groups composed of members of several other clans.

B. *House-in-the-Rocks People*
(Kiyaa'áanii) Genealogy

I. Segment 1

	Camp and Household Number	Residence
I. Cross Hills Lady (founder)	15–1	Independent
1. Son	Nonlocal	Uxorilocal
2. Son	15–2	Virilocal
3. Daughter (deceased)		
3.1 Daughter	Nonlocal	Neolocal
3.2 Son	Nonlocal	Neolocal
3.3 Daughter	54	Uxorilocal
4. Daughter (deceased)		
4.1 Son	23–3	Uxorilocal
4.2 Daughter	Nonlocal	Neolocal
4.3 Daughter	Nonlocal	Neolocal
5. Daughter	35–1	Independent (virilocal)
5.1 Son	34–2	Uxorilocal
5.2 Daughter	35–2	Uxorilocal
5.3 Daughter	35–3	Uxorilocal
5.4 Daughter	35–4	
6. Son	Nonlocal	Neolocal
7. Son	15–3	Virilocal
(one of daughters was Susie, daughter of Edna)		
8. Daughter	Nonlocal	Neolocal
9. Daughter		
9.1 Daughter	53	Uxorilocal
9.2 Daughter	21	Virilocal
9.3 Son	Nonlocal	Neolocal
II. Mrs. Buttons (sister of Cross Hills Lady)		
1. Mrs. Cross Roads	11–1	
1.1. Daughter (deceased)		
1.2 Son	Nonlocal	Neolocal
1.3 Son (Fred)	5	Independent
1.4 Stella's mother (deceased)		
1.4.1 Stella	49	Uxorilocal
1.4.2 Rebecca	32–2	Virilocal
1.4.3 Son	Nonlocal	Neolocal
1.5 Daughter	Nonlocal	Neolocal
1.6 Daughter	Nonlocal	Neolocal
1.7 Daughter	Nonlocal	Neolocal
1.8 Daughter	11–2	Uxorilocal
2. Mrs. Cross Road's sister		
2.1 Son	Nonlocal	Uxorilocal
2.2 Daughter	31	Uxorilocal
2.3 Son	Nonlocal	Neolocal
2.4 Son	Nonlocal	Neolocal
2.5 Son	Nonlocal	Neolocal
2.6 Daughter	Nonlocal	Neolocal
2.7 Son	Nonlocal	Neolocal
3. Son	30	Independent (virilocal?)
4. Son	Adjacent community	Independent (uxorilocal)

II. Segment 2

	Camp and Household Number	Residence
'Asdzáán Nez	36–1	Independent
1. Daughter	48–1	Independent (uxorilocal)
1.1 Son	1–3	Uxorilocal
1.2 Son	48–2	Virilocal
1.3 Daughter	36–2	Uxorilocal
1.3.1 Son	36–1	Virilocal
1.3.2 Daughter	Nonlocal	Neolocal
1.3.3–7: 5 Unmarried children	36–2	(With parents)
1.3.8 Son	36–3	Virilocal
1.3.9 Daughter	36–3	Uxorilocal
1.4 Daughter	38	Uxorilocal
1.5 Daughter	48–1	Independent (uxorilocal)
1.6 Daughter	39	Virilocal
2. Daughter (deceased)		
2.1 Son	33	Virilocal
2.2 Son (deceased)		
2.3 Daughter	40–4	Virilocal
3. Daughter (deceased)		
3.1 Daughter	37–1	Uxorilocal
3.1.1 Son	37–2	Virilocal
3.1.2 Daughter	Adjacent community	Independent
3.1.3 Son	Nonlocal	Neolocal
3.2 Daughter (deceased)		
3.2.1 Son	Nonlocal	Uxorilocal
3.2.2 Son	Nonlocal	Neolocal
3.2.3 Daughter	Nonlocal	Neolocal
3.2.4 Daughter	37–1	Same household
Other unmarried children		as MZ above

III. Segment 3

	Camp and Household Number	Residence
1. John Begay	28–1	Independent
4 grown children		
2. Nelly Begay	19–1	Virilocal
2.1 Son	17–3	Uxorilocal
2.2 Daughter	Nonlocal	Neolocal
2.3 Daughter	19–2	Uxorilocal
Unmarried sons and daughters		
3. Brother	29	Virilocal
(deceased during field work)		
4. Sister	Adjacent community	Virilocal
5. Sister	Nonlocal	Virilocal

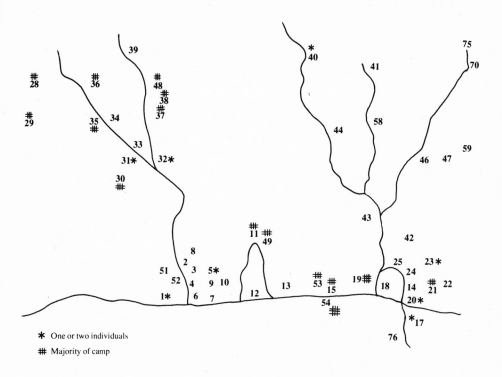

Map A 4.3 *House-in-the-Rocks people winter residences*

Settlement Patterns

In the winter, House-in-the-Rocks people were primarily located in two neighborhoods on the Flats, at Cross Hills and Cross Roads, and in a large area of the Gray Area flanking both sides of the road that crosses the mountains. This clustering is due both to the expansion of Segment 2 ('Asdzáán Nez's children) and to the independent settlement of members of Segments 2 and 3 in the area. See Map A 4.3.

The following is a summary of the moves made by first and second generation members of each segment and accounts for their location in 1966.

Camp of Present Residence	History of Movement
Segment 1	
Camp 15	Cross Hills Lady had been settled at Cross Hills for several decades. Two sons and a daughter lived outside Copper Canyon. With her lived two married sons and nearby lived two married granddaughters (daughter's daughters).
Camp 35	Another married daughter of Cross Hills Lady moved near her husband's relatives in the Gray Area. After the husband's father and brother died, the couple moved closer to the road where they lived with three married daughters.
Camp 21	Another daughter's daughter of Cross Hills Lady lived with her husband near his parents.
Camp 11	Mrs. Buttons was presumably Cross Hills Lady's sister, although descendants of the two sisters were not associated residentially or in terms of cooperation. Mr. and Mrs. Buttons used to live in the hills west of the trading post. One daughter, Mrs. Cross Roads, moved to Cross Roads with her husband. He was related to the Red-House people sibling group, which was not located near Mountain Rising, so his claim on their residence site is unclear. Most of her other children lived in California or on other parts of the reservation. One son, because of a complicated divorce and remarriage, lived near the trading post (Camp 5).
Camp 31	A daughter's daughter of Mrs. Buttons lived within a mile or two of the original Buttons homestead. (Other grandchildren by this daughter lived on other parts of the reservation.)
Camp 30	A son of Mrs. Buttons lived near the original site. A second son married into a family in the adjacent community and was living uxorilocally with married children a few miles south of his brother at Camp 31.
Segment 2	
Camps 36, 48, 38, 39	*'Asdzáán* Nez, her daughter, and granddaughters lived on both sides of an arroyo in the Gray Area. Their presence in this area was not related to the settlement of Camps 31 and 30. The daughter, and two of her daughters, were once married to the brothers and father of the husband in Camp 35 and all lived not far from the 1966 site of this camp.

C. *Mountain-Recess People (Dziłł'anii) Genealogy*

I. Segment 1

	Camp and Household Number	Residence
I. Ruby's grandmother (deceased)		
1. Ruby's mother (deceased)		
1.1 Ruby	43–1	Uxorilocal
8 unmarried children		
1.2 Marian	43–2	Uxorilocal
1.2.1–3: 3 unmarried children		
1.2.4 Daughter	43–2	Uxorilocal
1.2.5–7: 3 unmarried children		
1.3, 1.4, and 1.5 Sons (deceased)		
1.6 Daughter	Nonlocal	Independent

II. Segment 2

	Camp and Household Number	Residence
1. Desba (raised by Ruby's grandmother; not blood relative)	20–2	Independent
1.1 Son (deceased)		
- Amy*	17–1	Virilocal
1.1.1 Son	17–2	Virilocal
1.1.2 Daughter	17–3	Uxorilocal
1.1.3 Daughter	6	Neolocal
1.1.4 Son	Nonlocal	Neolocal
1.1.5 Daughter	Nonlocal	Neolocal
1.2 Evelyn	17–4	Independent (uxorilocal)
- husband (deceased)		
1.2.1 Son		
1.2.2 Son		
- husband		
8 unmarried children		
1.3 Edna	20–1	Uxorilocal
- Cross Hills Lady's son		
1.3.1 Susie		
- Mike		
1.3.2–6: 5 minor children		
1.4 Son	64–1	Uxorilocal
1.5 Son (divorced)	20–2	Virilocal
2. Desba's sister (also raised by Ruby's grandmother)	59–1	Independent
2.1 Son	59–2	Virilocal
2.2 Son	Nonlocal	Neolocal
2.3 Daughter		
3. Desba's brother (lived in community ten miles north, and was raised by member of Desba's husband's clan)		

*Hyphen indicates children of individual will follow. Following are Desba's son's children by Amy.

III. Segment 3

	Camp and Household Number	Residence
1. Sam's mother	42–1	Independent
1.1 Sam	50	Independent (Navajo policeman at trading center ten miles north of Copper Canyon)
2. Sam's mother's sister	49–1	Virilocal
- husband (separated)		
2.1, 2.2, 2.3: unmarried children	Live with father	
- husband		
3. Sam's mother's brother	Nonlocal	

IV. Segment 4

	Camp and Household Number	Residence
1. Old Lady Canyon (deceased)		
- Husband (deceased)		
1.1 Son	Nonlocal (near 55–1)	
1.2 Daughter	Nonlocal (near 55–1)	
1.3 Son	Nonlocal	
1.4 Old Lady Canyon's daughter (deceased)		
- Husband	55–1	Independent (uxorilocal)
1.4.1 Son	71	Independent
- wife		
1.4.2 Daughter	47–2	Virilocal
- husband		
1.4.2.1 Daughter		
1.4.3 Son	Near 55–1	
1.4.4 Daughter	55–2	Uxorilocal
1.4.5, 1.4.6, 1.4.7: 3 unmarried sons	55–1	

Settlement Patterns

Members of Mountain-Recess people belong to four genealogical segments, the first three having close residential (and possibly actual kin) connections in the Blue Mesa neighborhood. The fourth segment, the descendents of Old Lady Canyon, are primarily settled to the south of the Copper Canyon area near the wash.

Camp of Present Residence	History of Movement
Camp 43	Ruby's grandmother lived quite near the present camp site, and the ruins of her stone hoghan were still visible. She raised her own two children plus Desba and her sister (who were possibly relatives). Ruby's mother had died, but two of her four daughters still lived at the camp site along with their children.
Camp 20	Desba and her sister (59) were raised by Ruby's grandmother; a brother was raised by members of Desba's husband's clan in a community to the north. (He was no longer in contact with Desba). Desba first lived with her husband (who was originally from an area thirty miles to the southeast) at Black-Line-of-Hills, ten miles east of their present residence, Yellow Hills. Two of Desba's daughters lived uxorilocally, although one is technically across the road in Camp 17. A divorced son lived with her (virilocally) and another son (64) lived with his wife.
Camp 59	Desba's sister was living virilocally in a neighborhood dominated by her husband's siblings' camps.
Camp 42	Sam's mother and her sister, who lived with her husband at 49, probably grew up in the Blue Mesa neighborhood.
Camp 55	Old Lady Canyon and her husband settled south of Copper Canyon near the wash. Two of her children married into the southern section of the neighboring community. One daughter, who was deceased, had settled at 55, and of her children, two sons were living nearby and one married daughter lived in the camp at 55 with her father and unmarried brothers.
Camp 47	One granddaughter (daughter's daughter) of Old Lady Canyon was living in Blue Mesa, having moved there with her husband's relatives. Ruby's mother's brother (also Mountain-Recess people) lived in the same camp, having come there through his wife's ties. Thus, both were near other Mountain-Recess people though their camp's location was chosen by relatives of their respective spouses.

Summer Residences

Members of Segment 1 and Sam's mother (Segment 3) all lived in the same summer neighborhood. Sam's mother's sister lived near her father's land. Desba also used to live near Sam's mother, but moved her summer residence to "Rolling Area," which was Zonnie's summer site, after Desba started taking care of Zonnie. Desba's daughters, her daughter-in-law, and their children had summer places there also. Old Lady Canyon's descendents had a summer residence near "Water Running Down," fairly distant from where Segments 1 and 3, or Segment 2, were located.

Notes to Chapters

~~~~~~

Notes to Chapter 1

1. I am using the nonmathematical definition of "model" which has become commonly accepted by British and American anthropologists through the work of Lévi-Strauss (1953) and Leach (1954) and as expressed in some of the papers which appear in the ASA Monograph 1, *The Relevance of Models for Social Anthropology* (Banton 1965). Like Leach I believe that anthropologists construct "model systems" or structural models of the societies they study, that is, a hypothesized set of relations between persons, roles, and groups that helps them interpret the regularities they observe in social interaction. I also refer to a "cultural model," by which I mean an analysis of the relationship between the actors' categories, ideas, and beliefs. In this sense Schneider (1968) has presented a cultural model of American kinship. I distinguish between the "actors' model" and "observer's model" much in the same way Barbara Ward (1965: 113), following Lévi-Strauss (1953), contrasted "conscious models," or those that are constructs of the people themselves, and "unconscious models," or those of the outside observer.

2. This is true, of course, of kinship in Anglo-American society, where variant definitions of the terms "relatives" and "family" are prevalent and an important aspect of the way in which kinship operates (Schneider 1968).

3. Van Velsen derives his approach from Gluckman's use of the extended case method; his point of view is similar to that of Turner (1957), Mitchell (1957, 1966, 1969), and other Manchester-trained anthropologists.

4. In 1963 I was a member of the NSF Harvard-Columbia Summer Field Institute in Ethnology, under the direction of B.N. Colby. Results of a study of religious learning in a family are presented in Louise Lamphere, "Loose-Structuring as Exhibited in a Case Study of Navajo Religious Learning," *El Palacio* 71, No. 1 (Spring 1964): 37–44. During the summer of 1964 I was supported by a National Institute of Mental Health Fellowship (1 FI-MH-24, 103–01). Data on economics and kinship were collected for a study of residence patterns and published in Reynolds, Lamphere, and Cook (1967).

[203]

5. Although I was not aware of it at the time, Gary Witherspoon was working on Navajo kinship in Rough Rock about the time of my study. His ideas have been particularly useful in defining the cultural aspects of Navajo social groupings (1970, 1975).

6. Liquor is illegal on the reservation and Navajos often describe bringing cheap wine or beer onto the reservation either for consumption or for resale as "bootlegging."

7. Probably meaning that they were promiscuous, especially during a drinking spree.

8. The question frame method of interviewing was most useful in learning Navajo and in understanding Navajo categories. The method is described in D. Metzger and G. Williams, "Some Procedures and Results in the Study of Native Categories: Tzeltal Firewood," *American Anthropologist* 68, no. 2: 389–407.

9. The major service was transportation, though I often helped Navajos in dealing with the BIA, the State Welfare Office, or other bureaucracies. In addition, I loaned money, provided food, some clothing, and domestic labor.

10. During the 1930s the reservation was divided into eighteen land management districts to control grazing practices and administer the stock reduction program more easily. Several districts are under the jurisdiction of each of the Navajo BIA subagencies, with a central agency located in Window Rock, Arizona. School districts follow the land management boundaries.

11. Funds for this program are allotted by population and are to be utilized for such projects as home improvement, road repair, arts and crafts, cemetery construction, etc. Chapter members are hired for ten days at a time and earn one hundred dollars for work on these projects.

12. Since *dził* means "mountain," it can be applied to any mountainous area and even to the summit landscape; however, another term specifies the Top, and *dził* is reserved for the bench area.

13. By "distant clan ties," I mean that rather than being members of the same clan, the Navajos are either "born for" the same clan, one is "born for" the clan of the other, or their own clans are considered "related."

14. Based on data from a 1938 Soil Conservation Survey Map.

15. Young (1961: 228) estimates the average per capita income on the reservation as a whole as $521 not including $124 in benefits from Tribal and Government Health and Welfare programs. The figure for Copper Canyon is lower than Young's estimate because (1) I have not included agricultural and livestock products consumed at home, and (2) only 2 or 3 Copper Canyon residents are on payrolls of the BIA, Public Health Service, and Navajo Tribe. These payrolls contribute a much larger percentage of community income in service centers like Window Rock, Ft. Defiance, and Shiprock, and make up a larger proportion of the per capita tribal income.

Notes to Chapter 2

1. The terms "cooperative" and "uncooperative" are not used as logical opposites, but as convenient cover terms for Navajo words and phrases that, on one hand, describe "helping" and "caring for," and, on the other, indicate behavior that characterizes someone who does not help.
2. One informant explained in English the two words for jealousy.

> For instance, if some man sees that I have a butane tank out there and keep my house warm with gas or have a nice pickup truck or car, then maybe he is jealous (*'oołchįį*). There is another kind of jealousy. When a man and woman are married, maybe she knows another man and they get together; then the husband is jealous of his wife (*łe' nizin*). *Nizin* means "he's thinking"; *łe* means "he can't control his mind"—for example, *hait'áo nínizin* means, "What do you think about it?"

3. Although witches often deal with the dead, they are not to be confused with ghosts (*ch'įįdi*), a malevolent aspect of a deceased human which may cause sickness.
4. Handtrembling is one of the three forms of Navajo divination. The practitioner's hand and arm is possessed with a violent shaking and is passed over the patient's body, allowing the handtrembler to "see" or diagnose the cause of the illness and prescribe the appropriate ceremonial cure (Kluckhohn and Leighton 1946: 146–49).
5. The prefix *bi* or *ba* does not always indicate possession, but may refer to kin relationships as in *bamá* or *bizhé'é* (his mother, his father).
6. Children are not full-fledged members of the society and are considered ethically incompetent in some instances (Ladd 1957: 272). In other instances, notably the arrangement of a first marriage or the organization of a ceremony for the child, the parents are *bóholnííh* for the child. A Navajo child, however, has greater autonomy than in Anglo-American culture. A child may go where he wants without asking permission and may often choose which parent to live with if there is a divorce. In arranging a first marriage, if the girl objects strongly, the marriage probably will not take place.
7. The Enemy Way is a three-day ceremony to cure illness caused by the ghost of an alien or enemy. It requires the participation of two local groups (that of the patient and that of the Stick Receiver, who lives at some distance from the patient and his relatives).
8. As in the Navajo ideology of sickness and disease as it relates to witchcraft, this is a post hoc theory of causation. A woman with a "mean" personality may be said to have been mad at someone during her *kinaaldá*. Present behavior is explained in terms of a past event, and it is immaterial whether she actually was angry with someone during those four days. The breaking of an injunction did not *cause* the subsequent behavior; rather the behavior is *explained* because of a broken prescription.
9. No particular person is obligated to speak, so that the number and kinship or political status of speakers varies from occasion to occasion. If no one steps forward, there are no speeches on that particular night.
10. News or gossip is told to the anthropologist in much the same way as it is to other Navajos. Although I have evidence of some Navajos reporting only what they thought I wanted to hear and thus grossly distorting an episode of drunken fighting and driving, I have reason to believe that many other informants were telling me the same details they communicated to others. Much of my data on disputes and gossip were gathered by having an informant translate actual conversations where one Navajo was relating recent events to another of his own accord.

11. In my opinion the two points of view are complementary, since Gluckman concentrates on the latent or unintended functions of gossip for the group, while Paine elucidates the manifest and relatively conscious functions of gossip for the individual. In discussing gossip with respect to the Navajo cultural system, I have drawn on perspectives used by both authors.

12. A comparison of the Navajo with Colson's study of the Makah (1953) is instructive. Crucial differences between Makah back-biting and scandal and Navajo gossip are related to the importance of social ranking among the Makah versus the egalitarian quality of Navajo society. Navajo gossip is indirect, diffuse, and subtle by comparison with the Makah, where attacks on another's reputation are often made in face-to-face situations and gossip is much more vicious and more clearly related to defining one's social position as higher than that of others (Colson 1953: 228–30).

13. John and his wife were not well off economically. Their income came from his social security payments (sixty dollars a month) and his wife's weaving (approximately one thousand dollars per year). They had only a few sheep, no pickup truck, electricity, or other modern conveniences which the wealthier Copper Canyon households have.

14. Keith Basso's excellent analysis of Western Apache witchcraft also shows a relationship between behavior criteria and the concept of a witch (1969). The Apache clearly define a witch in the abstract on the basis of such concepts as stinginess, anger, and meanness, and make concrete accusations in light of disputes (1969: 40–59). Basso's data are much more detailed than mine, and I find he not only corroborates my point of view, but offers many suggestions for further investigation of witchcraft among the Navajo.

Notes to Chapter 3

1. If careful account were kept of exchanges of goods and services, then "who owes whom" would be more generally known and provide a system of credits and debits which could be negotiated in the request situation. Probability of refusal could be more accurately calculated before a request is made, and a refusal itself would be less damaging to the ongoing system of cooperation since there would be more legitimized ways of justifying a refusal (e.g., "He hasn't ever helped me," "I don't owe him that much," etc.). The more generalized nature of Navajo cooperative obligations and the lack of calculation make avoidance of refusals all the more necessary for the maintenance of the entire system of cooperation.

2. Imperatives take the same form as declarative sentences. Often the future tense is used in making a request, although the imperfective mode (action incompleted) is most common (Young 1962: 54).

3. Here the avoidance of gossip is a justification for proper behavior (i.e., cooperativeness) (see Ladd, 1957: 404–405), and gossip itself is seen by the speaker as a possible sanction to be used against those who are uncooperative. The informant's statement also defines meanness as refusing requests, thus making the connection between gossip and the definition of uncooperative behavior discussed in the previous chapter.

Notes to Chapter 4

1. There is some evidence that the husband-wife relationship is not separated from the general relation between male and female. The term of reference for "my husband" is *sha hastiin*, which literally means "my man," using the most common Navajo term for an adult male. Similarly, a man calls his wife *shi'esdzáán*, or "my woman."

2. Speeches are made by various relatives and chapter officers. At a wedding in Rimrock in 1963, the following gave speeches: the bride's father, the chapter vice-president (ex-husband of the bride's mother's mother's sister [MMZ]), the chapter president, a grazing committee member (the groom's father's brother's son [FBS], *bínaaí*, or classificatory "older brother"), the mother of the bride, and two unrelated women. At a Copper Canyon wedding I was told about, the groom's mother and mother's brother spoke, as did the bride's mother and mother's sister. Other relatives (including the bride's father's mother) and chapter officers may have also participated.

3. Another term relevant in delineating clusters of hoghans, but very unstable in its application, describes those who move together. Haile reports that *łago dah'oonééł* ("one group is on the move"), or *łahgo danda'inééh* ("one of several groups is on the move"), refer to the extended family (1948: 95). Young and Morgan also suggest this term and give the following sentence, *Nihí naabeehó danidlíini dikwíigo shíí dah yii'nééł* ("We Navajos exist as a number of camps or families,") using the progressive mode of the verb "on the move" (1951: 41). For one of my informants this sentence meant, "The Navajos are moving and don't know where they are going," suggesting that "moving" has nothing to do with defining social or spatial units. To another informant, however, the phrase *t'ááłá'ígo yii neeł* ("as one moving"), which is derived from the verb stem of previous examples, referred to the fact that her mother, her sister, and their households moved from the Flats to the mountains when she and her household did. Her use of the concept implied the whole residence group that, in this instance, "moves together," or at approximately the same time. In other cases, "moving together" does not designate the same people as those who would be classed together as a residence group on the basis of spatial proximity or membership in the same extended family.

4. Census material on which the statistics in Table 4.3 and subsequent tables are based was taken from a school census used at the boarding school nearest to Copper Canyon (administered by the BIA, Department of the Interior) and from the Copper Canyon copy of the 1963 Tribal Census conducted in each chapter area, in this case by the chapter secretary. These data were supplemented by information from informants. The census includes a number of couples and their children who were no longer living in Copper Canyon; however, the parents or siblings of at least one member of the couple lived there. Most such couples lived off the reservation and returned to Copper Canyon periodically for visits.

5. On the other other hand, Aberle has found that off-reservation wage work for males (e.g., employment on railroad work gangs) maintains uxorilocal-extended family patterns, since women find it more congenial to remain with their own relatives rather than the husband's kin when he is gone.

Notes to Chapter 5

1. A fifth relationship is *'aháshiilchíín*: "we two are born for each other," for example, when two men have exchanged sisters so that the children are double cross-cousins: MBD–FZD; MBS–FZS. Of course, the couples need not be consanguineal siblings, but only brothers and sisters of the same clan who intermarry.

2. "Should" or "should not" is not a literal translation of the Navajo which uses an imperative or negative imperative ("do" or "do not").

3. Thus one can say *Bit'ahnii dóó hashtł'ishnii dabik'éí 'it'é* ("Under-his-Cover people and Mud people are relatives"); or one can ask, *Haish dine'é yígíí danik'éi?* ("Which clans is your clan related to?"). A possible answer would be: *Tłízí łání, kinłichíi'nii, tsí'nad-jini, tsé'nahabiłni, deeschii'nii, dóó 'éí dashik'éí* ("Many-Goats People, Red-House People, Horizontal-Black-Tree-Line People, Rolling-Rock People, and Start-of-the-Red-Streak People, these are my relatives") (Haile 1941: 137).

4. Aberle suggested this phrase to me in 1965; he says it is used in the Piñon area to refer to a matrilineage. Information from my informants suggests that in Copper Canyon nonmatrilineal relatives (e.g., son's son) are included.

5. These terms are derived from *kééhat'į* or *kéédahat'į*, meaning "we [or] they reside"; *-kee* is not analyzed, *ha* is a place prefix combined with *'ast'į'*, "I do," or *'at'į*, "he does" (Haile 1948: 03).

6. Ross has also used the same concept but labeled it the Local Clan Segment (p. 55). He also discusses outfit.

7. Downs, in his 1964 monograph on animal husbandry, denies the existence of the outfit and the land-use community in the Piñon area. However, in a later article he refers to a "homestead group" (i.e., residence group) as an "outfit" (1965: 1388). This usage, at variance with so much of the published literature, only confuses the issue of definition and composition of the outfit, since the unwary reader is not likely to discriminate between the use of outfit meaning residence group and outfit meaning larger group of kin.

8. The notion that "everyone helps" is part of the ethic of generalized reciprocity discussed in Chapter 2. Since cooperation should be given freely and without expectation of return, Navajos are reluctant to suggest that some of their relatives do not help. Mary Shepardson and Blodwen Hammond indicate that they received similarly vague answers to the question of who should contribute to a ceremony at a Navajo Mountain (1970: 64).

9. Barnes even suggests that anthropological models used to describe African descent systems are too rigid to be applied appropriately to kinship and political organization in Highland New Guinea. Some of his objections are also appropriate to the Navajo case (1962).

10. See Fortes 1969, Chapters 13 and 14, for a full discussion of the differences between descent and filiation.

11. Mary Shepardson, in a personal communication, emphasized the ego-centered nature of cooperation and seemed to see the activation of an ego's matrilineage in the same way I conceptualize the activation of ego's set. She and Hammond also stress that the father's relatives and affines are important in Navajo Mountain cooperation (1970: 64–66).

Notes to Chapter 6

1. In fact, if there had been more sheep owned by Copper Canyon residents, I might have found it easier to define residence groups. The cases that presented difficulty in deciding whether a cluster of kin constituted one or two residence groups were those in which members of younger households had either none or only a few sheep to pool with the herd and where spatial and genealogical criteria were insufficient to decide if these households had completed the process of fission from a parent camp. Had such households owned more sheep, it would have been easier to distinguish if they had formed an independent camp.

2. In other parts of the reservation these tasks may be performed by kin recruited from several residence groups, such as in Klagetoh, or residence groups themselves may consist of more households, for example, Navajo Mountain. That members from different or larger groups perform the same tasks may be a function of the size of herds and the contribution livestock makes to community income.

3. Only one residence group hauled water for the herd in winter; they hauled water because the nearest water supplies were controlled by other residence groups, and using more distant sources would have meant crossing the grazing territory of others.

4. Nuclear camps with herds included, in addition to nuclear families, two camps with bachelors, two with widowers and children, a widow and children, and another widow who combined her herd with the herd of her daughter and son-in-law in another nuclear camp.

5. There were two exceptions to this type of composition: one widow had her granddaughter and small children living with her in the same household, while a son and daughter-in-law lived in the second household (Camp 32). Another widow had her son and his wife in the same household, while her sister's granddaughter lived in the other household in the camp (Camp 23).

6. The two exceptions were (1) a widow and granddaughter (Camp 32) who did most of the herding and did not receive help from the second household of a son and daughter-in-law, and (2) an older couple who did most of the herding and received little aid from a daughter and son-in-law in the second household (Camp 12). In both cases, there were two adults to do the herding in one household—enough to minimally accomplish this task, even though other Navajos utilized three or four in rotating herding duties.

7. At least two herds were sheared after the family moved to the Mountain. Since the nights on the mountain are much cooler, this delays shearing until two or three weeks after other families have finished.

8. In those camps where there was no married couple a variety of patterns were found: One bachelor was aided by his sister who lived in another residence group (Camp 33); an older widower was helped by his unmarried son who lived with him (Camp 2).

9. All the extended camps with larger herds had only two households, suggesting the need for outside help. It certainly would be possible for a residence group of five households to shear a herd of 250 or 300 sheep without aid. This, in fact, may be a pattern in other communities on the reservation.

10. Sheepdipping was instituted by the U.S. government, but since the mid-1950s has been under the jurisdiction and control of the Navajo Tribe and local grazing committees.

11. Out of forty-seven permits, twenty-three are in the name of a male, seventeen in a female name, and seven are joint permits.

Notes to Chapter 7

1. Twenty-eight residence groups had one pickup or car, eleven had two vehicles, and one had three cars; another had three pickups and three cars. Three camps had a wagon in addition to a pickup or tractor.
2. Nuclear residence groups include nuclear families, divorced or widowed parents and children, and isolated individuals. Extended camps contain two to five households, composed of nuclear families, or a widowed or divorced parent and children.
3. Four new shallow wells were completed on the Mountain during the summer of 1966, each near a residence group that had not been near an improved spring. This increased the number to twelve. Before the Shallow Wells Program was started on the reservation, Navajos in the Copper Canyon summer area used unimproved springs, of which there were many.
4. Three of these eighty-three households haul water by hand in both summer and winter; one used a wagon to haul wood and the other two owned cars, but all others called upon relatives outside the residence group for hauling wood.
5. Three nuclear families had two sets of furniture and, therefore, did not need to move the bulky items from one cabin to the other; this was unusual, however.
6. The cases are: (1) sister's husband for the isolated individual in Camp 9; (2) husband's mother's brother's son (MBS) for Camp 29; (3) wife's sister for Camp 56; (4) sister's daughter (ZD) of the isolated individual in 76; (5) nonresident daughter's husband for Camp 78; and (6) nonresident daughter for Camp 59.

Notes to Chapter 8

1. In Case 7, the father's relatives were unavailable, as they lived sixty miles from Copper Canyon.
2. Recent illness in the camp had been diagnosed as due to witchcraft; though particular witches had not been named, there was probably a distrust of social relations within nonkin and more distant kin.
3. They were called *naa'łaa'ii*, or "practitioner," a term which differs from that given by Aberle (1955: 378).
4. I have not performed tests of statistical significance on the data since the twenty-nine occasions do not represent a random sample, and since, in some cases, I was not able to identify all those who attended.
5. Clan relatives include those related to ego through one of four possible links: his own clan, his father's clan (i.e., the clan he is "born for"), children of his clan (i.e., those "born for" his clan), and those whose fathers are of the same clan as ego's father (i.e., those "born for" the same clan ego is "born for").
6. For large sings that require a great deal of effort, additional patients (and, hence, additional sets of kin) are added, instead of more clan relatives of the patient, spouse, or parents.

Notes to Chapter 9

1. Ladd, a philosopher, is one of the few to present a "middle-range" analysis—one that deals with the Navajo moral code on its own terms rather than imposing a system from the outside.

Bibliography

ABERLE, DAVID F.
  1961. "The Navajo." In *Matrilineal Kinship*, edited by David Schneider and Kathe-leen Gough. Berkeley and Los Angeles: University of California Press.
  1963. "Some Sources of Flexibility in Navaho Social Organization." *Southwestern Journal of Anthropology* 19: 1–8.
  1966. *The Peyote Religion Among the Navaho*. Chicago: Aldine Press.
  1967. "An Economic Approach to Modern Navajo Kinship." Paper presented at American Anthropological Association Meetings, Washington, D.C.
  1969. "A Plan for Navajo Economic Development." In *Toward Economic Development for Native American Communities*. Compendium of papers submitted to the Subcommittee on Economy in Government of the Joint Economic Committee of the U.S. Congress. Washington, D.C.: U.S. Government Printing Office.

ADAMS, WILLIAM Y.
  1963. *Shonto: A Study of the Role of the Trader in a Modern Navaho Community*. Bureau of American Ethnology Bulletin 188. Washington, D.C.: U.S. Government Printing Office.
  1971. "Navajo Ecology and Economy: A Problem in Cultural Values." In *Apachean Culture History and Ethnology*, edited by Keith H. Basso and Morris E. Opler. Anthropological Papers of the University of Arizona 21. Tucson: University of Arizona Press.

ALBERT, ETHEL
  1956. "The Classification of Values: A Method and Illustration." *American Anthropologist* 58: 221–48.

APPELL, G.N.
  1966. "Residence and Ties of Kinship in a Cognatic Society: The Rungus Dusun of Sabah, Malaysia," *Southwestern Journal of Anthropology* 22: 280–301.
  1967. "Observational Procedures for Identifying Kindreds: Social Isolates Among the Rungus of Borneo." *Southwestern Journal of Anthropology* 23: 192–207.

ARENSBERG, CONRAD
  1961. "The Community as Object and as Sample." *American Anthropologist* 63: 241–64.

[211]

BANTON, MICHAEL
    1965. *The Relevance of Models for Social Anthropology*. Association for Social An-
    thropologists Monograph 1. London: Tavistock Publications.
BARNES, J.A.
    1954. "Class and Committees in a Norwegian Island Parish." *Human Relations* 7:
    39–58.
    1962. "African Models in the New Guinea Highlands." *Man* 62: 5–9.
BASSO, KEITH H.
    1969. *Western Apache Witchcraft*. Anthropological Papers of the University of
    Arizona 15. Tucson: University of Arizona Press.
BASSO, KEITH H. and MORRIS E. OPLER, editors
    1971. *Apachean Culture History and Ethnology*. Anthropological Papers of the Univer-
    sity of Arizona 21. Tucson: University of Arizona Press.
BELLAH, ROBERT N.
    1952. *Apache Kinship Systems*. Cambridge: Harvard University Press.
BOTT, ELIZABETH
    1957. *Family and Social Network*. London: Tavistock Publications. Second edition
    paperback. New York: Free Press, 1971.
COLLIER, GEORGE and E.Z. VOGT
    1965. "Aerial Photographs and Computers in the Analysis of Zinacanteco Demog-
    raphy and Land Tenure." Paper presented at American Anthropological Associa-
    tion Meetings, Denver, Colorado.
COLLIER, MALCOLM CARR
    1966. *Local Organization Among the Navaho*. Human Relations Area Files (Flex
    Book, NT 13-001).
COLSON, ELIZABETH
    1953. *The Makah Indians*. Manchester: Manchester University Press.
DOWNS, JAMES F.
    1964. Animal Husbandry in Navajo Culture and Society. University of California
    Publications in Anthropology 1. Berkeley and Los Angeles: University of
    California Press.
    1965. "Social Consequences of a Dry Well." *American Anthropologist* 67: 1387–
    1416.
EDMONSON, MUNRO
    1966. "Kinship Systems." In *The People of Rimrock*, edited by E.Z. Vogt and E.
    Albert. Cambridge: Harvard University Press.
EPSTEIN, A.L.
    1961. "The Network and Urban Social Organization." *Rhodes-Livingstone Journal*
    29: 29–62.
EVANS-PRITCHARD, E.E.
    1937. *Witchcraft, Oracles and Magic Among the Azande*. Oxford: Clarendon Press.
    1940. *The Nuer*. Oxford: Oxford University Press. Reprint 1947.
FIRTH, RAYMOND
    1962. *Essays in Social Organization and Values*. London School of Economics
    Monograph 28. London: Athalone Press.
FORTES, MEYER
    1949. "Time and Social Structure: An Ashanti Case Study." In *Social Structure:
    Essays Presented to A.R. Radcliffe-Brown*, edited by F. Eggan and M. Fortes.
    Oxford: Clarendon Press.
    1958. Introduction to *The Developmental Cycle in Domestic Groups*, edited by Jack
    Goody. Cambridge Papers in Social Anthropology 1. Cambridge: Cambridge
    University Press.
    1969. *Kinship and the Social Order*. Chicago: Aldine Press.

FRANCISCAN FATHERS
1910. *Ethnologic Dictionary*. St. Michaels, Ariz.: St. Michaels Press.

FREEMAN, J.D.
1958. "The Family System of the Iban of Borneo." In *The Developmental Cycle in Domestic Groups*, edited by Jack Goody. Cambridge Papers in Social Anthropology 1. Cambridge: Cambridge University Press.
1960. "On the Concept of Kindred." *Journal of the Royal Anthropological Institute* 91: 192–220.

GEERTZ, CLIFFORD
1957. "Ritual and Social Change: A Javanese Example." *American Anthropologist* 59: 32–54.
1964. "Ideology as a Cultural System." In *Ideology of Discontent*, edited by D. Apter. New York: Free Press.

GLUCKMAN, MAX
1955. *The Judicial Process Among the Barotse of Northern Rhodesia*. Manchester: Manchester University Press.
1963. "Gossip and Scandal." *Current Anthropology* 4: 307–15.
1968. "Psychological, Sociological and Anthropological Explanations of Witchcraft and Gossip: A Clarification." *Man*, n.s. 3: 20–34.

GOFFMAN, ERVING
1967. "The Nature of Deference and Demeanor." In *Interaction Ritual*. Garden City, N.Y.: Doubleday & Company.

GOODY, JACK, editor
1958. *The Developmental Cycle in Domestic Groups*. Cambridge Papers in Social Anthropology 1. Cambridge: Cambridge University Press.

HAILE, FATHER BERARD
1938. *Origin Legend of the Navaho Enemy Way*. Yale University Publications in Anthropology 17. New Haven: Yale University Press.
1941. *Learning Navaho*. Vol. 1. St. Michaels, Ariz.: St. Michaels Press.
1943a. *Soul Concepts of the Navaho*. Annali Lateranensi, vol. 7. Citta Del Vaticana: Tipografia Poliglotta Vaticana.
1943b. *Origin Legend of the Navaho Flintway*. Chicago: University of Chicago Press.
1946. *The Navaho Fire Dance or Corral Dance*. St. Michaels, Ariz.: St. Michaels Press.
1947. *Learning Navaho*. Vol. 3. St. Michaels, Ariz.: St. Michaels Press.
1948. *Learning Navaho*. Vol. 4. St. Michaels, Ariz.: St. Michaels Press.
1954. *Property Concepts of the Navaho Indians*. Catholic University of America Anthropological Series 17. Washington, D.C.: Catholic University of America Press.

HALLOWELL, A.I.
1955. *Culture and Experience*. Philadelphia: University of Pennsylvania Press.

HARMON, ROBERT
1964. "Change in a Navaho Ceremonial." *El Palacio* 71: 20–26.

HENDERSON, E. B. and J. E. LEVY
1975. *Survey of Navajo Community Studies 1936–74*. Lake Powell Research Project Bulletin 6. University of California, Los Angeles.

HESTER, JAMES J.
1971. "Navajo Culture Change: From 1550 to 1960 and Beyond." In *Apachean Culture History and Ethnology*, edited by Keith H. Basso and Morris E. Opler. Anthropological Papers of the University of Arizona 21. Tucson: University of Arizona Press.

HILL, W.W.
    1936. *Navajo Warfare*. New Haven: Yale University Publications in Anthropology no. 5.
    1940. "Some Aspects of Navajo Political Structure," *Plateau* 13: 23–28.
HILLERY, GEORGE A. and FRANK J. ESSENE
    1963. "Navajo Population: Analysis of the 1960 Census." *Southwestern Journal of Anthropology* 19: 297–313.
HOBSON, RICHARD
    1954. *Navaho Acquisitive Values*. Papers of the Peabody Museum of American Archaeology and Ethnology 42, no. 3. Cambridge: Harvard University Press.
HOEBEL, E. ADAMSON
    1960. *The Cheyennes: Indians of the Great Plains*. New York: Holt, Rinehart and Winston.
JACOBSON, DORANNE
    1964. "Navajo Enemy Way Exchanges." *El Palacio* 71: 7–19.
JOSEPHY, ALVIN M., JR.
    1968. *The Indian Heritage of America*. New York: Alfred A. Knopf.
KAPFERER, BRUCE
    1969. "Norms and the Manipulation of Relationships in a Work Context." In *Social Networks in Urban Situations*, edited by J. Clyde Mitchell. Manchester: Manchester University Press.
KAPLAN, BERT and DALE JOHNSON
    1964. "The Social Meaning of Navaho Psychopathology and Psychotherapy." In *Magic, Faith and Healing*, edited by Ari Kiev. New York: Free Press.
KEESING, ROGER
    1966. "Kwaio Kindreds." *Southwestern Journal of Anthropology* 22: 326–53.
KEITH, ANN B.
    1964. "The Navajo Girl's Puberty Ceremony: Function and Meaning for the Adolescent." *El Palacio* 71: 27–36.
KELLY, LAWRENCE C.
    1968. *The Navajo Indians and Federal Indian Policy 1900–1935*. Tucson: University of Arizona Press.
KIMBALL, SOLON T. and JOHN H. PROVINSE
    1942. "Navajo Social Organization in Land Use Planning." *Applied Anthropology* 1: 18–30.
KLUCKHOHN, CLYDE
    1944. *Navajo Witchcraft*. Reprint. Boston: Beacon Press, 1967.
    1949. "The Philosophy of the Navaho Indians." In *Ideological Differences and World Order*, edited by F.S.C. Northrop. New Haven: Yale University Press.
    1956a. "Navaho Morals." In *Encyclopedia of Morals*, edited by Vergilius Ferm, pp. 383–90. New York: Philosophical Library. Reprinted in *Culture and Behavior*, edited by Richard Kluckhohn, pp. 168–76. New York: Free Press, 1962.
    1956b. "Some Navaho Value Terms in Behavioral Context." *Language* 32: 140–45.
    1958. "The Scientific Study of Values." University of Toronto Installation Lectures. Toronto: University of Toronto Press.
    1966. *The Ramah Navaho*. Bureau of American Ethnology Bulletin 196. Washington, D.C.: U.S. Government Printing Office.
KLUCKHOHN, CLYDE and D. LEIGHTON
    1946. *The Navaho*. Cambridge: Harvard University Press. Anchor paperback reprint. New York: Doubleday Publishing Company, 1962.
KLUCKHOHN, CLYDE and KATHERINE SPENCER
    1940. *A Bibliography of the Navaho Indians*. New York: J.J. Augustin.

KLUCKHOHN, CLYDE and LELAND WYMAN
    1940. *An Introduction to Navaho Chant Practice*. Memoirs of the American An-
    thropological Association 53. Menasha, Wisc.: American Anthropological As-
    sociation.
KLUCKHOHN, FLORENCE
    1950. "Dominant and Substitute Profiles of Cultural Orientation: Their Significance
    for the Analysis of Social Stratification." *Social Forces* 28: 376–93.
KLUCKHOHN, FLORENCE and FRED L. STRODBECK
    1961. *Variations in Value-Orientations: A Theory Tested in Five Cultures*. Evanston,
    Ill.: Row, Peterson and Co.
LADD, JOHN
    1957. *Structure of a Moral Code*. Cambridge: Harvard University Press.
LAMPHERE, LOUISE
    1964. "Loose-Structuring as Exhibited in a Case Study of Navajo Religious Learn-
    ing." *El Palacio* 71: 37–44.
    1969. "Symbolic Elements in Navajo Ritual." *Southwestern Journal of Anthropology*
    25: 279–305.
    1970. "Ceremonial Cooperation and Networks: A Reanalysis of the Navajo Outfit."
    Man, n.s. 5: 39–59.
LAMPHERE, LOUISE and E.Z. VOGT
    1972. "Clyde Kluckhohn as Ethnographer and Student of Navaho Ceremonialism." In
    Culture and Life, edited by Walter W.Taylor, John L. Fischer, and Evan Z. Vogt.
    Carbondale and Edwardsville, Ill.: Southern Illinois University Press.
LEACH, EDMOND
    1954. *Political Systems of Highland Burma*. Boston: Beacon Press. Reprint. London:
    Athlone Press, 1970.
LEE, DOROTHY
    1959. *Freedom and Culture*. Englewood Cliffs, N.J.: Prentice-Hall Spectrum Paper-
    back.
LEIGHTON, D. and CLYDE KLUCKHOHN
    1947. *Children of the People*. Cambridge: Harvard University Press.
LÉVI-STRAUSS, CLAUDE
    1953. "Social Structure." In *Anthropology Today*, edited by A.L. Kroeber. Chicago:
    University of Chicago Press.
    1963. *Structural Anthropology*. New York: Basic Books.
LEVY, JERROLD
    1962. "Community Organization of the Western Navajo." *American Anthropologist*
    64: 781–801.
MATTHEWS, WASHINGTON
    1887. "The Mountain Chant." *Annual Report of the Bureau of American Ethnology* 5:
    385–467. Washington, D.C.: U.S. Government Printing Office.
    1897. *Navajo Legends*. Memoirs of the American Folklore Society 5. New York:
    American Folklore Society.
    1902. *The Night Chant*. Memoirs of the American Museum of Natural History 6. New
    York: American Museum of Natural History.
MAYER, ADRIAN C.
    1966. "The Significance of Quasi-Groups in the Study of Complex Societies." In *The
    Social Anthropology of Complex Societies*, edited by Michael Banton. Associa-
    tion of Social Anthropologists Monograph 4. London: Tavistock Publications.
METZGER, DUANE and GERALD WILLIAMS
    1966. "Some Procedures and Results in the Study of Native Categories: Tzeltal
    Firewood." *American Anthropologist* 68: 389–407.

MITCHELL, J. CLYDE

1957. *The Kalela Dance: Aspects of Social Relationships among Urban Africans in Northern Rhodesia.* Rhodes-Livingstone Paper no. 27. Manchester: Manchester University Press for Rhodes-Livingstone Institute.

1966. "Theoretical Orientations in African Urban Studies." In *The Social Anthropology of Complex Societies*, edited by Michael Banton. Association of Social Anthropologists Monograph 4. London: Tavistock Publications.

1969. Editor. *Social Networks in Urban Situations.* Manchester: Manchester University Press.

MITCHELL, WILLIAM E.

1963. "Theoretical Problems in the Concept of the Kindred." *American Anthropologist* 65: 343–54.

MORGAN, LEWIS HENRY

1851. *League of the Iroquois.* Rochester: Sage and Brother, Publishers. Reprint. New York: Corinth Books, 1962.

MURDOCK, GEORGE P.

1960. *Ethnographic Bibliography of North America.* New Haven: Human Relations Area Files.

NEWCOMB, FRANC J. and GLADYS REICHARD

1937. *Sandpaintings of the Navajo Shooting Chant.* New York: J.J. Augustin.

PAINE, ROBERT

1967. "What is Gossip About: An Alternative Hypothesis." *Man*, n.s. 2: 278–85.

PARSONS, TALCOTT

1963. "On the Concept of Political Power." *Proceedings of the American Philosophical Society* 107: 232–62. Philadelphia: American Philosophical Society.

PARSONS, TALCOTT and EDWARD A. SHILS

1951. *Toward a General Theory of Action.* Cambridge: Harvard University Press.

PEHRSON, ROBERT N.

1954. "Bilateral Kin Groupings as a Structural Type: A Preliminary Statement." *University of Manila Journal of East Asiatic Studies* 3: 199–202.

RADCLIFFE-BROWN, A.R.

1952. *Structure and Function in Primitive Society.* London: Cohen and West.

REICHARD, GLADYS

1928. *Social Life of the Navajo Indians.* Columbia University Contributions to Anthropology 7. New York: Columbia University Press.

1939. *A Navajo Medicine Man.* New York: J.J. Augustin.

REYNOLDS, TERRY, LOUISE LAMPHERE, and CECIL COOK, JR.

1967. "Time, Resources, and Authority in a Navajo Community." *American Anthropologist* 69: 188–99.

RICHARDS, CARA

1963. "Modern Residence Patterns Among the Navajo." *El Palacio* 70: 25–33.

ROSS, WILLIAM T.

1955. *Navajo Kinship and Social Organization: With Special Reference to a Transitional Community.* Ph.D. dissertation, University of Chicago.

SAHLINS, MARSHALL

1965. "On the Sociology of Primitive Exchange." In *The Relevance of Models for Social Anthropology*, edited by Michael Banton. Association for Social Anthropologists Monograph 1. London: Tavistock Publications.

1968. *Tribesmen.* Englewood Cliffs, N.J.: Prentice-Hall.

SASAKI, TOM T.

1960. *Fruitland, New Mexico: A Navaho Community in Transition.* Ithaca: Cornell University Press.

SCHNEIDER, DAVID
  1968. *American Kinship: A Cultural Account*. Englewood Cliffs, N.J.: Prentice-Hall.
SERVICE, ELMAN R.
  1966. *The Hunters*. Englewood Cliffs, N.J.: Prentice-Hall.
SHEPARDSON, MARY
  1963. *Navajo Ways in Government*. Memoirs of the American Anthropological Association 63: 3, part 2. Menasha, Wisc.: American Anthropological Association.
  1971. "Navajo Factionalism and the Outside World." In *Apachean Culture, History and Ethnology*, edited by Keith H. Basso and Morris E. Opler. Anthropological Papers of the University of Arizona 21. Tucson: University of Arizona Press.
SHEPARDSON, MARY and BLODWEN HAMMOND
  1964. "Change and Persistence in an Isolated Navajo Community." *American Anthropologist* 66: 1029–50.
  1970. *The Navajo Mountain Community: Social Organization and Kinship Terminology*. Berkeley and Los Angeles: University of California Press.
SPENCER, KATHERINE
  1957. *Mythology and Values: An Analysis of Navaho Chantway Myths*. Memoirs of the American Folklore Society 48. Philadelphia: American Folklore Society.
SPENCER, ROBERT F. and JESSE D. JENNINGS et. al.
  1965. *The Native Americans*. New York: Harper and Row.
STACK, CAROL
  1974. *All Our Kin: Strategies for Survival in a Black Community*. New York: Harper and Row.
STEVENSON, JAMES
  1886. "Ceremonial of Hasjelti Dailjis." *Annual Report of the Bureau of American Ethnology* 8: 229–85. Washington, D.C.: U.S. Government Printing Office.
TURNER, VICTOR
  1957. *Schism and Continuity in an African Society*. Manchester: Manchester University Press.
VAN VELSON, J.
  1967. "The Extended-Case Method and Situational Analysis." In *The Craft of Social Anthropology*, edited by A.L. Epstein. London: Tavistock Publications.
VOGT, E.Z.
  1961. "Navajo." In *Perspectives in American Indian Culture Change*. Chicago: University of Chicago Press.
VOGT, E.Z. and ETHEL ALBERT
  1966. *People of Rimrock*. Cambridge: Harvard University Press.
WALL, LEON and WILLIAM MORGAN
  1958. *Navajo-English Dictionary*. U.S. Department of Interior, Bureau of Indian Affairs. Window Rock, Ariz.: Navajo Agency.
WARD, BARBARA
  1965. "Varieties of the Conscious Model: The Fishermen of South China." In *The Relevance of Models for Social Anthropology*, edited by Michael Banton. London: Tavistock Publications.
WITHERSPOON, GARY
  1970. "A New Look at Navajo Social Organization." *American Anthropologist* 72: 55–65.
  1975. *Navajo Kinship and Marriage*. Chicago: University of Chicago Press.
WYMAN, LELAND C.
  1957. *Beautyway: A Navaho Ceremonial*. New York: Pantheon Books.
  1970. *Blessingway*. With three versions of the myth recorded and translated from the Navajo by Father Berard Haile. Tucson: University of Arizona Press.

WYMAN, LELAND C. and CLYDE KLUCKHOHN
    1938. *Navajo Classification of Their Song Ceremonials.* Memoirs of the American Anthropological Association 50. Menasha, Wisc.: American Anthropological Association.

YOUNG, MICHAEL and PETER WILLMOTT
    1957. *Family and Kinship in Easton London.* London: Penguin Books, 1966.

YOUNG, ROBERT
    1961. *Navajo Yearbook*, 1951–61. Window Rock, Ariz.: Navajo Agency.

YOUNG, ROBERT and WILLIAM MORGAN
    1943. *A Dictionary of the Navaho Language.* U.S. Office of Indian Affairs. Reprinted as part of *The Navajo Language.* Young and Morgan 1962. U.S. Indian Service. Salt Lake City: Deseret Press.

    1951. *A Vocabulary of Colloquial Navaho.* Phoenix: U.S. Department of the Interior.

Index

[219]